Queens of
Georgian Britain

For Rob, the listening lister!

Queens of
Georgian Britain

Catherine Curzon

PEN & SWORD
HISTORY

First published in Great Britain in 2017 by
Pen & Sword History
an imprint of
Pen & Sword Books Ltd
47 Church Street
Barnsley
South Yorkshire
S70 2AS

ISBN 978 1 47385 852 7

A CIP catalogue record for this book is available from the British
Library

Typeset in Ehrhardt by
Mac Style Ltd, Bridlington, East Yorkshire
Printed and bound in the UK by TJ International, Padstow,
Cornwall, PL28 8RW

Pen & Sword Books Limited incorporates the imprints of Atlas,
Archaeology, Aviation, Discovery, Family History, Fiction, History,
Maritime, Military, Military Classics, Politics, Select, Transport,
True Crime, Air World, Frontline Publishing, Leo Cooper,
Remember When, Seaforth Publishing, The Praetorian Press,
Wharncliffe Local History, Wharncliffe Transport,
Wharncliffe True Crime and White Owl.

For a complete list of Pen & Sword titles please contact
PEN & SWORD BOOKS LIMITED
47 Church Street, Barnsley, South Yorkshire, S70 2AS, England
E-mail: enquiries@pen-and-sword.co.uk
Website: www.pen-and-sword.co.uk

Contents

Acknowledgements   viii
List of Illustrations   ix
Introduction   xi

Act I: Sophia Dorothea of Celle   1
Love at First Sight   1
Adolescent Fancies   3
Encountering the Count   4
The Boy from Brunswick-Wolfenbüttel   5
Making the Marriage   6
A Fatal Cannonball   9
Sophia Goes to Celle   11
Meeting the Husband   13
The Electoral Princess   14
Liaisons with Lassay   16
The Count and Clara   18
The Count Returns   19
A Fateful Glove   22
Towards the Future   24
Reunited   25
Discovery   26
The Cuckold   28
The Disappearing Count   29
Murder Most Foul   30
The Spider's Web   33
Goodbye to Hanover   36
Divorce   38
The Lady of Ahlden   39
The Return to Celle   41

The Cunning Count   42
The End of the Duchess   44

Act II: Caroline of Ansbach, Queen Consort of Great Britain
and Ireland   47
The Orphan of Ansbach   47
The Eligible Orphan   50
The Queen is Dead   52
Meeting Monsieur de Busch   54
Marrying Monsieur de Busch   59
Sons and Smallpox   60
Daughters and Mistresses   61
Succession   64
The Princess of Wales   65
A Catastrophic Christening   67
Separation   71
Claiming Custody   73
Reconciliation   75
The Scourge of Smallpox   77
A Happy Interlude   80
Hail to the Queen   81
Caroline the Illustrious   83
Farewell Henrietta, Hello Amalie   86
Battling Wales   90
The Porteous Riots   93
A Flight by Moonlight   95
The Queen is Dead   98

Act III: Charlotte of Mecklenburg-Strelitz, Queen of the
United Kingdom of Great Britain and Ireland   103
A Sheltered Childhood   103
Becoming a Bride   106
To England   108
Marriage by Moonlight   110
God Save the Queen!   113
The Prince of Wales   117
The Charitable Queen   119

Trouble at Home 122
The False Princess 123
Goodbye Augusta 125
The Lost Sons 128
The Regency Crisis 131
Marie Antoinette 137
The Madness Returns 138
The Nunnery 139
Breaking Hearts 144
Fading Away 146

Act IV: Caroline of Brunswick, Queen of the United Kingdom 150
A Shuttlecock at Court 150
The Mad Princess? 152
A Lonely Princess 154
The (Not Quite) Princess of Wales 156
Marrying for Money 159
Meeting the Husband 163
A Wedding to Remember 167
Into the Bridal Bed 169
The Heir to the Throne 171
The Lady from Blackheath 172
The Delicate Investigation 174
Into the Public Eye 180
The Princess of Orange 182
To the Continent 184
An Italian Caller 186
The Death of a Princess 189
Back to Britain 191
A Queen on Trial 194
If Your Name's Not Down… 197
'I Be Tired of This Life' 200

Afterword 203
Bibliography 204
Index 215

Acknowledgements

May the warmth of thanks radiate a rosy glow for all the team at Pen and Sword Books, especially Jon and Lauren. Thanks also to Lucy, the finest, fiercest editor an author could wish for.

For fudge, tea and a comfy bed, a big thank you is also due to the amazing folks of The Foxglove, Bex's, Beck Hall and T&Cake, the warmest establishments in the Yorkshire wilds. The kettle is always on for anyone who has ever taken a moment to read my eighteenth century ramblings. And for those who have stopped by the virtual salon, or have just encouraged and nudged me along in my pursuit of Georgian fabulousness.

For friends hither and thither, on this side of the world and the other, never, ever stop being amazing and Kathryn, keep your clapper handy.

Adrian and Caroline, you have rocked my world in a most eighteenth century sense!

To Pippa, Nel and Custard, how adorable can one trio get?

And especially for the Rakish Colonial – now you know *exactly* what a queen consort is!

List of Illustrations

1. Sophia Dorothea of Celle.
2. Caroline of Ansbach. Philip van Gunst.
3. Her Most Gracious Majesty Queen Charlotte. Thomas Ryder, after Sir William Beechey.
4. Caroline, Princess of Wales. John Murphy, after Thomas Stothard. 1795.
5. Bartolomo Bergami.
6. Queen Charlotte and George Prince of Wales. 1765, Robert Pile, after Richard Houston.
7. The murder of Count von Königsmarck.
8. Caroline of Ansbach. Alexander van Haecken, after Jacopo Amigoni, 1736.
9. Horace Walpole. Henry Hoppner Meyer, after Sir Thomas Lawrence. 1795.
10. HRH Caroline, Princess of Wales and the Princess Charlotte. Francesco Bartolozzi, after Richard Cosway. 1799.
11. George III and his Family. Richard Earlom, after Johann Zoffany.
12. His Majesty King George III returning to Town from Windsor with an Escort of 10th Prince of Wales' Own Light Dragoons. Charles Turner, after Richard Barret Davis. 1806.
13. Robert Walpole, First Earl of Oxford. Jacobus Houbraken, after Arthur Pond. 1746.
14. Henry Brougham, first Baron Brougham and Vaux. Charles Wagstaff, after Comte Alfred d'Orsay.
15. Charlotte, Queen of Great Britain.
16. Her Most Gracious Majesty Caroline, Queen of England. T Wageman, after Thomas Woolnoth. 1810.

17. Queen Caroline, wife of King George IV, is greeted by people from Marylebone. Theodore Edward Hook. 1820.
18. Caroline R (Queen of England). Abraham Wivell. 1820.
19. Her Majesty Queen Charlotte. Sir William Beechey. 1809.
20. The present royal family: George III, Queen Charlotte, Princess of Wales, Duchess of York. 1795.
21. Charlotte of Mecklenburg-Strelitz. Henrik Roosing. 1789.
22. Caroline of Ansbach. Leonard Schenk, after Adolf van der Laan. 1727.
23. The Prince and Princess of Wales. Francesco Bartolozzi, after H de Janvry, 1797.
24. Sophia Dorothea of Celle.
25. Funeral procession of a queen, probably Caroline of Brunswick, passing through Hammersmith in London. C Canton, after R. Banks.
26. Charlotte, Queen of Great Britain, and the Princess Royal. Valentine Green, after Benjamin West.
27. Queen Charlotte Sophia holding a baby.
28. The death bed of Queen Caroline. 1827.
29. The Royal Dozen.
30. Funeral procession of a Queen, possibly Queen Caroline. 1821.
31. Queen Charlotte. Richard Houston, after Johann Zoffany.
32. The grossly agitated King and Queen seated in a latrine to receive a message from the emaciated Pitt; satirizing the Royal reaction to news of the King of Sweden's assassination. James Gillray. 1792.

Introduction

Four kings, five wives, three queens

One divorce, one secret marriage… and all sorts of scandal.

It reads like a particularly saucy maths problem.

No doubt at least two of those monarchs had wished that a theoretical sum was all it had happened to be, but not even kings of Great Britain can make a troublesome wife disappear.

Electors of Hanover, of course, might be another matter…

Welcome to the world of the Georgian queen consorts. These are the women who occupied the throne beside the bad-tempered George II, the occasionally mad George III and the always notorious George IV. Their tales are far from fairy stories, romantic bliss all too often eluding our eighteenth century royal couples, but for better or worse, there was always *something* going on.

The one thing these women have in common is that none of them were born in the country that would eventually become their home. Their backgrounds and lives differed wildly, their stories lurched from *sort of* happy all the way to downright murderous but whether they hailed from Celle, Ansbach, Mecklenburg-Strelitz or Brunswick, their names have gone down in the history of the British Isles.

From canvasses by Reynolds, Kneller, Gainsborough and a dozen other illustrious names, the queens have been immortalized to peer down through the centuries. They are clad in velvet and ermine, self-possessed, knowing, wistful and sometimes just a little bit *insolent*, but who were the women behind the powder and pomp? Through tumultuous times, they steered the ships of marriage, family and even government, negotiating childhood, matrimony, pregnancy and the ever-challenging, ever-changing vagaries of the British court. In a world where a wedding could start a dynasty or end a war, shake a continent or splash scandals across the newspapers of Europe, the role of a queen was not one to be entered into lightly.

After all, it wasn't all state visits, boundless adoration and eating bonbons whilst lounging on a Chippendale couch. There was plenty of splendour of course, but whether you had one child or managed to produce enough offspring to start your own rather regal football team, a Georgian queen hadn't simply landed a husband, she had committed to a full-time job.

Prepare to meet the doomed Sophia Dorothea of Celle, the sharp-minded Caroline of Ansbach, the devoted Charlotte of Mecklenburg–Strelitz and the gadabout Caroline of Brunswick. Thrust into an unfamiliar land where intrigue, romance, drama and tragedy were the staples of life, these women occupied a spot at the very pinnacle of society. In *Queens of Georgian Britain* you will meet their crowned husbands, get to know their children and peek in on one or two *very* private moments. We shall take a scandalous trip to the continent, settle beside a stinking deathbed and endure some awfully public embarrassments, courtesy of some even more infamous sons.

The women you are about to meet lived fascinating, complex lives during one of the most turbulent periods in British history. So, find a seat in the salon, don your finest court dress and prepare to meet the queens of Georgian Britain.

Act I

Sophia Dorothea of Celle

(Celle, Germany, 15 September 1666 – Ahlden, Germany, 13 November 1726)

What are Rules if Not to be Broken?

You might not have heard of Sophia Dorothea of Celle, and you won't find her included on any lists of queens because, simply put, she wasn't one. She *was* an Electoral Princess and the wife of the man who became King George I of Great Britain and Ireland. Yet by the time her husband arrived in his new realm, their marriage was long since over.

Sophia Dorothea doesn't strictly belong in these pages at all but I'm happy to invoke authorial privilege, rules be damned. After all, without her there would have been no George II and the royal houses of the United Kingdom might have looked very different indeed.

Besides, it'd be a right royal shame *not* to tell the tale of why Great Britain never had a Queen Sophia Dorothea to call its own.

Love at First Sight

The first thing to know is that, once upon a time, it was not at all unusual to marry your cousin. In fact, when territory, money and title were at stake, it was positively encouraged.

And it didn't always go well.

In Celle in the distant 1660s, a storm was brewing. At the heart of it were brothers George William and Ernest Augustus, two of the four Dukes of Brunswick-Lüneburg. Together with their siblings, the pair ruled the family territories, each sitting in control of his own realm.

All of that was about to change.

In 1660, Ernest Augustus, the youngest of the four brothers from Brunswick-Lüneburg, became the father of a newborn boy. This boy, who would one day be King George I, was the only male heir to have been born to any of the brothers and that made him more valuable than the newborn could ever hope to comprehend. Little George, slumbering in his cradle, was *so far* the sole heir to the territories that his family possessed yet should any of his uncles also become father to a boy, he would stand to lose at least a share of his bounty.

George's father, Ernest Augustus, had no intention of letting that happen. He knew all too well the problems that brothers could bring. After all, he had even married the woman who might once have been his sister-in-law.

Early in his life, George William, Sophia Dorothea's father and the future George I's uncle, had been unwillingly betrothed to Sophia of the Palatinate. The thought of an arranged marriage chilled him to the marrow so he turned to his little brother, Ernest Augustus, for help. Ernest Augustus, of course, was delighted to comply. He would take Sophia off his brother's hands and marry her himself on two conditions.

And what conditions they *were*.

First, George William was to hand over the territory of Lüneburg to Ernest Augustus. Second and most importantly, he must promise *never* to marry, thus ensuring he would never be able to produce an heir to challenge ownership of those lands he had surrendered. George William must have been really keen *not* to hitch himself to Sophia because he agreed to the terms and handed his fiancée to his brother as though she were nothing but a pair of ill-fitting shoes. So far, so good, Ernest Augustus no doubt thought, but George William soon realized that a promise like that was exceedingly difficult to keep.

All might have gone well were it not for a fateful trip undertaken in 1664 when Éléonore d'Esmier d'Olbreuse, a noblewoman, who served as lady-in-waiting to the Duchess of Thouars, accompanied her mistress on a journey to Kassel. During the visit, Éléonore met George William and in true fairytale style, 'being of an amorous, though not of a marrying disposition, he fell in love at first sight'.[1]

---

1. Wilkins, WH (1900). *The Love of an Uncrowned Queen*. London: Hutchinson & Co, p.8.

Just a year after they met, George William asked his beloved Éléonore for her hand and she was delighted to accept. Due to her lesser social status their marriage was morganatic, meaning that Éléonore and any children born of the marriage would be unable to inherit the titles and privileges of the higher-ranking George William. Neither bride nor groom cared though; all they wanted was one another, and legitimately or otherwise, they were wed.

Just one year after the marriage, the couple's only child was born. She was Sophia Dorothea of Celle, the ill-fated future wife of George I.

Adolescent Fancies

Although Sophia, future Electress of Hanover and mother of George I, was one of the most ambitious ladies on the continental stage, Éléonore wasn't far behind her. She had big plans for her little girl and wasn't about to sit back and let her only child be sidelined. Instead she set about orchestrating a popularity campaign that would make any modern celebrity green with envy. With Sophia's dislike for her sister-in-law growing more pronounced with every new escapade, Éléonore encouraged her husband to purchase new territories that would be his to bequeath as he wished, regardless of his promise to his brother.

With Sophia working on a counter-attack intended to undermine and discredit the upstart Éléonore, behind the scenes, tales of intrigue and scandal were soon swirling. Although she no doubt heard the gossip of ambition and avarice, the unflappable Huguenot pressed on regardless with her efforts on her daughter's behalf. Determined to prove herself of the finest stock, Éléonore employed a genealogist to trace her family line back to French royal blood. She made regular forays out to meet her adoring public with her daughter in tow and, crucially, did all she could to endear her household to the powers that be in the dominating Holy Roman Empire.

Éléonore's hard work would pay off years later when Emperor Leopold consented to recognize her marriage to George William, thus legitimizing young Sophia Dorothea. For the time being though, although Sophia Dorothea was a young lady of grace, humour and beauty, she was not one of rank. Princess or not, she *was* sole heiress to a fortune, which meant that

Sophia Dorothea could still enjoy the very best of everything, including scandal.

When she was only 12-years-old, it was discovered that Sophia Dorothea's governess had allowed her young charge to receive love notes from a court page. Although such youthful indiscretions would barely raise an eyebrow these days, the consequences at the time were enormous. Both page and governess were exiled and Sophia Dorothea, perhaps having displayed a little more spirit than her parents would have liked, was temporarily moved into her mother's quarters.

In the years to come, secret notes would cause all *sorts* of trouble…

Encountering the Count

The little girl who so enchanted the people of Celle would not stay a child forever and as the years passed, the pretty youngster began to mature into a beauty with glossy dark hair and milk white skin. Good looks, money, land and influence were quite a combination and the young men of Europe and their ambitious families began to take note of this most eligible young lady. Gadding about the palace gardens of Celle, however, Sophia Dorothea had some romantic ideas of her own.

When she was little more than a girl, whilst strolling in the grounds, she met a young man who was in her homeland training for the military. Just one year older than Sophia Dorothea, Count Philip Christoph von Königsmarck was the son of a wealthy and respectable family, and he and the young lady became firm friends. In time that teenage friendship would end in murder and heartbreak but for now, life was innocent and the balmy days were long.

The young man was as handsome as Sophia Dorothea was beautiful and it was the start of a partnership that was intense and abiding. Whether they dreamed of a life beyond childhood and innocent friendship we cannot know, but given what came later, it's tempting to speculate that an adolescent fancy had blossomed between them. Whatever the truth of the matter, when Sophia Dorothea and Königsmarck danced together at a ball, the excitable court came alive with gossip. After all, Sophia Dorothea was already approaching marrying age and with Philip's finances and pedigree, his family too would be looking for the right woman to further their line. Marriage to the ruling house of Celle would be a good catch for them, but yoking her daughter to mere minor nobles fell short of Éléonore's ambition.

Although her own marriage had been of questionable legitimacy, Éléonore looked to the senior ranks of nobility for her future son-in-law. Her influence over George William seemingly knew no bounds and what she wanted, she usually got, so decisions over their only child's marital future were naturally left to her. Whatever games Sophia Dorothea and Philip were playing in the garden, they were about to come to a shuddering halt.

The Boy from Brunswick-Wolfenbüttel

Anthony Ulrich, Duke of Brunswick-Wolfenbüttel, the man the Duchess of Orleans rather unkindly called 'an ugly baboon',[2] had long been a favourite of the ambitious Éléonore. What he lacked in looks he made up for in intelligence, diplomatic ability and that same empire-building savvy that could make or break a seventeenth century noble.

As cousin to Éléonore's husband, he looked on with interest as the years passed and the lady's influence over her husband and his court grew. Nobody wielded more power than she, and George William trusted no one as he did his wife, the woman to whom it seemed that every decision fell. With one eye on Éléonore and the other on the rather stuffed coffers of Celle, the Duke of Brunswick-Wolfenbüttel let his imagination run wild with dreams of what he might make of his own territories if he could get his hands on some of that money. For the cash-strapped duke, uniting his family with that of George William might just be the making of him.

Initial correspondence with Éléonore was favourable and when Anthony Ulrich made a trip to Celle, he found that he and the lady were kindred spirits indeed. Each was ambitious, canny and keen to progress and in the other, both saw the stepping stones to do just that. Éléonore's bargaining chip was the dowry of 100,000 thalers that she could offer to Sophia Dorothea's future husband and Anthony Ulrich's selling point was the royal prestige of his eldest son, Crown Prince Augustus Frederick.

Let the negotiations commence.

---

2. Ibid., p.21.

Although all the parents involved liked the sound of the prospective marriage, there was a considerable obstacle in the way of the supposed happy ending. Augustus Frederick was bona fide royalty, a *crown prince*. For all her money and finery, Sophia Dorothea had been born into a morganatic marriage and Sophia, the woman who had married Ernest Augustus, was always quick to *helpfully* remind her sister-in-law of that fact. Their initially cool but steady relationship blossomed, thanks to gossip and intrigue, into all-out hatred and the women mounted something of a battle of wits, each striving to outdo the other.

If Éléonore could ensnare the crown prince, it would be a social poke in the eye for Sophia and Ernest Augustus, whom she believed had contrived to deprive her husband of his rightful inheritance. Indeed, though Éléonore's left-handed marriage to George William had annoyed the Hanoverian couple to start with, the decision to legitimize it and break the promise made all those years ago completely, would no doubt have enraged Sophia and Ernest Augustus.

Tough.

Keen for the marriage to progress, Anthony Ulrich proposed a solution. He suggested that the morganatic marriage between Éléonore and George William should be legitimized. This would elevate Éléonore to the rank of duchess and give Sophia Dorothea the longed-for title of princess, neatly clearing the way for her to wed a crown prince without raising too many eyebrows. Unsurprisingly, Éléonore loved the idea and took it to her compliant husband, who gave the plan his blessing.

Making the Marriage

In 1676, the Bishop of Osnabrück, aka Ernest Augustus, who had inherited the title, was presented with the request to sanctify and legalize the marriage that his brother had once promised never to pursue. Although one might expect him to be dubious, Ernest Augustus was rather heartened by the fact that a document had been drawn up that protected his own rights, making it inarguably clear that his interests would not suffer. George William was heartened for another reason, for that same legal contract would ensure beyond a doubt that his family could only *benefit* from the stringent conditions.

The document stated, amongst other clauses:

' 1. The Bishop [Ernest Augustus] promises not to oppose the said marriage, but will acknowledge and countenance the said Countess [Éléonore], and the children that may be born of this marriage; and also the daughter now living, Sophia Dorothea, agreeing to uphold her in the possession of her estates, and in her state and rank conferred upon her, and which may be conferred upon her, by the Emperor, and his Serene Highness Duke George William, in so far as such may not be to the prejudice of the heirs of the Bishop, as regards the sovereignty of this Duchy and its appurtenances.

2. The heirs of the Bishop are bound to respect the Duke's settlement on the Countess and her heirs.

3. The Duke promises that this marriage shall not be to the disadvantage of the Bishop or his male heirs [...]

4. Should one or more children be born in this marriage, they are to remain satisfied with the property the Duke, with the consent of the Bishop, may leave them at his decease and renounce any pretension to the Duchy and its appurtenances, as long as male heirs exist in the Bishop's family.

5. Neither sons nor daughters born of this marriage can be permitted to make use of the Ducal coat of arms; but should Sophia Dorothea marry a prince of ancient family, she will be allowed to use the title and coat of arms of a princess by birth of Brunswick-Lüneburg.

[...]

12. Should the lady be further blessed with offspring, the Duke agrees to publish to all his subjects, that, after his death the succession must rest with the Bishop, and descend from him, from father to son, according to an arrangement made when the Duke first entered upon the government as his own offspring will be otherwise provided for at his decease.

In the foregoing stipulation, a great deal is stated respecting the Duke's anxious desire for the peace and welfare of his people having led him to enter into this arrangement, and his hope that after his decease they will be faithful and obedient to the successor whom he has appointed them.

[...]

Lastly, the Duke will write to his brother Duke John Frederick, and to his cousin Duke Rodolph Augustus, the necessary information for the benefit of their princely family, with a request that, for the preservation of peace and the good of the country, this agreement may be respected.'[3]

Although this certainly satisfied Ernest Augustus, what might have happened in the future should any male heirs have been born, we can't really guess. A later agreement makes this even more explicit, containing the clause that:

'Any other children who may be hereafter born in this wedlock must content themselves with the titles of Counts and Countesses of Wilhelmsburg, and they can make no pretences to the succession to the duchy, which is bestowed on Ernest Augustus Bishop of Osnabrück and his heirs male.'[4]

Certainly it rather brutally dismisses any rights, claims and privileges that any future heirs might believe themselves to hold. If it seems like a blunt instrument designed solely to facilitate the smooth path of the marriage, that's exactly what it was. Of course, the final contract, drafted in poker-faced legal jargon, doesn't tell the full story of the no doubt hard-fought discussions that went into finalizing something that would be palatable for both brothers, but the deed was done for now.

With both George William and Ernest Augustus putting their signatures to the contract, a second was drawn up to ensure that Sophia Dorothea was

3. Williams, Robert Folkestone (1845). *Memoirs of Sophia Dorothea, Consort of George I, Vol I*. London: Henry Colburn, pp.36–40.
4. Wilkins, WH (1900). *The Love of an Uncrowned Queen*. London: Hutchinson & Co, p.23.

given that all-important title of princess. Anthony Ulrich, Ernest Augustus and George William signed their names and the deal was agreed. After years of a rather questionable status, the marriage of George William and Éléonore was legal, the lady was finally a duchess and Sophia of Hanover, Éléonore's courtly enemy, had egg all over her rather disapproving face.

'That the children born of this marriage shall be called Counts and Countesses of Wilhelmsburg, but should Sophia Dorothea marry into a princely family, she should enjoy the title of Duchess of Brunswick-Lüneburg. All that the Duke has bequeathed to them from his allodial estates, and to which no one can prevent their succeeding, to belong to them as their property. Furthermore, ten thousand thalers are to be paid to the Duchess at the decease of her husband ; and she is also to have as a dowry the Castle of Lüneburg, and an annual income of eight thousand thalers. All this, at her death, is to revert to the sovereign; but her unsatisfied claims are to be paid to her heirs.'[5]

So that was that. The marriage was legal and Sophia Dorothea was set for life as the wife of Crown Prince Augustus Frederick.

How fate can turn.

A Fatal Cannonball

On 9 August 1676, Augustus Frederick took a cannonball to the head at the Siege of Philippsburg and died of his catastrophic injuries. Never mind, said the duke, because he had *another* son who could step into the breach, so the plans could continue after a respectable period of mourning. Though Éléonore was heartily behind the idea, George William was less keen. A man of superstition, he regarded the violent death of the crown prince as an ill omen and was reluctant to accept the proffered substitute. The best he would give was a half-hearted promise to think about it, asking the duke to return to Celle on Sophia Dorothea's sixteenth birthday. Then,

5. Williams, Robert Folkestone (1845). *Memoirs of Sophia Dorothea, Consort of George I, Vol I*. London: Henry Colburn, p.41.

he promised, he would be in a better position to decide whether or not to accept the proposal.

In Hanover, rather scheming wheels were turning, and at the head of affairs sat Sophia, wife of Ernest Augustus, mother of the future George I and sworn enemy of Éléonore. Although she disliked Sophia Dorothea's mother with a passion, Sophia wasn't so blinkered that she would let her personal feelings stand in the way of her dynastic ambition. Plans to marry George off to England's Princess Anne had come to nothing and now the search was on for another suitable girl. Though George William didn't know it, the House of Hanover had a valuable mole in Celle in the shape of Prime Minister Bernstorff, a man of limitless ambition. He saw the value in uniting the duchy of Celle with Hanover and was determined to use every opportunity to make a case for Sophia's son, George.

His opposite number in Hanover, at least in terms of ambition and influence, was Clara Elisabeth von Meysenburg, Countess of Platen and Hallermund, the long-time mistress of Ernest Augustus and wife of the Prime Minister of Hanover. She was also the sister of one of George's many mistresses, so it might be said that she had plenty of fingers in plenty of pies. Nothing at the Hanoverian court escaped her attention, no matter how seemingly insignificant.

Clara too wanted to ensure that nothing could threaten the dominance of Hanover and was keen to unite with Celle. Seeing in Bernstorff a man whose ambition mirrored her own, she invited him to work on George William and sweetened the request with the gift of a gold snuffbox, studded with diamonds. As Clara whispered Sophia Dorothea's many good points into her lover's ear in the bedroom, her husband did the same in the debating chamber whilst across in Celle, Bernstorff worked to convince George William of the benefits of the young Hanoverian.

That young man, later the first king of the House of Hanover, was born in 1660 and was destined for great things. Hanover was on track to become the ninth electorate of the Holy Roman Empire and thanks to his father's ruthless ambition and self-promotion, George would one day inherit all of the territories currently shared by his uncles. Sophia Dorothea was, of course, his cousin, and what better way to lessen the chances of future trouble or unwanted claims to the territory of Hanover than to keep any marriages strictly in the family?

Time was of the essence though as once again Duke Anthony Ulrich of Brunswick-Wolfenbüttel was knocking at the door of Celle, yet another son at his side. Though Bernstorff was influential in securing the delay until Sophia Dorothea's sixteenth birthday, they couldn't wait forever. If Sophia wanted her boy to marry the young princess then there was no time to lose, she had to move *now*, so that's exactly what she did.

Sophia Goes to Celle

Years after George William rejected Sophia and passed her onto his brother, the matriarch of Hanover came once more to Celle. Now though, she was no longer the pawn in a game of marriage, but a key player. She was the one who could negotiate, bargain and change the path of her family's fate forever.

The imperious duchess travelled through a storm-lashed night to beat the Duke of Brunswick-Wolfenbüttel to her brother-in-law's home on the day that his daughter was due to turn 16. Dismissing the ceremony and propriety that had dictated her whole life, she stalked through the castle and into George William's chambers where, as dawn broke, she surprised both the duke and duchess by her unexpected appearance.

Conducting herself in Dutch, a language of which Éléonore had no knowledge, Sophia told George William that she was here to negotiate a marriage between his only daughter and her eldest son. It was time to mend the bridges that had been burned, she implored, and to put right all that had gone wrong between Celle and Hanover once and for all.

It was time for a happy ending.

George William was so thrilled by the olive branch that promised to reunite him with his brother that he utterly lost his head. Rather than properly consult his wife, the woman who had been his rock for years, he rather foolishly accepted Sophia's offer there and then.

After so many years spent courting Duke Anthony Ulrich of Brunswick-Wolfenbüttel, so many years in which the courts of Hanover and Celle had endured a war of attrition, the news hit Éléonore as hard as that cannonball had hit the crown prince. In vain, she begged her husband to reconsider yet George William had had enough. He wasn't getting any younger and his family, with its territorial splits, had been riven with division for too long.

With the duke due later that very day and Sophia Dorothea looking forward to celebrating her birthday, it was to be a far from a happy occasion.

It was left to Éléonore to tell her daughter of the fate that awaited her. With a heavy heart, she told the young lady of the forthcoming marriage and no doubt waited for the fireworks.

She was not to be disappointed.

Sophia Dorothea snatched up George's miniature and glared at it, railing against the man who had been chosen for her. Furiously she told her mother, 'I will not marry the pig snout!'[6] and she smashed the trinket against the wall, splintering it into fragments. If we were being fanciful, we might ascribe this unwillingness to her adoration for Count Philip Christoph von Königsmarck, by now off on manoeuvres elsewhere, or even wonder whether she had already fallen for the *second* offering from Brunswick-Wolfenbüttel. Of course, the truth is somewhat more prosaic.

Think of Sophia Dorothea: spoiled, pampered, adored, the apple of her parents' eyes. For sixteen years she had grown up in Celle, hearing grim stories of the austere and strict court of Hanover, the place where duty and ceremony trumped everything. She had been raised to believe her mother was loathed by Sophia and that Sophia, in turn, was a cold-hearted monster, her eldest son a joyless, humourless sourpuss despite his young age. Now that ill-humoured young man was to be her husband, his battleaxe mother was to be her mother-in-law and her own father, the man she had wrapped around her little finger, was doing nothing to stop the union.

It must have seemed like the very world was ending for the beautiful young princess, and when Duke Anthony Ulrich of Brunswick-Wolfenbüttel arrived just as Sophia of Hanover was settling in for morning refreshments, it was she who was at George William's side to welcome the visitors. Both mother and daughter were indisposed and unable to receive callers, George William explained, moments before the triumphant duchess shared the news of the *happy* betrothal. Perhaps the visitors from Brunswick-Wolfenbüttel might like to stay in Celle, she asked benevolently, and celebrate the birthday and engagement with dinner?

---

6. Morand, Paul (1972). *The Captive Princess: Sophia Dorothea of Celle*. Florida: American Heritage Press, p.23.

The duke's reply was to get back into his carriage and leave as fast as his horses could carry him.

In fact, Duke Anthony Ulrich later got a rather public revenge when he adapted the events into his 1708 work, *Roman Octavia*. Although the names had been changed, there can have been no doubt whom the characters were intended to represent, nor his take on the key players. Duchess Sophia's fictional counterpart is a single-minded harridan, her son a brutish oaf whilst the unfortunate Sophia Dorothea is little short of an angel. Perhaps the duke felt better for getting it off his chest, but it would be too late to help the unfortunate young woman.

Meeting the Husband

Of course, if Sophia Dorothea had spent a lifetime being told that the courtiers of the House of Hanover were not to be trusted, then George had been told exactly the same thing about those who lived in Celle. A young man who liked to mix and match mistresses, he had no wish to be saddled with even a wealthy bride, and when he arrived at Celle the day after his mother's audacious swoop, he found a far from happy house.

Both Éléonore and Sophia Dorothea were muted and unhappy, whilst George William was annoyed at the two of them for making things so darned difficult. Quite by contrast, George's father, Ernest Augustus, was delighted at what his wife had achieved yet the young man was as sullen as could be.

Sophia Dorothea's adoring and occasionally florid biographer, WH Wilkins, leaves the reader in no doubt that she was quite a catch. He cannot imagine what George found to dislike, commenting lovingly:

'She was brunette, with dark brown, almost black hair, large velvety eyes, regular features, brilliant complexion, and the veriest little red rosebud of a mouth. Her figure was perfectly proportioned: she had an exquisite neck and bust, and slender little hands and feet. She had nothing in common with the large-waisted, flat-footed German princesses of the period [...]'[7]

---

7. Wilkins, WH (1900). *The Love of an Uncrowned Queen*. London: Hutchinson & Co, p.54.

George had mistresses, of course, and he was really in no rush to marry so it's perhaps a little one-sided to assume he was the villain in this particular piece. Although there can be no doubt that he would gain far more from the marriage than his wife, it wasn't a match he had conspired to achieve, but one that they were both stuck with. In case he had any doubts about his prospective bride's opinion, Sophia Dorothea fainted clean away on their first meeting, quite overcome with despair.

She couldn't stay out cold forever, of course, and the marriage plans carried on regardless. The groom's ambitious mother handled the arrangements with aplomb and told her friend:

'[…] George Louis [is] the most pigheaded, stubborn boy who ever lived, and who has round his brains such a thick crust that I defy any man or woman ever to discover what is in them. He does not care much for the match itself, but one hundred thousand thalers a year have tempted him as they would have tempted anybody else.'[8]

Ouch.

On 22 November 1682, the unhappy cousins were joined in marriage. The festivities went on for days, continuing long into December when the newlyweds arrived in their new home in Hanover.

There was to be *no* fairytale ending.

The Electoral Princess

Despite Sophia Dorothea's despair at the marriage, at first things didn't go as badly as we might suspect. No doubt her integration into life in Hanover was helped by the fact that her new father-in-law, Ernest Augustus, found the young lady to be diverting company. In fact, he became quite a champion of his daughter-in-law and winning his approval was part of the battle won. At least the princess had an ally at a court full of strangers, if nothing else.

Sophia Dorothea had much to learn of court life and set herself to it with some devotion at first, though her enthusiasm quite understandably began

---

8. Ibid., p.57.

to wane as the long months of stifling protocol passed. Used to having things all her own way, to being the sole child of parents who adored her, Sophia Dorothea was no longer the centre of everyone's attention, but an incomer who had to hit the ground running. Not unlike Marie Antoinette when she negotiated the bewildering world of Bourbon etiquette at Versailles, Sophia Dorothea found herself bombarded and bewildered by the rules that now governed her life.

Although earlier biographers stressed the mutual dislike that existed between bride and groom, Ragnhild Hatton took a different view. She relates a letter Duchess Sophia wrote in which she described her son's passion for his new wife, painting a picture of a couple very much in love. Of course, this might have been lip service but perhaps the newlyweds had decided to make the best of things and see if they could salvage something from the situation into which they had been plunged. After all, Sophia Dorothea had been raised by Éléonore to be a social climber and we might suspect that her reluctance to allow her daughter to marry into the Hanoverian court had less to do with parental protection and more to do with getting one over on Sophia, her sworn enemy. Hatton speculates that the ambitious and spoiled Sophia Dorothea rather enjoyed her new position and the promise of power the marriage brought with it. In truth, she probably *did*, for she had been raised as a realist and was hardly going to stay unhappy forever.

Still, one can only imagine that the young bride must have allowed herself to hope that life wasn't going to be as bad as she had feared and the first stepping stone was giving the family an heir. News that Sophia Dorothea was with child caused great rejoicing, and when she gave birth to a boy, on 9 November 1683, the whole of Hanover celebrated. Destined to one day rule as George II, the little boy was in a unique position, as Ernest Augustus was about to announce.

With so many brothers sharing his dynastic territories, Ernest Augustus had navigated rather choppy waters to get to where he was today. He knew that if he was ever to achieve his dreams of seeing Hanover made an electorate, then things had to change. It needed to be strong, both politically and militarily, and any number of brothers tussling over the dukedom and its shared territories was never going to work.

Had George been an only child this wouldn't have been a problem but he wasn't, and Ernest Augustus was determined that his eldest son wouldn't face the same obstacles that had blighted his own ambition. He had half a dozen sons and all would one day be hungry for power, so something had to be done to stop the squabbles before they started.

The answer, which Ernest Augustus first considered in 1682, was primogeniture. This would mean that George would one day inherit everything, with his younger brothers offered rich payment should they agree with the decision. Although it wasn't until 1684 that the House of Hanover accepted primogeniture, no doubt Sophia Dorothea was aware of what this would mean for her newborn son. As George's brothers battled and feuded with their father, the future of his firstborn was being decided. Soon it was a foregone conclusion that the little boy who slumbered in his cradle would one day stand to inherit Hanover.

With the birth of a son, relations between the princess and her mother-in-law became rather more cordial and when Sophia Dorothea followed George to Italy where he had been fighting, she was happy to leave her child with the duchess. Entrusted to Katharine von Harling, who had cared for the older George in childhood, the infant was in safe hands.

He would soon be joined by a sister and a whole lot of domestic discord.

With George often away and his wife never one for governing her tongue, who should come scheming out of the woodwork but Clara, Countess of Platen and Hallermund. The woman who had once conspired to ensure that Sophia Dorothea and George were wed was in the mood for mischief and when Sophia Dorothea took up with a lively and notorious Frenchman, Clara could not have been more delighted!

Liaisons with Lassay

When Sophia Dorothea arrived in Italy with her father-in-law, she found herself in the midst of carnival celebrations. For one so full of enthusiasm and zest as the young princess, such colour and life must have seemed dazzling after the stifling court and she threw herself headlong into the fun.

The rather cold-blooded George found his wife's enthusiasm a little trying and if Sophia Dorothea hoped he might gad about with her, she was to be disappointed. Instead George left her to make her own entertainment and as the delightedly scandalized Hanoverian gossips whispered, she *certainly* did that.

Also enjoying the carnival was one Marquis de Lassay, a well-known rake and all-round saucy sort. Lassay, never one to be shy when being indiscreet would do, began boasting all over the city that he had bedded Sophia Dorothea and in Hanover, the supposed couple was soon the talk of the court.

Perhaps surprisingly, the meddlesome Clara told Duchess Sophia not to fret, suggesting that a man like Lassay was a far from trustworthy source. Years later he published the love letters he had sent to Sophia Dorothea yet it's worth noting that there appeared to be no response from the lady herself. Lassay's list of lovers is as long as it is unlikely and contains some great beauties and famous names that he collected as other men might collect stamps. George never spoke of this gossip, but it seems difficult to believe he hadn't heard it. For now at least, the couple was not completely at odds; in fact, they were on good enough terms to ensure that when Sophia Dorothea returned to Hanover, she was pregnant once more.

But things took a distinctly darker turn as Clara played her masterstroke. She did nothing more mischievous than make an introduction or two but that was all it took. For a man as vain and pompous as George a kind word from an attractive woman could do wonders and Clara knew that full well when she welcomed two friends into the heart of the House of Hanover. With one fell swoop, into George's life came a pair of women who would be at his side for decades, the notorious duo of *the Elephant* and *the Maypole*.

The Elephant was none other than the daughter of the scheming Clara, Sophia von Kielmansegg. Rumours that she might also be the child of Ernest Augustus swept the court as her friendship with George grew as close as any sister or even, if one were a little more bawdy, lover. Though gossips whispered that he was sleeping with his own half-sibling, neither proof of an affair nor her paternal parentage were ever satisfactorily established. More damaging to the marriage of George and Sophia Dorothea was Clara's friend, Melusine von der Schulenberg, whose skinny frame earned her the nickname, *the Maypole*.

Melusine was a Maid of Honour to George's mother and when Clara introduced her to George, the attraction was immediate.[9] As the affair burgeoned with the couple making no effort to hide it, Sophia Dorothea was horrified. Pregnant and increasingly isolated as the influence of Clara and Melusine grew unchecked, there was nothing the young mother-to-be could do other than withdraw into herself and the company of her friend and lady-in-waiting, Eléonore von dem Knesebeck. Sophia Dorothea had Ernest Augustus's admiration but in the hothouse of the court, even that was of limited use.

No doubt Sophia Dorothea hoped that things might still be set right because she threw herself on her husband's mercy and asked if their marriage could be saved, begging him to tell her if she had caused him some upset. George furiously dismissed her and went back to the loving arms of Melusine.

Sophia Dorothea delivered a daughter who shared her name in 1687 and from that day to her last, bore no more children. Now the strained relationship between husband and wife began to fracture and split, and the seeds of tragedy started to take root. Things were not helped when Sophia Dorothea once again begged her husband to tell her what had come between them and he seized her violently, almost throttling her. After this assault, there would be no more overtures from the young bride, only a swift descent into misery and isolation.

The Count and Clara

Years after they had played in the gardens of Celle, with marriage, military service and adventuring having come between them, Count Philip Christoph von Königsmarck strutted back into Sophia Dorothea's life. In the years that had passed since their friendship began, the count had enjoyed a distinguished military service and had cultivated a rather dashing reputation as a man of action, a chap who was cultured, charming and had no shortage of female admirers.

---

9. The couple eventually had three children.

The pair renewed their friendship at a glittering masked ball when Sophia Dorothea was in the deepest depths of unhappiness thanks to the conduct of her husband, and the count offered her a chance to feel adored once more. She wasn't the only one to be charmed by him though, as everywhere the rich, urbane young man went, he was feted by the ladies who threw themselves in his path.

One of those ladies was, of course, the rather keen Clara. She no doubt recognized that there was an attraction between Sophia Dorothea and the count but for now at least, the princess was attempting to resist it. The alluring Clara had no such scruples and after she showered Königsmarck with praise for his ability on the dance floor, it was just a matter of time before she would be showering him with praise in the bedroom too.

Sophia Dorothea was horrified to hear from gossips that Clara and Königsmarck were lovers, though perhaps not surprised given the older woman's influence at court and rumoured sexual prowess. However, what was intended to be an uncomplicated bit of fun soon proved to be anything but as Clara became her lover's constant shadow. There was no escape from the countess, it seemed, and no doubt Sophia Dorothea thought Königsmarck deserved his fate but he wasn't about to accept it. Instead he joined a military campaign in the Balkans, leaving Hanover far behind. Although Clara was furious at his desertion, Sophia Dorothea wished her friend well. Such kind sentiments meant more to Königsmarck than any of Clara's furious remonstrations ever would, and the countess was not about to forget that.

The Count Returns

With George off fighting for Hanover in Flanders, in 1690 news reached home that the dashing Count Königsmarck was lost, believed killed alongside George's brother, Karl Philipp. As the court was plunged into mourning for their lost prince, Sophia Dorothea pined for the friend she had thought lost forever. Before his disappearance, the couple had exchanged friendly letters and perhaps now, with hope seemingly gone, she realized that she wished to be more than a friend to him.

Although news of Karl Philipp's death was confirmed, for Königsmarck the future was brighter. He was neither dead nor captured, but alive and well. The friendship between the couple now burst into flames and their letters, though their authenticity has been hotly debated, leave us in no doubt that their relationship was about to progress far beyond platonic.

At first the declarations of adoration are couched in somewhat chivalrous terms, suggesting a little touch of Hanoverian courtly love as Königsmarck tells Sophia Dorothea that he is the most sombre chap whilst on manoeuvres. Not for him the drinking and whoring of others; he was keen for Sophia Dorothea to know that he longed only for 'a corner where I could daydream in comfort while the others danced, undressed and jumped up on the table.'[10]

Sophia Dorothea hid the letters in her rooms, sewing them into curtain linings and squirrelling them away wherever she might find a suitable spot. Mindful of discovery, the couple communicated via the intermediary of Königsmarck's sister, Aurora, and Sophia Dorothea's confidante, Eléonore von dem Knesebeck. Notes were left in hats and gloves, and the judicious women passed them along, yet for all the subterfuge, which eventually extended as far as writing in code, the court knew *exactly* what was afoot. Deciphered in the years that followed, Wilkins provided royal watchers with the following handy legend:

'All the personages mentioned in the letters are disguised under different names; as, for instance:

L'Aventuriere: Countess Aurora Konigsmarck.
Le Reformeur: Prince George Louis.
Don Diego: The Elector Ernest Augustus.
La Romaine: The Electress Sophia.
Le Grandeur: The Duke of Celle.
La Pedagogue: The Duchess of Celle.
La Perspective: The Countess Platen.

[…]

---

10. Morand, Paul (1972). *The Captive Princess: Sophia Dorothea of Celle*. Florida: American Heritage Press, p.97.

Some of these nicknames are not very complimentary to the persons for whom they are intended, but they are comparatively easy to decipher. The task is much more difficult when we come to the other code which was in figures. Speaking roughly, numbers of one hundred and upwards signify names of men; two hundred and upwards, names of women; three hundred and upwards, names of places.

As for example :

100: Elector Ernest Augustus.
101: Duke of Celle.
102: Prince George Louis.

[…]'[11]

The correspondence that began in 1691 continued for just shy of three years. Sophia Dorothea proved a graceful author, whereas Königsmarck's written French didn't match his spoken word and his letters were untidy, badly spelled and littered with errors. More solid evidence of the change in their relationship can be determined by something that required no words: an evocative wax seal.

At the start of the relationship, Königsmarck sealed his letters with the image of a flaming heart on an altar, lit by the blazing sun. In keeping with his rather florid attempts at courtly love, the words read, 'rien impure inallurne,' translated as 'nothing impure can set me on fire.' Yet by the time the seal had become one heart inside another and the words, 'cosi fosse il vostro dentro il mio,' ('thus might yours be inside mine'), we can probably assume that they were no longer simply discussing the weather!

Unless the weather in Hanover looks like this, of course:

'Oh God, if I ever saw you kiss anyone with as much passion as you have kissed me, and ride astride with the same desire, I never want to see God if it would not drive me mad.'[12]

---

11. Wilkins, WH (1900). *The Love of an Uncrowned Queen*. London: Hutchinson & Co, pp.126–127.
12. Morand, Paul (1972). *The Captive Princess: Sophia Dorothea of Celle*. Florida: American Heritage Press, p.85.

Young lovers they might be, but for Clara, this was all a little bit much. She knew better than to go straight to George with her suspicions and instead contrived a little intrigue and entertainment of her own.

All she needed was a glove…

A Fateful Glove

Returning to Hanover from military manoeuvres in 1691, Königsmarck celebrated his survival with a grand masked ball to which the great and good were invited.

And Clara was obviously there.

George had also returned of late, this time from Flanders, and he brought his wife the gift of a pair of lavishly embroidered gloves. Clara helped herself to one of them and, tucking it safely into her bosom, set off in pursuit of the count. This time, however, her motives were more wicked than wanton.

Königsmarck, dashing, arrogant and always a sucker for the attentions of a lady, allowed the masked Clara to tempt him away from the crowd and into the grounds of the palace. Here she set about her flirtatious pantomime, having already asked her husband to ensure that he and George arrived in that secluded spot before too much time had passed.

Hearing the sound of Count Platen and George approaching, the countess fled the scene, ditching Königsmarck and the glove there in the grounds. Seeing the rather fine figure of a lady in full flight abandoning her would-be paramour, the no doubt amused George asked Count Platen who she might have been. Platen pretended ignorance yet in a twist worthy of Cinderella, conveniently found the glove the woman had dropped. Innocently he handed it to George, who recognized the gift he had given his wife and said nothing, though rage seared in his heart. Just as Clara had intended, he believed himself betrayed, and it was a slight that he would not soon forget.

Königsmarck and Sophia Dorothea knew nothing of this and continued their affair, yet they did mention in correspondence that Clara's spies were watching. Though suspecting they were under surveillance they did little to allay any suspicions that might be growing. Instead their letters are full of a mutual and, it must be said, somewhat florid paranoia. Each seems convinced that the other is just *waiting* for a chance to stray, filling the pages with pleas to remain true, to forgive jealousies and suspicions with Königsmarck even appending his signature with the promise that his letters were *written in blood*. If nothing else, the dramatic couple seemed well-matched, at least!

In fact, when Königsmarck did finally share his bedroom with someone else, it wasn't a woman at all, but a rather more hairy proposition – a bear.

With his love away at the rural retreat of the Hanoverian court, the count wrote:

'I must tell you that I have a consolation here, close to me; not a pretty girl but a bear, which I feed. If you should fail me I will bare my chest and let him tear my heart out. I am teaching him that trick with sheep and calves, and he doesn't manage it badly. If ever I have need of him – God help me! I shall not suffer long.'[13]

As the gossip grew louder, Sophia Dorothea's mother implored her daughter to let things cool. Deaf to the warnings, the princess couldn't battle her passion for the count and after a particularly long break in which the two exchanged sometimes laughably jealous and suspicious letters, there is evidence of what can only have been an intimate liaison.

'I slept like a king, and I hope you did the same. What joy! What rapture! What enchantment have I not tasted in your sweet arms! Ye gods! What a night I spent! The memory of it blots out all my troubles, and for the moment I count myself the happiest man on earth. You see, it rests wholly with you to make me happy, and when I am sad you are the cause. Adieu, dear heart. How long the day will seem to me without seeing you! Adieu.'[14]

13. Wilkins, WH (1900). *The Love of an Uncrowned Queen*. London: Hutchinson & Co, p.148.
14. Ibid., p.165.

Towards the Future

For all the obstacles, both real and imagined, that might have torn the lovers apart, war was perhaps the most deadly. Alongside George, Königsmarck fought for Hanover in fierce battles that kept him from Sophia Dorothea for months at a time and left her in an agony of waiting for news of his fate. No doubt those around her thought her distraction and anxiety was for the husband who faced those same dangers, but in Sophia Dorothea's long and emotional missives to the count, George is relegated to eye-rolling, sigh-heaving annoyance.

> 'My father and mother have just interrupted me. I was writing this letter, and it was all I could do to hide it; it would have astonished them if they had seen it. They are very considerate and kind, but are always preaching to me to behave properly to the Prince. My father will not hear any jokes or ridicule at his expense, and therefore I do not speak to him as much as I should otherwise do. If you only knew how weary I am, you would never have the cruelty to leave me again. But I must not think of this; I must make up my mind to divide your heart with your love of glory. You have all mine. There is no room in it for anyone or anything – the desire to please you fills it entirely. I love you far more than you love me.'[15]

In truth, there is an immaturity in these letters that is as trying as it is surprising. The relationship is so mutually needy that the constant accusations, reproaches and endless self-flagellation become somewhat wearing. When Königsmarck admits to taking supper with Clara, Sophia Dorothea reacts as though he has absconded with the countess and married her! With letters written in blood, furious recriminations and passionate encounters, the affair truly did have something for everyone. Yet for George, there was only humiliation and the memory of that glove, so conveniently dropped at the location of a passionate liaison between two masked figures.

---

15. Ibid., p.212.

Reunited

It cannot be often that politics comes to the rescue of star-crossed lovers but when Königsmarck and George both returned from battle, that's exactly what happened. The court was gripped by political intrigue and feverish discussions of the possibility of Hanover becoming an electorate. This may seem like a rather dull subject given the drama that was unfolding in Sophia Dorothea's bedroom but the illustrious influence of the likes of Clara and her husband stood to skyrocket if the emperor accepted Hanover into the Holy Roman Empire.

So it was that George was required to travel to Berlin, leaving his wife happily at home to enjoy the attentions of her adoring lover. Alas, these distractions could only be temporary and, with the deed done and the celebrations out of the way, it was back to business as usual. Once again George, now an Electoral Prince, went to war in Flanders but this time, Königsmarck did not go with him. The count owed large gambling debts to creditors in Flanders and couldn't risk going there, so he remained safe in Hanover and again, the gossip mill began to churn.

Königsmarck's coffers were emptying rapidly, yet he would accept no office that meant he had to leave the electoral princess. Even worse, the Swedish king, by now at odds with Hanover, threatened to confiscate Königsmarck's lands in his homeland of Sweden unless he distanced himself from the electoral household. Still he continued to meet Sophia Dorothea, donning a disguise to enjoy nocturnal liaisons with his lover under the very noses of those meddling Hanoverian courtiers.

If the couple had hoped to spend uninterrupted time together they were to be disappointed and, with an eye on stopping the scandal in its tracks, Sophia Dorothea was removed from Hanover and the presence of her lover. Under the watch of her mother-in-law there was no hope of any intrigue and soon the princess began to grow suspicious of the Electress Sophia's interest in the count.

'She praises you so highly and with such pleasure that if she were younger I could not help being jealous, for really I think she is fond of you. She could not give me more evidence of it than she does. It even makes me uncomfortable.'[16]

No doubt the cunning Sophia thought she might be able to draw Sophia Dorothea into somehow giving herself away, but there was no chance that might happen. It hardly mattered anyway, the affair was by now an open secret and tragedy was drawing ever closer. Perhaps if they had been less *adolescent*, less *impassioned*, things might have passed unremarked. If the relationship had not been so very flamboyant and overt it might even have been overlooked. After all, George had no great love for his wife, it was simply the very public humiliation that left him furious and with women like Clara around there was always someone to throw fuel on the fire.

The net was closing in on the lovers.

Someone, most likely Clara, conspired to have Königsmarck's sister exiled from Hanover, removing one of the couple's champions. Yet even now Clara *still* managed to pull the wool over the eyes of the princess and after a long heart to heart, Sophia Dorothea declared that she and the countess had resolved their differences and were friends at long last. Königsmarck continued to be kept from Sophia Dorothea either by his being forced to travel in the service of Hanover or the watchful gaze of the entire household. One less blinded by passion might have taken a moment to regroup but instead the pair hurtled headlong into disaster.

Discovery

Without the company of her lover, Sophia Dorothea grew desolate. Perhaps dreaming of somehow escaping Hanover she combed through her marriage contract, seeing now how disadvantaged she truly was, with barely a penny to call her own unless her husband allowed it. Perhaps this sudden interest in money and marriage suggests that Sophia Dorothea was plotting to leave George and to start life anew, certainly she was tired of being watched, of being kept from her lover, of being the *electoral princess*. Desperate, she

---

16. Morand, Paul (1972). *The Captive Princess: Sophia Dorothea of Celle*. Florida: American Heritage Press, p.119.

appealed to her mother and father for permission to establish a home away from George. She had the backing of her lover, who promised that he would go anywhere to be with his adored princess:

'But I should be wrong to doubt you after the proposition you made to me – that you are willing to leave all this pomp and splendour and retire with me to some corner of the world. After that I have nothing to fear. I accept your offer with joy. You have only to say the word and I am ready.'[17]

Yet flight costs money and the lovers found that the coffers of Celle had little to spare. Caught up in territorial disputes and conflict, Sophia Dorothea's father had no cash to give her and she can hardly have been heartened to receive letters like this from her Königsmarck, a curious mixture of confession and shade:

'The life I have been leading since the court returned must, I fear, give you cause for much jealousy, for I am playing every night with ladies, and, without vanity, they are neither ugly nor of mean rank. I crave your pardon, but I cannot live without a little pleasure, and one of them is so much like you that I cannot help being in her society. [...] La Platen has appeared dressed in a ridiculous yellow cloak.'[18]

George notably cooled in his friendship with Königsmarck, and Clara now swooped once more on her former paramour. She offered him the hand of her own daughter in marriage, the renewed favour of the House of Hanover as well as money, influence and security. Königsmarck rejected the offer. Now Clara's wrath knew no bounds and she set herself firmly on the path of mischief.

Of this, Königsmarck had no suspicion. Indeed, when a man who owed him a *lot* of money became Elector of Saxony, it looked as though his fortunes

---

17. Wilkins, WH (1900). *The Love of an Uncrowned Queen*. London: Hutchinson & Co, p.162.
18. Ibid., p.284.

were on the up. With the ready permission of George and Ernest Augustus, who was keen to see the back of him, Königsmarck left for Saxony, hoping to extract the money that was owed to him from the newly-capped Frederick Augustus I. It was here that after all their letters, all their passionate intrigue and secret meetings, the couple was eventually undone by a boozy night out.

Drunk, loud and rather enjoying the attention, Königsmarck regaled the Dresden court with stories of life in Hanover. He spoke of the electoral prince's temper, the conniving Clara, the ill-served Sophia Dorothea, the whole sorry lot of them. One of his listeners just happened to be friends with the illustrious Countess Platen and told her of the count's indiscretions; she in turn went to her lover, the Elector of Hanover, and let him know of this careless, humiliating and unforgivable talk.

When the gossip reached George, the endgame began.

The Cuckold

George Louis, future elector, future king and, let us not forget, father of three children with his mistress, was not a man to trifle with. The mystery of the glove was one he had been willing to try and overlook, but with his name being mocked as a cuckold across the Holy Roman Empire, it was too much. Furious, gripped by rage and anger, he burst into Sophia Dorothea's chambers and challenged her to explain away the gossip that had enthralled the courts of Europe.

It was as though the floodgates had been opened on both sides, as out poured recriminations and long-festering resentments. Sophia Dorothea shrieked of her hatred of her husband's mistress, Melusine, George bellowed of his wife's intrigue with the Swedish count.

Always free with his fists, George let fly once more. He pounced upon his wife, throwing her to the floor and strangling her. It was only the quick intervention of Sophia Dorothea's lady-in-waiting that prevented tragedy. With a howled demand for a divorce extracting a ready agreement from her husband, the princess fled for Celle and the safety of her parental home.

What she found there was surprising.

Although her mother, Éléonore, was sympathetic, her father was a little more circumspect. George William simply couldn't afford to have bad blood with Hanover now, when his own territories were threatened by challenges from all sides. With the conniving Bernstorff quietly whispering in one ear, George William encouraged Sophia Dorothea to go home and put things right yet the unhappy young lady would not or, perhaps, could not. She was utterly exhausted, worn into the ground by the intrigue, the emotion and sheer overwhelming weight of it all. Only now was George William moved to agree that his daughter might stay in Celle, but it was on the promise that she would go home as soon as her health allowed.

Mindful of the scandal that might unfold, the elector and electress agreed to this arrangement, and though Sophia Dorothea attempted to delay, eventually the day came when her father would not hear of it. Marshalling what little dissent she could, Sophia Dorothea set out for home where the entire court had assembled to welcome her. According to protocol, she would be received by the elector and electress and nobody imagined for a moment that she would dare do otherwise. Instead, Sophia Dorothea shunned the powerful family and went straight to her apartments, where she sent word that she was ill and would see nobody.

Such a deliberate snub would not go unpunished.

The Disappearing Count

Just days after Sophia Dorothea's return to Hanover, along came Count von Königsmarck ready to play his part in their flight. They would flee to Wolfenbüttel, the couple decided, and the shelter of the duke who had once almost become Sophia Dorothea's father-in-law. It was an audacious and treasonous plan and one that, with palace spies out in force, they could not hope to keep a secret. Rather than take care, the couple continued to arouse gossip and suspicion and somewhere in those hallowed halls, someone was plotting against them.

On 1 July 1694, Königsmarck received a note that he believed to have come from his lover, summoning him to a meeting. When he arrived at the Leineschloss however he found that the princess had not written the note at all. She immediately laid the blame at Clara's feet, believing that it had merely been a bait to bring the two together.

With Eléonore von dem Knesebeck keeping watch for them, the pair shared a final evening together. Of course the forged letter should have raised red flags but, as we have learned, our couple was far from sensible. We know they were aware of the danger and the consequences yet still they persisted on the path to discovery and with it, tragedy.

Murder Most Foul

As the night went on, Königsmarck and Sophia Dorothea remained lost in one another's company at the Leineschloss, little caring for who had written the fake note, let alone what it might mean for the future. No doubt Eléonore von dem Knesebeck breathed a sigh of relief when her mistress's illicit paramour finally departed in the darkest hours of the night, hardly suspecting that things were about to take a violent turn. Sophia Dorothea readied herself for escape and as her thoughts turned to packing and making her farewells to the children she would leave behind, elsewhere others were conspiring to put a rather hefty spanner in the works.

In fact, once Königsmarck left Sophia Dorothea's chambers, he vanished forever. It is a tantalizing mystery that remains unsolved yet there is one name that keeps cropping up in every single report, Clara Elisabeth von Meysenburg, Countess of Platen and Hallermund, lover of the elector of Hanover and a woman who wielded almost unlimited influence at court.

Reports of Königsmarck's fate are scandalous, prurient and shot through with passionate drama and violence, yet few ascribe any blame to George. Although none of these reports can claim to be borne out by the virtually non-existent evidence, let us consider the most obvious and popular explanation of the fate of Count Philip Christoph von Königsmarck.

Step forward, Clara

For months if not years Clara had been warning her lover, Ernest Augustus, of the danger posed by the affair between Königsmarck and Sophia Dorothea. The count could not be relied upon to remain faithful to Hanover, just as Sophia Dorothea was not faithful to George, and should the elector's daughter-in-law flee to Wolfenbüttel, the cost to Hanover might be high. The fact that Königsmarck had read and responded to the forged note was proof positive that he and Sophia Dorothea were intriguing; after all, he had jumped to it when he thought his lover sought his company. The time had come, Clara urged Ernest Augustus, to finally put a stop to it once and for all.

Ernest Augustus agreed that Königsmarck should be arrested and Clara, in the company of four courtiers, went along to *supposedly* ensure that he was. In fact, Clara's companions that night were enemies of the count and there was never any intention that he would leave the Leineschloss alive. All of the accounts seem to agree that Königsmarck found the door he usually frequented locked and it was then that the four men accosted and attacked him, Clara having concealed herself in a neighbouring chamber. Whether Königsmarck was armed and fought back we'll never know; though wearing a sword was second nature to him, whether he would do so during a midnight trip to Sophia Dorothea is doubtful. After all, he usually visited her wearing a disguise of humble clothes, so the addition of a sword might well have raised eyebrows should anyone see him on his mission.

The count stood no chance against his attackers. Grievously injured by a blow to the head, he summoned the breath to beg for the life of the princess before losing consciousness. The insensible soldier was dragged into the presence of the vengeful countess who peered into his bloodied face as he blinked awake. As he spat out a bitter oath, she drew back her dainty foot and kicked him hard in the mouth that she had once kissed so fervently.

Moments later, Königsmarck was dead.

Just as the circumstances of the count's death are a matter of conjecture, so too is the fate of his corpse. If the tale of Clara's involvement in his killing is true, then no doubt she and her comrades fell into a panic once the cold truth of their deeds sank in. After all, the elector had given his permission for her to have Königsmarck arrested, not killed, and the future for the courtiers involved might be very bleak indeed if Ernest Augustus discovered what they had done.

Perhaps the elector was summoned to the sorry scene and told that Königsmarck had resisted arrest, perhaps he knew nothing of what had happened at all, perhaps he sanctioned the disposal of his body, it is a mystery that remains unsolved. Historian Ragnhild Hatton believes that the most likely answer is that the body was weighted and thrown into the Leine River. For this, she turns to the investigations of Professor Georg

Schnath, who conducted an exhaustive study of the Königsmarck affair. Schnath's investigations found that none other than Duke Anthony Ulrich of Brunswick-Wolfenbüttel[19] had received intelligence from Hanover that even named one of the four murderers, the courtier Don Nicolò Montalbano. So far, so inconclusive until one considers that, not long after the fateful night, Montalbano received a payment of 150,000 thalers from Ernest Augustus. This would have been quite an unexpected bonus for a man whose salary was set at 200 thalers.

The cash, Schnath and Hatton conclude, was hush money and payment for grisly services rendered. Now the court intrigue began afresh. As a panicking Eléonore von dem Knesebeck readied herself to flee, mindful of her part in the affair, Sophia Dorothea was placed under house arrest. Unfortunately for her retainer, Eléonore left her own escape too late and she too was arrested and prevailed upon to bear witness against the woman who had once been her closest friend.

Horace Walpole, that inveterate and rightly esteemed chronicler of Georgian court life, threw fuel on the fire when he wrote that, many years later, 'the body of Konigsmark [sic] was discovered under the floor of the Electoral Princess's dressing-room – the Count having probably been strangled there the instant he left her, and his body secreted.'[20]

We can be doubtful of the veracity of this statement. Though bones certainly were found beneath floorboards all over Europe, to be able to definitively identify Königsmarck's remains more than thirty years after his murder would be quite a feat for an eighteenth century archaeologist. Likewise, secreting the body of a man in the room of his lover would be a rather bizarre move when there was a whole country in which to quietly dispose of the evidence.

Of course, Walpole might have been right, but I doubt it. Likewise, Thackeray's highly dramatic retelling of the story ends with the burning of

---

19. Duke Anthony Ulrich of Brunswick-Wolfenbüttel would later use the sorry events at Hanover as the basis for a volume of his work, *Die Römische Octavia*, changing names and locations to avoid any unpleasant fallout.

20. Walpole, Horace (1840). *The Letters of Horace Walpole, Earl of Orford: Vol I*. London: Richard Bentley, p.61. There is no evidence to support Walpole's fanciful assertion.

the count's body. Once again, it has a certain *grand guignol* grisliness about it, but the claim is entirely without evidence.

And so history draws a veil over the fate of the raffish Count Königsmarck, yet Sophia Dorothea's misery was only just beginning.

The Spider's Web

The disappearance of Königsmarck left Sophia Dorothea shattered, her dreams of escape and a new life in tatters. Meanwhile, Ernest Augustus appeared to be dragging his heels over investigating the matter. After all, the count was known to be an adventurer and his appetites had led him into debt and trouble before, so there might be any number of reasons for his absence, not all of them involving criminality. Even the Elector of Saxony, Königsmarck's long-time friend and gambling partner, did little to intervene, mindful of keeping things on an even keel with his fellow electors.

Königsmarck's quarters were searched and the letters recovered there were passed to Ernest Augustus. Even then, he clung to the hope that his beloved daughter-in-law was innocent, and that her passionate missives were nothing more than the romantic dreams of a neglected wife. After all, her husband was openly living with his mistress, it wasn't impossible that Sophia Dorothea might have entered into the correspondence with Königsmarck for the sake of her flagging spirits, with no physical side to the relationship. In all honesty, this feels like distinctly wishful thinking and as the correspondence turned from declarations of love and adoration to the treasonous plot to flee for the opposing state of Wolfenbüttel, Ernest Augustus's rather forgiving opinion of his daughter-in-law began to harden.

Despite the unpleasant conditions in which she was held, Eléonore von dem Knesebeck refused to speak against her mistress.[21] Instead she declared Sophia Dorothea innocent of the claims that were being laid at her door.

---

21. Eléonore remained in prison at Scharfels Castle until November 1696, when she made a dramatic escape with the help of sympathetic friends. She was given sanctuary by Duke Anthony Ulrich of Brunswick-Wolfenbüttel, who simply couldn't keep out of Sophia Dorothea's story for long. Although she was never recaptured, an order existed for her to be arrested should she ever set foot on Hanoverian territory again. Sadly, she and Sophia Dorothea were never reconciled and Eléonore always believed she had been

In the years of her incarceration she became convinced that Königsmarck was still alive and being held alongside her in Scharfels Castle. Indeed, she was certain that she had heard him singing a lilting song on more than one occasion but no evidence exists to suggest that Königsmarck had survived beyond that summer evening in 1694. After all, there would have been no reason to keep him alive but imprisoned and Eléonore, mindful of the capital of her tale, embroidered it richly when she claimed sanctuary in Wolfenbüttel.

What though, of George's part in the sorry story?

On the night of Königsmarck's disappearance the electoral prince wasn't in Hanover, and all things considered, it seems unlikely that he had any involvement in the murder. He had a hot temper and a violent nature when angered, but the impetuous nature of his violence leads me to doubt he played any part in the crime. He wasn't a man whose cruelty was premeditated; instead he lashed out like an angry child when offended. Königsmarck's disappearance was more likely to be the work of someone hungry for vengeance and in love with power; someone, in fact, like Clara.

The countess might well have been motivated by furious spite, still smarting at the man who had abandoned her after their liaison, but would that really have led her to plan a murder? She was a woman of experience and, crucially for one so ambitious, influence. As long-time lover of the Elector, she had installed her own daughter, Sophia von Kielmansegg, as confidante to his son. Indeed, as we have already discovered, Sophia may have been George's half-sister and if she wasn't *that*, she might even have been his lover. Not only that, but Clara had been the one to introduce George to his beloved Melusine von der Schulenberg and she and Clara remained firm friends. Clara wasn't the sort of woman to put her power and influence in jeopardy in the name of vengeance but if she *was* behind the plot, what was her motive?

Put simply, I believe it was the continuation of that influence at all costs. Her lover, the elector, was in his sixties and of course wouldn't live forever. Whilst Sophia Dorothea and Königsmarck were trysting it was nothing but

---

betrayed by her friend, who had done nothing to secure her release. The faithful lady-in-waiting died in 1717.

a source of gossip and scandal but once they decided to abscond, things took a more serious turn. Should the couple flee and it emerge that Clara knew that they had been intriguing as surely it *would*, then this might not bode well for her fortunes with the elector. By telling Ernest Augustus what she knew, Clara maintained her position as the loyal lover in the know, sparing the electoral family the shame and scandal that would surely come should the couple make their escape. The agreement to have Königsmarck arrested sealed his fate, because to leave him alive might risk all sorts of unpleasant truths seeping out.

If Clara did indeed kick the dying man in the mouth, this suggests a rather more personal motive. For one acting out of court loyalty, this is a curiously intimate, if violent, gesture. It is an action borne of passion, of hatred, of disdain; it is the action of a woman who knew that the final victory was hers.

Yet if history is written by the victors, for those who plot a murder there is no such allowance. Mired in secrecy and shadow as Königsmarck's fate was, Clara could do nothing but endure the gossip that whirled around her. In the years that followed, the historical record branded her as a wanton woman, a Lady Macbeth driven by jealousy, the predator seeking her hapless prey. She is immortalized by Sophia Dorothea's champions as a woman hell-bent on mischief and revenge, remembered only as the villainess whose inhumanity led to tragedy.

> 'Excited by rage, jealousy, and hatred, she had sufficient stimulants at work to bring out all that mischievous talent which had so helped her forward during her career, and moreover, she had at her hand agents of all kinds, of whose readiness at any bad purpose she had ample evidence. She well considered her plans, and when they were mature, satisfied of their success, she kept like a bloated spider, out of sight of her victims, but ready to pounce upon them the moment they got entangled in the intricate web she had spun for their destruction.'[22]

---

22. Williams, Robert Folkestone (1845). *Memoirs of Sophia Dorothea, Consort of George I, Vol I*. London: Henry Colburn, p.207.

Goodbye to Hanover

Devastated by the loss of her lover and the arrest of her friend, Sophia Dorothea came under pressure from the Electress Sophia to tell all that she knew. Separated from her two children, the young electoral princess had never been more isolated and though she cried day and night for freedom, for divorce, the House of Hanover was sure it could still reach a more respectable conclusion.

Clara's husband, Prime Minister Count von Platen, was by now Sophia Dorothea's unwelcome and far from impartial shadow. It was he who was on hand to advise Ernest Augustus and George on their next steps and he was present, alongside the family, when Sophia Dorothea took the sacrament and made a declaration of innocence. Spying the count's smirk, she invited his wife to step up and take the same oath of fidelity; history does not record Clara's response.

In fact, Sophia Dorothea had no wish to reconcile with her husband and longed only for her old home of Celle. She was proud, after all, and had been most grievously wronged. Indeed, she chose to occupy the moral high ground, a somewhat dangerous place since her letters had fallen into her father-in-law's hands.

'If what I am accused of is true, I am unworthy of his bed; and if my accusation is false, he is unworthy of me; I will not accept his offers.'[23]

When Sophia Dorothea reached out to Prime Minister Bernstorff in Celle for help she had no idea that he was a confidante of the von Platens. Years after he had accepted that diamond-studded snuffbox for his part in the arrangement of George and Sophia Dorothea's marriage, he once again picked up his wooden spoon and began to stir. He knew that, should Sophia Dorothea return to Celle, then George's inheritance of her dowry might be in jeopardy. He also knew that her father-in-law was keen to avoid a public embarrassment and that, the more she pushed and needled to go home,

---

23. Coxe, William (1816). *Memoirs of the Life and Administration of Robert Walpole*. London: Longman, Hurst, Rees, Orme & Brown, p.261.

the more likely she would be to face censure. More worryingly, should she ever publicly tell her side of the story, it could be the source of much embarrassment in Hanover.

Bernstorff encouraged Sophia Dorothea to keep pushing to be allowed to go back to Celle telling her that, above everything else, she should continue to protest her utter innocence. In reply, lawyers were summoned and soon a divorce was on the table, yet it was to be a divorce that would ensure that the young woman would enjoy no freedom for the rest of her days. Over and over, Sophia Dorothea was prevailed upon to admit to her wrongs and to return to the company of her husband. Over and over, she refused.

> '[…] we still adhere to our oft-repeated resolution never to cohabit matrimonially with our husband, and that we desire nothing so much as that separation of marriage requested by our husband may take place.'[24]

Finally, in December 1694, the decision was made. If Sophia Dorothea would not consent to live with her husband, then she was guilty of desertion. No mention of the unfortunate Königsmarck was made during the legal hearing and Sophia Dorothea was charged only with 'incompatibility of temper, added to some little failings of character'.[25]

In Celle, Sophia Dorothea's family reeled from the blow to their honour and their hopes. George William was disgusted and though his wife, Éléonore, begged him to show their daughter some kindness, he had no forgiveness in his heart for her. No matter how much Éléonore implored him to invite Sophia Dorothea home to Celle he would not hear of it, well aware that this would give the impression that her behaviour had been forgiven or condoned.

Sophia Dorothea had longed to escape Hanover and now, finally, that moment had come. Still only in her twenties she was taken to Ahlden House in Celle and there, the House of Hanover hoped, would be forgotten. Yet

---

24. Ibid., p.259.
25. Doran, Dr John (1855). *Lives of the Queens of England and the House of Hanover: Vol I*. New York: Redfield, p.100.

she was not forgotten, as across Europe, gossip began to ring out and in response, the spin began.

An official explanation was issued that laid the blame at the feet of Eléonore von dem Knesebeck. The lady-in-waiting had exploited a little bit of domestic discord until what began as something as minor as Sophia Dorothea being a touch cool towards her husband had become full blown loathing. The dispatch has Count Platen's fingerprints all over it and casts Sophia Dorothea as a manipulated innocent. Most innocent of all, however, the man to whom no blame can be attached is George. He emerges as a loving husband, far removed from the fellow who had fathered children with his mistress and throttled his wife without a second thought.

For now, of course, Sophia Dorothea and George were still legally husband and wife; that wouldn't be the case for much longer!

Divorce

For a time, the disgraced Sophia Dorothea was removed to Lauenau where she was incarcerated, her life neither that of a prisoner nor that of a princess, but somewhere in between. The living conditions were by no means physically unpleasant yet she enjoyed no freedom whatsoever. All letters in or out of the castle, whether to Sophia Dorothea or domestic staff, were vetted and all visitors, who were allowed only by prior arrangement with George, were searched.

Sophia Dorothea was placed under the constant watch of the Seigneur de la Fortiere, who was entrusted with reporting and observing her every move. Even her walks in the garden were to be restricted to a particularly isolated area and always in the company of the Seigneur. Her children, and even her mother, were denied permission to see the lonely electoral princess, whilst her father had no wish to do so.

Finally, with all hope of reconciliation lost, it was agreed that the couple would divorce. Sophia Dorothea would receive a stipend from George for her upkeep and by the close of 1694, the marriage was officially over. In her haste to be free, Sophia Dorothea had gladly agreed to any demand her husband's family made of her, naively believing that she would be awarded her freedom should she do so.

Charged with desertion and held up as the culpable party, Sophia Dorothea's fate was never going to be a happy one. The court ruled that the marriage would be dissolved and that she would be forbidden from ever remarrying, though George remained free to do so. The one thing that Sophia Dorothea did not suspect, and had no warning of, was that she would never see her two young children again.

Once again, she was spirited away to Ahlden, whilst in Hanover, Clara ironically found herself the target of the sort of gossip that she had once revelled in. Even as the court rallied to support her and denounce whispers of her involvement in the count's disappearance and the unfortunate circumstances of the princess, George simply continued on as ever. He had not loved his wife and he did not miss her; after all, he had Melusine – what more could a man need?

For Sophia Dorothea, the intrigue and romance of her life in Hanover with Königsmarck was nothing but a distant, darkened memory. Watched, followed and confined, she was permitted only to ride out in the grounds of Ahlden under full guard and never further than the limits of the driveway. How she must have longed to escape, must have looked back on the years since those happy days in the gardens of Celle before George, before Clara and long before respectable, stultifying married life.

> 'Local tradition among the peasants of Ahlden still hands down the picture of the mysterious great lady of the castle always beautifully dressed, and with diamonds gleaming in her dark hair, galloping up and down the road, followed by an escort of cavalry with drawn swords.'[26]

She would have thirty-two long years to contemplate the life she had lost.

The Lady of Ahlden

And so, in her gilded cage, Sophia Dorothea began life as the newly-minted Duchess of Ahlden and was, the House of Hanover hoped, forgotten.

---

26. Wilkins, WH (1900). *The Love of an Uncrowned Queen*. London: Hutchinson & Co, p.395.

As the years passed, she had no choice but to accept the cruel hand that she had been dealt. In Hanover the world kept turning; Ernest Augustus died[27] and George became Elector, with Clara, the woman who had been at the heart of so much trouble, outliving her lover by just two years. In Ahlden, Sophia Dorothea assumed the administration of her limited local territory, and spent her days managing her household. She had not been left a pauper and enjoyed a full household staff, as well as some limited company during her captivity. She missed her mother and youngsters dreadfully but there was no concession made; Sophia Dorothea would never see her children again, and her adoring mother would have a long, long wait.

There could be no question of romance of course, but Sophia Dorothea was eventually allowed to receive visitors from the village and local nobles. She could not make house calls in turn and the monitoring of her correspondence continued. Yet no matter what her life might be, she was never less than immaculate in her appearance and during the final years of Ernest Augustus's life, she petitioned constantly for her freedom.

Perhaps the elector would have eventually acquiesced but his death in 1698 ended her chance of release forever. With power now resting in the hands of her former husband, Sophia Dorothea realized that she would never taste freedom. Still she begged George and his mother, the Dowager Electress, for the opportunity to see her children once more. Neither party replied to her letters but the thought that the dowager would allow the woman she regarded as a 'little clot of dirt'[28] even a moment of kindness is, sadly, laughable.

Sophia Dorothea's entreaties received no reply but one small concession was made and it was agreed that her mother, her lifelong champion, would be permitted to see her daughter. Four years from their last meeting, the two women were reunited and with her, the Duchess of Celle brought news of her grandchildren. Sophia Dorothea learned that her son and daughter were well and happy, yet forbidden to ever speak her name. Indeed, though rumours of young George II swimming the moat at Ahlden to see his

---

27. His mistress, Clara, followed him in 1700.
28. Wilkins, WH (1900). *The Love of an Uncrowned Queen*. London: Hutchinson & Co, p.204.

mother might be fanciful, he did hang her portraits once more when his father finally passed away.

The Return to Celle

Clara, the author of so much mischief and by now 'hideous to behold and deprived of her sight',[29] died a miserable and painful death. She supposedly gave a deathbed confession of the count's murder, as did a servant from Hanover, but perhaps that has more to do with the need for a neat conclusion than the truth. Sophia Dorothea's reaction to her passing was not recorded; instead she was preparing to go home to Celle.

In spring 1700, just a few months after the death of the scheming Clara, Sophia Dorothea left Ahlden House for the first and last time as invading forces were closing in on her prison. At the request of her mother, George grudgingly allowed his former wife to return to her childhood home of Celle, but only under the strictest conditions.

Here she returned to the rooms where she had spent her carefree girlish years and for several months, long after the supposed danger had passed, she sheltered at Celle. Every time Hanover demanded her return, word was sent via Sophia Dorothea's mother that her daughter was too ill to travel. When they had run out of excuses, the people of Celle were forced to bid an unhappy farewell to their favourite princess and once again, she was confined to Ahlden.

In Sophia Dorothea's former marital home of Hanover, big changes were afoot thanks to events in Great Britain, where the 1701 Act of Settlement forever changed the life of her former husband. This Act ruled that if no heir was born to William III, the current incumbent of the English throne, or his sister-in-law, the future Queen Anne, then Sophia, Dowager Electress of Hanover, would be named queen of England. Should Sophia die before she came to power, her son, George, would be crowned sovereign in her stead. The Act wiped away the succession rights of over fifty Roman Catholics who might lay claim to the crown ahead of the family from Hanover; and the problems the succession caused would rumble on for decades.

---

29. Ibid., p.414.

In the twilight years of his life, Sophia Dorothea's estranged father began to soften towards his only child. He amended his will to leave her a vast fortune and spoke of her frequently, yet his thawing had come too late. In 1705, George William died, never having been reconciled with his daughter.

As the years rolled past, Sophia Dorothea was shown no kindness, no respite. She was kept from the weddings of both her son and daughter[30] and eventually the players in her sorry tale were dwindling at a considerable rate. Her mother-in-law, Sophia of Hanover, died in 1714, shortly before the death of Queen Anne. These two royal deaths, of course, catapulted George I onto the throne of England.

No doubt Sophia Dorothea received the news with a sense of grim amusement. Under different circumstances, she would be a queen, yet instead she was a prisoner, kept from her children and friends and for so long despised by the father who had once adored her.

Sophia Dorothea passed her days in quiet contemplation. She wrote, walked, rode and prayed, receiving her mother's visits with utmost joy. When Éléonore died in 1722, her daughter was left utterly bereft and no doubt wondered what new calamity life might find to hurl at her. This was the one person who had *always* believed in Sophia Dorothea, had never withdrawn her kindness and now, suddenly, she was gone.

The Cunning Count

In the depths of her grief and despair there was still one place where Sophia Dorothea could turn for comfort. She had started a forbidden and secret correspondence with her daughter, also named Sophia Dorothea, who was by now married and living in Prussia. Of course, George would have been furious if he had known but he *didn't* know, and nobody was about to tell him. Sadly, when the young woman recommended that her mother put her financial affairs in the hands of the Prussian Count de Bar, it proved to be a disastrous bit of advice.

---

30. George married Caroline of Ansbach in 1705; his sister, Sophia Dorothea, married Frederick William I of Prussia in 1706.

Sophia Dorothea's son-in-law, Frederick William I of Prussia, encouraged his wife to renew her acquaintance with her mother, yet his motives were far from honourable. He knew that Sophia Dorothea was one of the richest women in Europe and he intended to keep one eye on that bounty. After all, she wasn't getting any younger and would no doubt be looking for someone to bequeath her fortune to.

As soon as Frederick William learned that his wife was guaranteed to receive half of Sophia Dorothea's wealth upon her death, he ordered the correspondence to cease, having admirably achieved his aim. It did, though the younger Sophia Dorothea warned her mother to be wary of Count de Bar, whom she had come to distrust after her initial recommendation. It was advice that the unfortunate Duchess of Ahlden unwisely chose to ignore.

Sophia Dorothea had placed the management of her finances in the hands of the count and he was more than happy to play along. As time passed, the imprisoned woman began to hatch plans to escape Ahlden once and for all and she came to believe that Count de Bar might be able to make her dreams of freedom into reality.

Her daughter begged her to wait, promising that she would seek mercy for Sophia Dorothea once she had concluded some tricky marriage negotiations for her own children. She would be able to finish this business all the quicker, she admitted, if Sophia Dorothea might lend her some money for the task. The duchess felt that she had waited long enough; all she wanted now was to be far, far from Ahlden. She refused to lend her daughter the cash and, unsurprisingly, the burgeoning relationship between the two women swiftly began to cool. When she learned that her daughter had been to Hanover and *not* paid her a visit, Sophia Dorothea felt more alone than ever, and her determination to escape only grew.

Although Sophia Dorothea's daughter did try to make amends, her mother would hear nothing of it. All she wanted was to be free, and if the Prussian queen wouldn't help, then she would turn to her new favourite, the scheming Count de Bar. Despite the warnings, Sophia Dorothea persisted in trusting him with her enormous fortune, sure that he would secure her freedom.

Count de Bar, however, had no intention of helping the unfortunate woman to escape her prison. Instead, he had been dipping into Sophia

Dorothea's fortune as though it were his own, spending her money whilst keeping her hanging on, and believing that he had only her best interests at heart. When she discovered his treachery, it was one betrayal too many for the fragile woman and she sank into a depression.

The last days of Sophia Dorothea had come.

The End of the Duchess

After three decades in captivity, little trace remained of the beautiful, passionate, vibrant woman who had once lit up the castles of Celle and Hanover. Exhausted by loneliness, despair and the sheer weight of misery, the fight had finally gone out of the 60-year-old Sophia Dorothea and she took to her bed, her health failing at a rapid rate.

Here the once vibrant woman languished between life and death, her strength lasting as long as it took to pen a final, furious letter to the husband who had so cruelly deserted her. As she lay on her deathbed, she cursed the man to whom she had been wed, mourning the life that he had stolen from her.

On 13 November 1726, Sophia Dorothea died at Ahlden House, after more than half a life spent in captivity. On receipt of the news, George was chilled to the bone, for he remembered only too well a prophecy given years earlier and now, in the twilight years of his own life, he felt it drawing near.

'A female of that vocation [a prophet] warned George I to take care of his wife, as he would not survive her a year.'[31]

Sophia Dorothea's body was placed in a lead coffin and removed to the depths of Ahlden House, where it remained for weeks. Her will, rumoured to bequeath her fortune to her children, was destroyed and her worldly goods passed to George I. Formal mourning was not ordered and when George learned that his daughter's court *had* observed mourning for the late duchess, he was furious. Efforts to bury Sophia Dorothea at Ahlden were

31. Walpole, Horace (1840). *The Letters of Horace Walpole, Earl of Orford: Vol I*. London: Richard Bentley, p.64.

vexed by flooding and in England, Melusine, ever the bearer of glad tidings, told her lover that she had been visited by the vengeful spirit of the dead woman in a dream. She must be buried at Celle, the unquiet ghost had told her, or she would *never* let her former husband rest.

In May 1727, Sophia Dorothea was finally interred in Celle's ducal burial vaults. It was done without ceremony, her interment as low-key as her life had been forced to become.

Whether one believes the words of prophets is, of course, a matter of opinion, but George I did indeed die within a year of Sophia Dorothea. On 11 June 1727, he passed away on a visit to Osnabrück. The crown went to his son, George II, 'and the morning after the news of the death of George the First had reached London, Mrs. Howard observed (in the antechamber of the king's apartment) a picture of a woman in the electoral robes, which proved to be that of Sophia'.[32]

Years later, George II visited Herrenhausen, the summer palace of the Hanoverians, where he quite unexpectedly found himself awarded the custody of Sophia Dorothea's personal papers.

Finally the unfortunate woman's son was able to read her story in her own words and what he found there, we will never know. He had always believed Sophia Dorothea was innocent of adultery and defended her name, yet the information he learned in Herrenhausen changed that forever. The contents of those papers shattered the king and he had them burned. From that day on, he never spoke of his mother again.

And so history draws a veil over the sad story of Sophia Dorothea, the woman who might have been the first British queen of the House of Hanover. But for its unhappy ending the story of her life is one that could have come from the annals of romantic fiction. Much of the correspondence between Sophia Dorothea and Königsmarck has been lost or destroyed, yet enough remains to suggest that there was at least an intrigue, more likely a full blown affair.

Sophia Dorothea's role in the story of Great Britain cannot be underestimated. She was the wife and mother of a king and without her, the

---

32. Coxe, William (1816). *Memoirs of the Life and Administration of Robert Walpole*. London: Longman, Hurst, Rees, Orme & Brown, p. 262.

history of the nation would have looked very different indeed. The cruel fate she endured is enough to make even the most hardened cynic flinch, for the finest cage is still a prison and to spend thirty years within the same walls with no hope of freedom, with few friends to call your own, is punishment indeed.

Historians tend to look kindly on Sophia Dorothea, perhaps because of her grim fate, and her story certainly casts a dark shadow over her husband. Led by his mother, by self-interested courtiers and by scheming nobles, George's wounded pride would not allow him to show his wife even the barest hint of mercy. Instead he tried to forget his imprisoned bride, his efforts to lay the ghost of her memory enjoying some small amount of success as the years sped past.

Even today, Sophia Dorothea is little remembered yet the Duchess of Ahlden's story is one that deserves to be told, and her memory is one that should not fade into history.

Act II

Caroline of Ansbach, Queen Consort of Great Britain and Ireland

(Ansbach, Holy Roman Empire, 1 March 1683 – London, England, 20 November 1737)

George I did not bring a queen with him when he arrived in his new realm, so Great Britain had to wait a while to meet the first royal bride who would sit at the side of a king from Hanover. That esteemed lady was Wilhelmina Charlotte Caroline of Ansbach, a woman whose marriage started as a fairytale and turned into a tale of political influence, pioneering medical treatment, family breakdown and a very grisly death.

Caroline was not the sort to dally with nobles, write heartfelt love letters and end up behind gilded bars. She was the quintessential eligible young lady and became a most political queen indeed. During Caroline's lifetime the venom that began to bubble with George I and George II continued its slow drip down through the generations of the House of Hanover, a legendary prime minister rose to prominence and the Georgian era boomed.

The Orphan of Ansbach

The scourge of smallpox threw a long and deadly shadow over eighteenth century life. Whether princess or pauper, saint or sinner, nobody was safe from the dreaded infection and it claimed hundreds of thousands of lives across the world. Those who survived might be left disfigured or blind and for Caroline of Ansbach, it was a disease that struck close to home far too often.

Caroline's first encounter with the infection that blighted the era came at the age of three when smallpox claimed the life of her father, John Frederick,

Margrave of Brandenburg-Ansbach. Aged just 31, John Frederick left behind not only the tiny German state that he had ruled but also his wife, Princess Eleonore Erdmuthe of Saxe-Eisenach, and their children, Caroline and William Frederick. Seeking a fresh start, Eleonore gathered her children and fled home to Eisenach and what she hoped would be a new life, yet it was to prove a disastrous decision.

At their new home in Crailsheim, the little family's fortunes suffered a sharp downward turn. Money was tight and conditions were hard and soon the widow was desperate for help. With all avenues of assistance exhausted, in 1692 she reluctantly agreed to be married to John George IV, Elector of Saxony. Although this would spell the end to her financial woes, when she and her youngsters arrived in Saxony, life didn't get any happier. Here she suffered a humiliating and unhappy marriage as her new husband openly cavorted with his mistress, Magdalena Sibylla von Neidschütz, known as *Billa*. He lived with her as though *she* were the electress whilst the lady who bore the title went neglected and ignored.

Just as George I and Sophia Dorothea's union had descended into violence, so too did that of Eleonore and John George. During one of their many confrontations the elector attempted to stab his wife and she became convinced that, if she stayed by his side, she would end up in an early grave. After all, with Billa promoted to countess and waiting none too subtly in the wings, John George already had a preferred candidate for the role of royal consort. Fearing for her life, Eleonore fled the court with her children and established a residence in the Saxon town of Pretzsch, where she prayed that she might be safe from the machinations of her husband.

In fact, John George did indeed have a softer side, though his wife never experienced it. When his beloved Billa contracted smallpox, he vowed that he would not leave her side. It was a promise he kept and it proved to be the death of him. The elector was soon showing the classic symptoms of smallpox too and, within a month of Billa's death, John George died. The newly widowed Eleonore didn't mourn his loss and she little cared that the court of Dresden showed no interest in her fate now she was no longer married to its elector. Instead, Eleonore retired to Pretzsch, her future uncertain but her life, at least, no longer in jeopardy from knife-wielding husbands.

All of this coming and going didn't bode well for young Caroline. Shuffled from pillar to post, from tragedy to disaster, her education was neglected and even in later years, her husband commented that she wrote 'like a cat'.[1] Perhaps she was already beginning to recognize the importance of establishing oneself as more than just a wife.

In a life already beset with uncertainty, the next devastating blow came with Eleanor's death when Caroline was just 13. After a brief stay with her half-brother, George Frederick II, Margrave of Brandenburg-Ansbach, Caroline was sent to Lützenburg, where she was given into the care of her mother's friends, Sophia Charlotte and Frederick, the Electress and Elector of Brandenburg.

Sophia Charlotte was the sister of George I and by 1701, she and her husband would be king and queen of Prussia. It was with their encouragement that the unfortunate Eleonore had entered into her disastrous marriage to John George and now, entrusted with the care of her daughter, they swore to bring the girl up as their own, and to raise her well. The couple honoured the name of Eleonore and the elector promised Caroline that, 'I will never fail as your guardian, to espouse your interests, and to care for you as a loving father, and pray your Highness to have in me the same confidence as your mother always had, which I shall perpetually endeavour to deserve.'[2]

It was a promise that he kept.

In this glittering new home, Caroline found herself living a life she could only have dreamed of when in the care of her unhappy, ill-treated mother. Sophia Charlotte adored the girl and under the loving eye of this seasoned electress, Caroline began to develop into the politically-minded queen she would one day become. She delighted in the maternal care of Sophia Charlotte, who couldn't have been a better mother to Caroline. Here in the Hohenzollern court, the young lady was introduced to the great thinkers of the age and plunged into an exciting, new world. Her lack of formal education forgotten, Caroline was soon embroiled in deep conversations

1. Borman, Tracy (2010). *King's Mistress, Queen's Servant: The Life and Times of Henrietta Howard*. London: Random House, p.37.
2. Arkell, Ruby Lillian (1939). *Caroline of Ansbach: George the Second's Queen*. Oxford: Oxford University Press, p.7.

with philosophers and policy makers, nurturing the love of politics that would later make her an able regent.

Young Caroline found a particularly adoring champion in the shape of Gottfried Wilhelm Leibniz, a celebrated scholar and philosopher who became her unlikely friend and mentor. Indeed, in some ways Leibniz became almost a father to the young orphan, recognizing and nurturing the natural intelligence that she possessed. Under Leibniz's tutelage, she began to expand her studies and interests, joining him in the salons that were so much a part of court life.

By now ripe for marriage and one of the most eligible young ladies in Europe, the tide had turned for the orphan of Ansbach.

The Eligible Orphan

Caroline of Ansbach was, by all accounts, a beauty. With her dazzling blue eyes, rosy cheeks and waves of blonde hair, she had a poise and grace that turned heads wherever she went and a bosom that set noble hearts aflutter. She was also smart, witty and known for her pitch perfect, witheringly arch impersonations of courtiers. By the time Caroline reached 20, speculation over her future was rife, and would-be suitors came calling from the continental courts, keen to snatch this astute, well-connected stunner for themselves.

Dowager Electress Sophia of Hanover, that most formidable lady, called Caroline 'the most agreeable Princess in Germany',[3] and it seemed that one man who certainly agreed was Archduke Charles of Austria. This was a man with connections, a man who would make any politically ambitious girl a fine husband, set as he was to eventually become the Holy Roman Emperor.[4] Although informal negotiations had been going on for some years, it was not until 1703 that the official approach was made; would Caroline, Charles wondered, consider becoming his bride?

---

3. Ibid., p.18.
4. He became Holy Roman Emperor Charles VI in 1711. His eventual bride was Elisabeth Christine of Brunswick-Wolfenbüttel, who agreed to convert to Catholicism for the marriage.

Caroline's adoptive father, by now King of Prussia, knew exactly what he wanted his charge's answer to be. This was the sort of proposal that a young lady, especially one whose surrogate family had far-reaching dynastic ambitions, couldn't afford to turn down. The one small spanner in the works was the fact that Caroline wasn't only a Lutheran, she was *vehemently* a Lutheran. Charles was Catholic and so, if the marriage was to be contracted, one of them would have to change their persuasion.

Guess which one?

Right first time.

Although devout in her faith, at first, Caroline agreed to consider conversion and Father Ferdinand Orban, a Jesuit priest, was sent to school the young lady in her possible change of faith. In fact, this proved to be a decisive moment in the negotiations and far from convincing her that Catholicism was the way forward, Orban actually did precisely the opposite. After her lessons with him, Caroline was often distressed, unable to reconcile the idea of converting to Catholicism with her pious devotion to her own faith.

Eventually, perhaps with not such a heavy heart, Caroline decided that she wouldn't be able to accept Charles's proposal if it meant changing her faith. Together, she and Leibniz composed a letter explaining the decision. Caroline would later shine as a beacon of Protestantism in her adopted country, and memorably told John Robinson, the Bishop of London, that he was 'very impertinent to suppose that I, who refused to be Empress for the Sake of the Protestant Religion, don't understand it fully'.[5]

Caroline's decisions and ideals, however, were subjected to intense scrutiny from both the priest and those who looked on. Her grandmother-in-law, Dowager Electress Sophia, wrote:

'First the Princess of Ansbach says "Yes" and then "No". First she says we Protestants have no valid priests, then that Catholics are idolatrous and accursed, and then again that our religion is the better. What the result will be I do not know. The Princess is shortly leaving here, and

---

5. Cowper, Mary (1865). *Diary of Mary, Countess Cowper, Lady of the Bedchamber to the Princess of Wales, 1714 -1720.* London: J Murray, p.41.

so it must be either "Yes" or "No". When Urban [sic] comes to see the Princess the Bible lies between them on the table, and they argue at length. Of course, the Jesuit, who has studied more, argues her down, and then the Princess weeps.'[6]

Although Sophia Charlotte had refrained from passing judgement and had allowed Caroline to make up her own mind on the matter of marriage, Frederick was furious. As far as he could see Caroline had thrown away a perfect match for a point of principle that she could ill afford to indulge. Had she forgotten, he wondered, that she had *nothing*, and that all her good fortune stemmed from his own generosity in taking her into his house and raising her as his own in the first place?

Caroline wisely decided that it might be good sense to let the dust settle in her adoptive home and quietly withdrew to her brother's care in Ansbach. Safe in the shelter of her sibling, Margrave William Frederick, she wrote to Leibniz to tell him:

'I do not think the King of Spain is troubling himself any more about me. On the contrary, they are incensed at my disinclination to follow the advice of Father Urban [sic].'[7]

Incensed they might be, but Caroline had been ruled by her heart *and* her head. She had made her choice and, armed with her faith and her fortune, Caroline of Ansbach was back on the market.

The Queen is Dead

On 1 February 1705, Sophia Charlotte of Hanover, Queen consort in Prussia, died.

The woman whose court had been so vibrant, so intellectually stimulating and so full of life passed away at the age of just 36, a victim of pneumonia.

---

6. Wilkins, William Henry (1901). *Caroline, the Illustrious Queen-Consort of George II and Sometime Queen-Regent: A Study of Her Life and Time, Volume I*. London: J Murray, pp.29–30.
7. Ibid., p.31.

She died in Hanover, the land of her birth, having fallen ill whilst travelling there. Suffering from a debilitating cold and possibly a tumour in her throat, the queen had turned down the services of a priest and took to what she knew would be her deathbed. Always a passionate devotee of philosophy, as Sophia Charlotte approached the end of her days, she told her attendants:

> 'I am at last going to satisfy my curiosity about the origin of things, which even Leibniz could never explain to me, to understand space, infinity, being and nothingness; and as for the King, my husband – well, I shall afford him the opportunity of giving me a magnificent funeral, and displaying all the pomp he loves so much.'[8]

It was one of the great tragedies of Caroline's life that she was never able to say goodbye to the woman who had raised her, introduced her to philosophy and science, and allowed her to follow her own heart when it came to the matter of marriage. In fact, the seriousness of Sophia Charlotte's condition had been greatly underestimated and by the time it was discovered, it was too late.

The future George I was with his sister when she died and felt her loss keenly. Her decline and death was so swift that for a time, there were rumours of poisoning.

> '*Mahomed* [the king's servant] entertained us with the Praise of the Queen of Prussia, sister to the King, who died at Hanover of two Days' sickness, suspected of having been poisoned, before she left Berlin, with Diamond Powder, for when she was opened her Stomach was so worn, that you could thrust your Fingers through at any Place, as did Mahomed. The King, he said, was in such Sorrow, that he was five Days without eating or drinking, or sleeping, but kept walking and wailing all the Time, and by hitting his Toes against the Wainscot (which he ever does when he walks), he had worn out his shoes till his Toes came out two Inches at the Foot.'[9]

---

8. Kiste, John van der (2013). *King George II and Queen Caroline.* Stroud: The History Press, p.12.
9. Cowper, CS (ed.) (1865). *Diary of Mary, Countess Cowper, Lady of the Bedchamber to the Princess of Wales, 1714–1720.* London: John Murray, pp.149–150.

We'll never know if she was really poisoned and certainly no official verdict was ever recorded to suggest that there had been foul play, but the mud, as they say, stuck.

Sophia Charlotte's death plunged the court into mourning. The doughty Dowager Electress Sophia was utterly bereft at the loss of her daughter, yet none felt her departure more keenly than young Caroline. Mired in grief, she wrote to Leibniz in strong terms, sure that nothing could fill the void Sophia Charlotte had left other than death itself.

> 'Heaven, jealous of our happiness, has taken away from us our adored and adorable Queen. The calamity has overwhelmed me with grief and sickness, and it is only the hope that I may soon follow her that consoles me.'[10]

In the event, death did *not* claim Caroline and nor would it for many, many years. Before that day, she had plenty more adventures awaiting her.

Meeting Monsieur de Busch

As the Dowager Electress Sophia mourned the death of her daughter, the constitutional wheels of Hanover didn't stop turning and events in England conspired to catapult the House of Hanover into touching distance of the throne. Their claim to the British crown was secured by the 1701 Act of Settlement, a spectacular bit of politicking which changed the course of history forever.

Realizing that the current Stuart monarch, King William III, was unlikely to father an heir, Parliament knew that something had to be done. After all, no Protestant heir waiting in the wings would leave the road clear for a Catholic restoration and this couldn't be allowed to happen, no matter what. The result was the Act of Settlement and it ruled that, should no Stuart heir be born, then the crown would pass to Sophia, Electress of Hanover or her successor. Crucially, the Act also stated that no Catholic could sit on the

10. Wilkins, William Henry (1901). *Caroline, the Illustrious Queen-Consort of George II and Sometime Queen-Regent: A Study of Her Life and Time, Volume I*. London: J Murray, p.38.

English throne and, should the heir or monarch ever *marry* a Catholic, then they would be removed from the line of succession.

The Act of Settlement effectively wiped out the claims of over fifty heirs to the throne including James Francis Edward Stuart, *the Old Pretender*. As the Catholic half-brother of Queen Anne, the Pretender could secure the throne by converting to Protestantism. He refused to convert for the crown, just as Caroline refused for the sake of marriage, and he was swiftly and unceremoniously shoved out of the line of succession.

This meant that one day soon, either Sophia, the Dowager Electress of Hanover, or her son, George, would make the trip to Great Britain. Such an unexpected expansion of the power of the electorate offered great opportunities for the family and Sophia was set on maximizing the potential of her forthcoming new role. With her grandson, George Augustus, still unmarried, the time had come to seek a mate and she could think of nobody better than Caroline of Ansbach.

Caroline was by now 22, and all over Europe, ambitious households and eligible chaps were more than capable of recognizing her many assets. From the grandeur of her adoptive family to her good looks and excellent childbearing prospects, she would be quite a catch.

> 'Her hand and arm were greatly admired for their whiteness and elegance; she had a penetrating eye, an expressive countenance, a fine voice, and much sweetness and grace, particularly when she spoke.'[11]

This was not, of course, all about her arms. Though Caroline's interest in matters philosophical might have come in for mockery and a gentle pat on the head among some gentleman, intelligence was a commodity highly prized in the marriage market:

> 'In some respects, however, Caroline would have been a promising subject for a satirist; for she affected to combine the characters of a

---

11. MacFarlane, Charles, and Thomson, Thomas (1792). *The Comprehensive History of England; Civil and Military, Religious, Intellectual and Social, from the Earliest Period to the Suppression of the Sepoy Revolt, Vol III*. London: Blackie & Son, p.219.

philosopher and princess royal (and proudly royal), a beauty and a wit, a metaphysician and a divine.'[12]

Caroline's adoptive father, Frederick I of Prussia, had other ideas. With Sophia Charlotte's death, Caroline had lost her greatest champion and Frederick fully intended to capitalize on it. Still smarting from her guardian's fury over her refusal to convert and marry Archduke Charles, Caroline decided to remain in Ansbach with her brother for the time being. Undeterred, in Berlin, the king began to make overtures that might result in the possible reopening of negotiations with Charles or even, as a last resort, see Caroline hitched to Frederick's own son. Although this plan had been discussed with his late wife, her death had halted the planning; now, however, it could begin again.

No doubt Caroline was considering her own future too when she travelled to Triesdorf to spend the summer with the brother who had become her rock. Still mourning for the woman who had been as good as a mother to her, she passed calm days in the peace of the summer palace, slowly adjusting to life without Sophia Charlotte.

Into that tranquil idyll rode a party of Hanoverian gentlemen led by a most notable noble, who was introduced to the young lady as *Monsieur de Busch*. Though not particularly handsome, his aspect was pleasing enough, he was excellent company and, crucially, the heir to a throne.

For Monsieur de Busch was no travelling nobleman at all, but George Augustus, heir to the House of Hanover, one day to rule as George II.

Mindful of his own disastrous marriage to Sophia Dorothea, when the time came to find a wife for his son, George Louis knew that he must give the young man some say. Although the dowager electress was singing Caroline's praises from the rooftops, it was vital that the perspective groom also be involved in the decision. On the other hand, any young lady faced with a chap with George Augustus's illustrious lineage might well employ a little subterfuge of their own to win his hand. It was important, therefore, that the lady in question did not know exactly who her suitor was; only that way would she show her true self. Sophia knew nothing of the scheme and, when she learned of it, was as stunned as she was delighted.

---

12. Ibid., pp.219–220.

George fell for Caroline at first sight, 'seized with such an affection and desire for her that he is most eager to marry her without delay'.[13] Happily, she appeared to be enchanted by him too; but was she really taken in by the subterfuge? Whether this rather fairytale romance was as wide-eyed as it appeared, when Caroline was finally told of the true identity of her suitor by his envoy, Baron Von Eltz, she certainly *seemed* surprised.

Eltz arrived in Ansbach armed with strict instructions from the elector on exactly how to handle the conversation, with each point ensuring that *nothing* was left to chance.

'When our Envoy is admitted to the Princess, he must explain to her that the young friend who accompanied him on his last visit to the Court of Ansbach was our son, the Electoral Prince, who had been so much impressed with the reports of the Princess's incomparable beauty and mental attributes that he arranged to appear incognito, and have the honour of seeing and speaking with the Princess without her knowing his electoral rank and station. As he had succeeded in doing this, and had found that the reports were more than verified, our son is so charmed and delighted with her that he would consider it the height of good fortune to obtain her for his wife, and has asked our permission to seek this end. As we, the Elector, have always held the Princess in highest esteem and repute, we are not a little rejoiced to hear that our son cherished these sentiments towards her, and we should be even more glad if he could attain the object of his mission.

Our Envoy must then declare to the Princess who he himself is, and by whose authority he has come, and he must sound her as to whether she be free from all other engagements, and if so he must discover if her heart be inclined towards our son.

[…]

If the Princess should reply that she is engaged to another, or if she should behave in such a way as to lead our Envoy to suppose that she was desirous of avoiding the proposal of marriage from our son, our

---

13. Trench, Charles Chenevix (1973). *Charles II*. London: Allen Lane, p.8.

Envoy is charged to beg the Princess not to make the slightest mention of the matter to anyone, and, under pretext that he has received news that his travelling companions have at last reached Nuremberg, he is to take leave of the Court of Ansbach, and return hither at once as secretly as he left.

[…]

The Princess will probably require time to consider the matter, in which case our Envoy will request her to think over the question by herself. Should the Princess delay in coming to a decision, our Envoy, in the most polite and delicate manner possible, will remind her that he must guard in every way against the Princess having any kind of communication with the Court of Berlin until such time as this project of marriage is so far established as to prevent any possibility of its being upset; and to this end our Envoy will most strongly urge that only trustworthy persons favourably disposed towards this marriage be employed in the drawing up of the contract.

[…]

Our Envoy can suggest to the Princess that an explanation could easily be given to the Court of Berlin later (with apologies for not having acquainted it before), to the effect that she was so hard pressed by our Envoy for a decision, she could not well refrain from accepting at once, the more especially as it was an offer she had no reason to refuse. Her brother, the Margrave, could say that he knew nothing of the matter until the Princess announced that she had chosen our son.'[14]

In fact, the powers that be from Hanover needn't have feared either a refusal or indiscretion. Caroline was quick to accept the proposal and receive consent

---

14. Wilkins, William Henry (1901). *Caroline, the Illustrious Queen-Consort of George II and Sometime Queen-Regent: A Study of Her Life and Time, Volume I*. London: J Murray, pp.44–48.

from her brother. Only then, was Sophia informed that the young lady she adored would soon be wife to the electoral prince, George Augustus.

It was the start of a powerful partnership.

Marrying Monsieur de Busch

Frederick I of Prussia was, understandably, most 'out of humour with the House of Lüneburg for sending so late to notify the conclusion of the marriage… but he [was] more angry with the Court of Ansbach who are a branch of his family and he a guardian to the Princess'.[15] There was nothing that he could do, but stamp his feet and on 2 September 1705, Caroline and George Augustus were married at Herrenhausen.

Ever the romantic, George Augustus slept through the ceremony. Caroline was wide awake, already dreaming of the glittering prizes that awaited her. Receiving her suitor at Triesdorf, Caroline had been the perfect wide-eyed innocent, as she played her part as a romantic lead. Yet this was the lady who resisted the attempts of Father Orban to covert her, who stuck to her guns even when the King of Prussia himself challenged her to do otherwise.

Caroline of Ansbach was not the innocent she might appear.

Courtier Lady Mary Wortley Montagu had her own suspicions about Caroline. She saw in the new electoral princess not a sweet orphan made good, but a shrewd, cunning woman who clumsily did all she could to gain the upper hand in her relationships with her husband and his family. Lady Mary charged her with:

> '[…] a low cunning, which gave her an inclination to cheat all the people she conversed with, and often cheated herself in the first place, by showing her the wrong side of her interest, not having understanding enough to observe that falsehood in conversation, like red on the face, should be used very seldom and very sparingly, or they destroy that interest and beauty that which they are designed to heighten.'[16]

15. Arkell, Ruby Lillian (1939). *Caroline of Ansbach: George the Second's Queen*. Oxford: Oxford University Press, p.23.
16. Wharncliffe, Lord (1837). *The Letters and Works of Lady Mary Wortley Montagu: Vol I*. London: Richard Bentley, p.118.

George Augustus wasn't quite the fairytale Prince Charming who had ridden into Triesdorf those short months earlier, either. Hot tempered and given to tantrums, he would hurl his wig to the ground and stamp on it, ranting and raving about whatever had caused his latest offence. Caroline endured his tempers with a serenity that endeared her even further to him.

Unlike Sophia Dorothea, who attempted to meet fire with fire when George I railed at her, Caroline knew better than to face George Augustus head-on. Instead, Lady Mary tells us that the new bride connived to distance her husband from his father and grandmother so that she alone might rule his head and heart. Indeed, she describes the scheme by which Caroline lamented her wedding gifts and, not at all by accident, drove a stake through George Augustus's already fractious relationship with his family.

> '[Caroline] could not help taking notice that the presents made to her on her wedding were not worthy of his bride, and at least she ought to have had all his mother's jewels. This was enough to make him lose all respect for his indulgent father. He downright abused his ministers, and talked impertinently to his old grandmother the Princess Sophia; which ended in such a coldness towards all his family as left him entirely under the government of his wife.'[17]

Of course, it wasn't *only* down to Caroline that George Augustus contrived a coldness for his father. *That* had been nurtured in childhood with the imprisonment of Sophia Dorothea, and the House of Hanover had hardly been a happy family since then. Still, Caroline was smart enough to know exactly how to handle her husband; it would help to make her one of George II's most trusted advisors and even, in time, his Regent.

Sons and Smallpox

At first the newlyweds were happily cosseted in the Leineschloss, but George Augustus was beginning to feel restless. He longed to go into battle, yet his father flatly refused to consider it until his son had done his duty and produced an heir.

---

17. Ibid., p.119.

His prayers were answered in the spring of 1706 when Caroline began to suspect that she might be pregnant. She was experiencing symptoms and her body was changing yet, oddly, her physicians tended to disagree. Instead they theorized that her pregnancy was nothing but wishful thinking, whilst the true cause of her symptoms was simply dropsy.

How wrong they were.

At the thought that she might not be pregnant, Caroline withdrew and began to suffer from anxiety that was scarcely relieved in 1707 even when she proved her physicians wrong. That February she gave birth to Frederick, one of only two sons that would survive to adulthood.[18] Finally George Augustus was able to go to war, leaving the sickly boy at home with his mother.

Or so he thought.

In fact, Caroline had been so weakened by the delivery of the rather large boy that her health was shattered and she fell ill with pneumonia and smallpox. George forgot his desperation to go into battle and pledged to remain at her bedside, no matter what the risk was. His grandmother, Sophia, fretted for the granddaughter-in-law she adored and perhaps unsurprisingly, George's devotion resulted in him contracting smallpox just as his bride was on the road to recovery.

Both survived the infection yet the experience made a deep impression on Caroline, serving as absolute proof of George Augustus's commitment to her. His father, George Louis, could hardly understand why he would have placed himself in such danger, yet to the electoral princess, his motive was clear. He adored her and during the occasionally fractious years of their marriage, he always would. Through the coming decades, they might not always have been the best of friends, but they remained very much a couple, united in ambition, in politics and in power.

Daughters and Mistresses

Little Frederick, aka *Fritz* to some and *Fred* to others, was not a well boy, having fallen victim to rickets in his early years. Thankfully he survived,

---

18. Caroline delivered eight live children, three boys and five girls. One son, Prince George William, did not survive infancy.

but with George Augustus finally allowed onto the battlefield and Fred a far from strong child, the pressure was on to add a *spare* to the *heir*.

In fact, this seemed to be a far taller order than anyone had expected and though Caroline gave birth to three daughters between 1707 and 1713,[19] there were no more sons for now. Caroline recognized the importance of ensuring the succession but was more than a little preoccupied with politics and, alongside her husband and his family, watched events in England keenly. Of course, the succession of the elector to the throne *should* be a forgone conclusion thanks to the Act of Settlement, yet Hanover and England were a long way apart and Caroline and George Augustus were both worried that something might yet happen to upset the plans for a Protestant succession.

When Queen Anne conferred on George Augustus the Order of the Garter and the title of Duke of Cambridge, Caroline thought that their moment had come. She went to his father and suggested that it might be a good idea to send her husband to England, where he could take his seat in the House of Lords. With Queen Anne and her government already slightly fearful of a Hanoverian takeover, George Louis dismissed the very idea of it, keen not to stir up any diplomatic drama. One can only wonder what he made of this bold daughter-in-law, married to the son whose relationship with him was so difficult.

The ambitious Caroline of Ansbach hadn't been raised to sit quietly in the corner and was ready to begin life in England. She employed an English servant to converse with and to read to her, determined to make the most of whatever opportunities came her way. The electoral princess was shrewd, smart and, as circumstances were about to show, a realist.

Ambition was not limited to Hanover, after all.

In Great Britain, everyone knew that Queen Anne was far from well and to those who had an eye on the future that meant only one thing: travel. From across the sea they came to Hanover, the families who meant to ingratiate themselves *now*, to win the favour of the soon-to-be-king and his family, no matter what it took. Among them was a woman who had strived, struggled and suffered to get here, who had sold everything she owned[20] and who,

---

19. They were Anne, Princess Royal (1709), Amelia (1711) and Caroline (1713).
20. Henrietta even looked into the possibility of selling her hair.

married to a brute, was seeking protection, security and the future she knew she could not have if she remained in England.

She was Henrietta Howard, and she was to be George Augustus' mistress for decades.

Orphaned at a young age and torn from an idyllic life, young Henrietta Hobart had sought security in marriage to Charles Howard, son of the Earl and Countess of Suffolk, and from that day on, had rued her decision. A womanizing gambler and a violent drunk, Charles took what money they had and abandoned his wife in London. If not for her quick thinking uncle, who placed Henrietta's inheritance in trust, things might have been even worse. Her fortune would not be released to be squandered by her husband, but would be kept safe for whatever children she had, robbing Charles of his chance to make a grab for his bride's cash. Her money might be safe, but Henrietta had nothing to call her own and life had become a living hell.

Whenever she had a spare penny, Henrietta hid it away. Sometimes Charles found the pot and spent it anyway but, slowly, surely, Henrietta began to accrue a travelling fund. She looked to Hanover as a land of plenty, a place where she and her husband might begin again, might escape their creditors, shed the shame that had attached to their name, and rediscover their respectability.

Finally, after long and agonizing months of struggle, Henrietta and Charles reached Hanover. Here it seemed that Henrietta's dreams were finally about to come true as the English couple swiftly found favour with the dowager electress and, through her, Caroline. The two women shared an interest in philosophy and both Sophie and Caroline promised Henrietta that, whichever one of them came to the throne of England first, they would appoint her as a Woman of the Bedchamber.

And then came George Augustus.

Henrietta and the electoral prince got on like the proverbial house on fire and though their relationship began as friends, at some point over the years, it blossomed into something more. Caroline was perfectly relaxed about all of this; she knew the reality of life as a royal wife, after all, and that reality included mistresses. Besides, as Lady Mary Wortley Montagu scathingly noted:

'[Caroline was] so devoted to [George Augustus's] pleasures, (which she often told him were the rule of all her thoughts and actions,) that whenever he thought proper to find them with other women, she even loved whoever was instrumental to his entertainment, and never resented anything but what appeared to her a want of respect for him.'[21]

Such was the bargain of the royal wife.

Succession

On 8 June 1714, whilst Dowager Electress Sophia was taking the air in the gardens of Herrenhausen with Caroline, a rainstorm forced the women to find shelter. Waiting for the downpour to subside, Sophia collapsed into the arms of her beloved granddaughter-in-law. She died later that day, going peacefully to her grave in the tranquil surroundings of the home she loved.

This meant that the Elector, George Louis, now stood to inherit the throne of Great Britain and nobody expected Queen Anne to last long, including the queen herself. In fact, she died less than two months after Sophia, and George I got ready to travel to England and assume his new position.

With him George took a vast selection of courtiers and domestic staff, among them was George Augustus, destined for a new life as Prince of Wales. For Caroline, this was the moment she had been waiting for. She envisioned a life in England of power and influence, of glamour and privilege and a canvas far broader than Hanover could offer.

Caroline didn't immediately leave with her husband, but instead remained on the continent until October. She was heartbroken to say goodbye to her brother, William Frederick, who had stood by her through thick and thin, and the two never met again.[22] Caroline's companions on her voyage to England were Anne and Amelia, with Caroline, her youngest child, set to follow on when she had recovered from an illness. For seven-year-old Fred, however, there was to be no such move.

---

21. Wharncliffe, Lord (1837). *The Letters and Works of Lady Mary Wortley Montagu: Vol I.* London: Richard Bentley, p.118.
22. William Frederick, Margrave of Brandenburg-Ansbach, died in 1723.

George Louis, now George I, decided instead that Fred should remain in Hanover. Cared for by his great-uncle, Ernest Augustus, the boy was destined to serve as the ceremonial figurehead of the House of Hanover in his homeland. Caroline was devastated to leave her son behind yet she was given no choice. As the years passed and Fred grew further and further apart from his family, her grief at their parting would turn into loathing for the young man but for now, the Princess of Wales had business to do.

The Princess of Wales

With his former wife captive at Ahlden and his mistress a wife in all but the legal sense of the word, George I found himself in a peculiar situation. He had no queen to call his own so for duties that required one, he called upon Caroline, the new Princess of Wales.

When Caroline and her daughters arrived at Margate they were reunited with the Prince of Wales before, amid great pomp and rejoicing, the family progressed on to London. Settled at St James's Palace, they were soon the talk of the town. The elector, grim-faced, ill-humoured and introverted, could not have been more different from his son and the cheery wife and children who accompanied him to London. They strolled in St James's Park, plunged into the social whirl of the city, and made new friends wherever they went, among noble and poor alike.

Caroline was, it seemed, too good to be true.

> 'The whole Conversation of this Place turns upon the Charms, Sweetness, and good Manner of that excellent princess, whose generous Treatment of everybody that had the Honour to approach her was such that none came from her without being obliged by some particular Expression of her Favour.'[23]

The couple dined in public every evening and when Caroline attended drawing rooms, everyone flocked to see her. All of this did nothing to endear the couple to George I. He did what he could to lessen the influence of

---

23. *Daily Courant* (London, England), Tuesday, 19 October, 1714; Issue 4052, p.3.

his son yet still his popularity continued. Unlike the king, the Prince and Princess of Wales could speak English well enough to be understood, and they were quick to shrewdly court their new British friends, telling them they would 'as soon live on a dunghill as return to Hanover'.[24]

With his love of all things Hanoverian, this was *not* what George I wanted to hear.

Caroline and George Augustus were having far too much fun to care.

In 1716, the Prince and Princess of Wales moved to Hampton Court to prepare for the imminent arrival of the child Caroline was carrying. Dedicated to her duties and to the guidance of her husband, much to the humour of his contemporaries, Caroline took some convincing to slow down until, in the middle of November 1716, she went into labour. The midwife and physician were summoned and, almost immediately, things began to go wrong.

Countess Cowper, Caroline's Lady of the Bedchamber, details the whole, long labour in her memoirs, documenting each dramatic twist as it happened. Although the first day passed without incident, when the second came, Caroline wasn't at all well. She was seized by a shivering fit and that was enough for the midwife to take fright. Lady Cowper tells us:

'The Midwife had refused to touch the *Princess* unless she and the *Prince* would stand by her against the English "Frows", who, she said, were high Dames and had threatened to hang her if the *Princess* miscarried.'[25]

George Augustus was furious at the fact that his wife's fragile state was being further compounded by such arguments and that hot temper burst forth once more. If he caught anyone meddling or causing upset, he declared, he would fling the wrongdoer from the window. Immediately the mood changed and the courtiers jumped to it, with Lord Townshend quick to smooth the midwife's ruffled feathers whilst the princess's ladies fluttered to her side, promising all the assistance she might need.

---

24. Graves, Charles (1963). *Palace Extraordinary*. London: Cassell, p.98.
25. Cowper, Countess Mary (1865). *Diary of Mary, Countess Cowper, Lady of the Bedchamber to the Princess of Wales, 1714–1720*. London: J Murray, p.127.

Despite their efforts, Caroline's son was stillborn. The strain of the birth left her near death. Frail and weak, she remained at Hampton Court as the nation held its breath, waiting for news of the unhappy princess.

In fact, Caroline of Ansbach would live to fight on and by December, the press was filled with notices of her recovery. It was the perfect opportunity for enterprising Georgians to cash in.

'This Day is published, The Great Happiness of a Faithful Princess in Child-bearing. Set forth in a thanksgiving Sermon upon the entire Recovery of her Royal Highness the Princess of WALES from Her late Illness in Child-bed.'[26]

Recovered she might be, but the stillbirth reminded Caroline of the son she had left behind in Hanover. She longed for another child to embrace in place of the little boy she had been forbidden to see and now, hardly giving herself time to recover, she fell pregnant again.

The fallout would almost shatter the House of Hanover.

A Catastrophic Christening

When Caroline gave birth to a seemingly healthy baby boy in November 1717, the Prince and Princess of Wales were delighted. Across Britain, the people rejoiced and at court, the atmosphere was one of celebration.

'*Whitehall*, Nov. 4. On Saturday the 2nd Instant, a little before Six a Clock in the Evening, her Royal Highness the Princess of Wales was safely delivered of a Prince, in the Royal Palace of St. James's; there being there present in the Room, His Royal Highness the Prince of Wales; the Lord Archbishop of Canterbury; the Duchesses of St. Albans, Montague, and Shrewsbury, the Countess of Dorset, the Lady Inchinbroke, the Lady Cowper, being the Ladies of Her Royal Highness's Bed-Chamber; the Duchess of Monmouth, the

---

26. *Post Man and the Historical Account* (London, England), 13 December, 1716–December 15, 1716; Issue 11520, p.2.

Countess of Grantham, the Countess of Picbourg, the Governess of their Highnesses the young Princesses; all the Women of Her Royal Highness's Bed Chamber; Sir David Hamilton, and Dr. Steirgerdahl Physician to His Majesty.

Their Royal Highnesses dispatched the Lord Harvey to Hampton-Court, to acquaint His Majesty with it, and to make their Compliments; and His Majesty was pleased to send immediately the same evening the Duke of Portland, with His Compliments to their Royal Highnesses. Her Royal Highness's safe Delivery being soon made publick by the firing of the Cannon in St. James's Park, and at the Tower, a universal Joy was seen that Evening among all Sorts of People throughout London and Westminster, of which the greatest Demonstrations were shown by Ringing of Bells, Illuminations, and Bonfires.

[…]

Her Royal Highness and the young Prince, are (God be praised) in very good Health.'[27]

The baby, who would be named George William, was the first British royal son to be born in years. The last had been James Stuart, *the Old Pretender,* that thorn in the side of the Hanoverians. This new baby would cause problems of an altogether different kind.

The christening would be conducted in Caroline's bedchamber by William Wake, Archbishop of Canterbury. Wake was a great favourite of the princess but as soon as the planning began, George I just had to stick his oar in. He was king, after all, and what he wanted, he got.

What he wanted *this* time was to choose the name and the godparents; this was *not* negotiable.

Caroline favoured the name William yet when the king suggested that the boy be called George, the Prince and Princes of Wales readily acquiesced. On the matter of godparents, however, things got a little more stuck and

---

27. *London Gazette* (London, England), 2 November, 1717–5 November, 1717; Issue 5587, p.4.

when a newspaper innocently reported that discussions were taking place regarding the christening, they can little have guessed what was happening behind the scenes.

> 'We hear that his Majesty and his most Serene Highness the Margrave of Anspach [sic], Brother to her Royal Highness the Princess of Wales, will be Godfathers, and the Queen of Prussia, his Majesty's Daughter, Godmother to the young Prince, and the Duke of Newcastle,[28] will stand Proxy for the Margrave and Duchess of St Alban's[29] for her Prussian Majesty.'[30]

This report belies the heartache and drama that would follow, let alone the arguments that had gone before. In fact, neither the Prince nor Princess of Wales wanted Newcastle and had instead envisioned George William's great-uncle, Ernest Augustus, as godfather. Yet the king was set on a role for Newcastle, whom the new parents loathed, and the king *always* got his way.

George I knew that his son didn't want Newcastle anywhere near the ceremony, yet he persisted anyway. The relationship between the two Georges, always marked by antagonism and one-upmanship, was about to explode. Since the king had insisted on the separation of Frederick from his parents, George Augustus believed that George I had worked to undermine his influence on the boy, to mould him in his own image. Perhaps George I saw in George Augustus his errant former wife, perhaps he simply resented the younger man's popularity. Whatever it was, the monarch was not about to step back and take Newcastle with him.

At the christening ceremony tempers flared, voices were raised and the prince, driven to anger, warned Newcastle, 'you are a rascal, but I shall find you', meaning that he would show everyone just what a bad sort the duke

---

28. Thomas Pelham-Holles, 1st Duke of Newcastle, was an influential Whig politician and brother to Henry Pelham, Prime Minister. He was a member of Robert Walpole's powerful faction.
29. Diana Beauclerk, Duchess of St Albans, was considered a great court beauty in her youth, and was now employed as Mistress of the Robes to Caroline.
30. *Weekly Packet* (London, England), 9 November, 1717–16 November, 1717; Issue 280, p.3.

was. Newcastle told the king that George Augustus had said, 'I shall fight you', which the prince utterly refuted. He blamed his German accent for the misunderstanding, suggesting that perhaps Newcastle had not been able to fully understand his words. The inflamed duke wasn't backing down; he had been threatened, and something must be done.

And it was.

Henrietta Howard was shocked to discover that, by the following morning, the prince had been placed under house arrest.

'What was my astonishment [...] when going to the Princess's apartment the next morning, the yeomen in the guard-chamber pointed their halberds at my breast, and told me I must not pass! I urged that it was my duty to attend the Princess. They said, 'No matter; I must not pass that way.'[31]

The Prince of Wales was ordered to leave St James's Palace and not return. He was to be deprived of his royal guard and should any courtiers choose to go with him, then they too would be banished from the king's presence.

This was a gamble that didn't wholly pay off. The king wasn't getting younger, after all, and many chose to keep favour with the incoming monarch rather than the irascible existing one. When George learned that Caroline wished to go too, he told her that she was more than welcome to do so, yet it would mean surrendering her children to his custody. The heartbroken princess held true to her word but 'went into one faint after another when her weeping little princesses said goodbye'.[32]

Hardly recovered from the birth, the exhausted Caroline fell into a swoon as soon as she and her husband arrived at the home of Lord Grantham, where they were to stay until they could find more a permanent abode. Hearing of her indisposition the king sent word that she would still be welcome at court

31. Walpole, Horace (1842). *Letters of Horace Walpole, Earl of Orford, Vol I*. London: Lea and Blanchard, p.83.
32. Kroll, Marie (ed.) (1842). *Letters from Liselotte*. London: Allison & Busby, p.207.

if she renounced her husband. Despite her despair she replied unequivocally that her children 'were not a grain of sand compared to him'.[33]

So now, with her eldest son lost to her and living an increasingly indulged life in Hanover, Caroline had willingly removed herself from her children, including the newborn George William whose baptism had started the drama. Perhaps she thought the king would relent but if she did, Caroline was mistaken. George I had form for this sort of thing, after all.

In fact, so set was the king on the path he had chosen that he told his son there might be a chance for the prince and princess to be received back into the royal bosom, but only if they agreed to certain conditions. They must sign a guarantee that they would never befriend, employ or associate with anyone whom the king found distasteful. The couple understandably balked at this and the battle lines were drawn.

Separation

As George Augustus and his father entered into a war of attrition, Caroline stood firmly at her husband's side. Awarded the nickname of 'cette diablesse Madame la Princesse', by the king, she was the Prince of Wales's rock now as she had always been. Yet for all her devotion and strength, the separation from her children proved as painful as a wound to the Princess of Wales.

The estranged royal couple established a home at Leicester House, where opponents of the king were regular visitors. Here Caroline was lauded as a political force to be reckoned with, *Caroline the Illustrious* reigning at the head of her alternative court. Among those who visited were Alexander Pope and two of Caroline's greatest friends, the waspish commentator, Lord Hervey, and political giant, Robert Walpole. Walpole would remain a powerful ally throughout her life, often to her husband's chagrin.

The daily drawing rooms and regular evening receptions at Leicester House soon became the hottest ticket in town and when they weren't entertaining at home, the prince and princess were putting in appearances

---

33. Wilkins, William Henry (1901). *Caroline, the Illustrious Queen-Consort of George II and Sometime Queen-Regent: A Study of Her Life and Time, Volume I*. London: J Murray, p.279.

at the most fashionable events in London. They relaxed at Richmond Lodge, where Caroline indulged her passion for architecture in the building of follies and grottos that were intended to delight the eye and engage the mind. She loved wandering the grounds and plotting ever more elaborate improvements to the gardens, soon making them the talk of the town.

For all her influence and style though, the princess was increasingly feeling the strain of her emotional distress. She pined for her children and they desperately missed her, with neither party taking much comfort from the daily visits of an envoy from the palace, who brought news of how the little ones were faring. Secret notes were exchanged, clandestine meetings with friends and ladies-in-waiting held in garden hideaways and, with those at the palace aware of the suffering of both mother and children, Caroline began to think about sneaking back into St James's Palace.

For all her ambition, her guidance, her strong will and hard head, Caroline had perhaps reckoned without the pain the separation would cause. Petitions to the king fell on deaf ears, yet it was the plaintive pleas of a child that finally swayed him, if only a little.

Anne, the eight-year-old Princess Royal, was the oldest of the children under the king's care and she did all she could to keep in contact with her parents. The little girl sent gifts via intermediaries and lamented: 'We have a good father and a good mother and yet we are like charity children',[34] adding that the king rarely came to see his grandchildren because, 'he does not love us enough for that'.[35]

When George I heard this he made a concerted effort to see the youngsters more often and found, perhaps to his surprise, that he enjoyed their gentle company. Surely he realized now how much their parents must miss their little ones, and when he discovered that the Prince and Princess of Wales had made a clandestine trip to the palace, the king made the barest concession he could.

As you might imagine, that secret visit to the children had been emotional. Caroline swooned and George Augustus wept yet the stolen moment was over too quickly and at the end of it, both the parents and their children were plunged once more into unhappiness. No anger can boil forever though and

---

34. Arkell, Ruby Lillian (1939). *Caroline of Ansbach: George the Second's Queen*. Oxford: Oxford University Press, p.107.
35. Ibid.

swayed by his own time in the royal nursery, George I eventually agreed that Caroline could visit her children freely and without notice. She could not, however, take them to live at Leicester House.

The princess was delighted yet delight turned to despair in February 1718 when George William, who was less than three-months-old, fell dangerously ill with a polyp on his heart. With Caroline in regular attendance, the king had the little boy and his sisters moved to the clean yet damp confines of Kensington Palace. Mercifully his mother was allowed to visit as often as she wanted over those terrible, final days.

> 'Last Wednesday in the Evening the Princess (being informed Prince George-William was ill) went to St. James's to see him; and, after some little stay there, she return'd to Leicester-Fields, and the young prince, with his three Sisters were soon after sent to Kensington, whither the Prince and Princess went to see them. The young Prince continuing dangerously Ill, the next Day they came again to Kensington, and found him much worse; their Royal Highnesses continu'd with him till about Half an Hour of his Death, which was between six and seven o' th' Clock on Thursday in the Evening. The Concern their Royal Highnesses shew'd upon this Occasion is unexpressible [sic]. The young Prince, whilst he was at Kensington, was attended by the Doctors, Mead, Stone, Hamilton and a German Physician.'[36]

Soon after the death of her youngest son, Caroline suffered another miscarriage. Lower than she had ever been, she now fixated on one thing: to have the custody of her daughters once more.

And for that, she would need Walpole.

Claiming Custody

In 1719, George I decided that a trip to Hanover was in order to revisit the land he so loved. Perhaps showing a slight thawing in his demeanour, he

---

36. *Weekly Journal or Saturday's Post* (London, England), Saturday, 8 February, 1718; Issue 61, p.4.

wrote to Caroline and invited her to come to Hampton Court and spend the summer there with her children. She replied that she would be happy to, should her husband be allowed to join her.

Needless to say, that was the end of that.

By 1720 George Augustus and Caroline had been at daggers drawn with George I for more than two years. Caroline took her revenge on the king by establishing her home as the most glittering and influential opposition gathering place in the country, yet it was nothing compared to the children she still longed for. Under the influence of the Prince and Princess of Wales, Leicester Fields was transformed into a place where Whig grandees and up-and-coming talents could be seen gallivanting with decorous young ladies at all hours of the day and night, whilst scholars, bluestockings and celebrities were regular visitors. Even Isaac Newton, who Caroline had admired since her early days in Berlin, became a familiar sight, as he attended audiences with the princess.

In spite of all of these visitors, the faces that Caroline was most desperate to see were those of her children. Perhaps inevitably, the case eventually came before a panel of ten judges and it was left to the might of the law to decide the fate of the little princesses. The answer that came back from Lord Chief Justice Parker was unequivocal and for Caroline, it was shattering.

The children, he ruled, would not be returned to their parents. The king was awarded the sole right to decide on their education and was given full reign over their upbringing, including the power to grant or deny visitation to the distraught prince and princess. Lord Cowper, the Lord Chancellor, felt so strongly that this was the wrong decision that he resigned his position, while Parker, for his supposedly independent judgment, was made an earl.

'I see how all these Things go; I must be the Sufferer at last, and have no Power to help myself,'[37] wrote Caroline and across England, gossip about the discord at the heart of the royal family was rife. Robert Walpole, that inveterate schemer, saw in this the opportunity to sow the seeds of reunion as well as pave the way for an improvement in his fractious relationship with George Augustus. After all, George I wouldn't live forever and if Walpole

---

37. Cowper, Mary (1865). *Diary of Mary, Countess Cowper, Lady of the Bedchamber to the Princess of Wales, 1714-1720*. London: J Murray, p.131.

wanted his glittering career to continue, he had to be well in with the incomer, not just the incumbent.

Life, however, was about to deal another devastating blow.

Reconciliation

As Caroline of Ansbach knew only too well from her own childhood, smallpox was a cruel and all too common part of life in the eighteenth century. She had lost her father to the infection and for those who lived through the Georgian era, the devastation it caused was never too far away. When little Anne fell victim to smallpox in 1720, her illness played directly into Walpole's hands. As soon as she was taken ill, Caroline was granted leave by the king to visit her. Still she was told that she must bring no physician, as the care of the children remained in the hands of the monarch.

Caroline often spent nine devoted hours or more at her daughter's side each day as her condition began to improve. Although she would bear the scars of smallpox for the rest of her life, Anne survived. Yet it had given the king a scare and the last thing he wanted was another dead grandchild on his hands. After all, the public already took a dim view of him and the thought that Anne might have died whilst in his custody was a step too far.

For the Prince and Princess of Wales, reconciliation might have a more financial benefit too. Their household was deep in debt and renewing familial ties would increase the likelihood of those debts being paid off. Walpole, seeing his chance to increase his standing with George Augustus, made it his mission to reunite the families once and for all. For her part, Caroline left him in no doubt that this must be accomplished not for money, but for the sake of her children. She told him, 'this will be no jesting Matter to me; you will hear of me and my Complaints every Day and Hour, and in every Place, if I have not my Children again'.[38]

Walpole knew of the influence that Caroline exerted over her husband and determined to bring about the reconciliation, thus placing the Princess of Wales and future queen firmly in his debt. The time had come, Walpole determined, to knit the royal household together once more.

---

38. Ibid., p.132.

Accordingly, Walpole asked Caroline if George Augustus might be prevailed upon to write a formal letter of apology to the king. Though her husband balked at the thought of it, Walpole 'engrossed and monopolized the Princess to a degree of making her deaf to everything that did not come from him',[39] and she pushed and nudged at the prince, urging him to reconsider.

Lady Cowper, who wrote extensively on the comings and goings at Leicester House, noted that Walpole also let George Augustus have a fling with his own wife.[40] Indeed, she notes, Caroline knew of the relationship and took no action. Of course, we wouldn't expect her to; she was a princess, after all, mistresses were part of the territory. She numbered Henrietta Howard among her confidantes and attendants, so she wasn't about to cause a scandal over the presence of Mrs Walpole.

The hard-headed prince declared to his wife that he would be happy to write to the king and demand his children, his right to be regent, his palaces and his official guard. Soothing as ever, Caroline continued to work on her husband until he agreed that Walpole could request an audience on his behalf. At that meeting, George Augustus didn't press the point of custody but instead focused on the matter of clearing his debts. Upon hearing of what he had negotiated, Caroline was horrified. She considered that she had been betrayed, believing that George Augustus had sold the girls to their grandfather in return for a financial settlement.

Yet what was done was done and when George Augustus was summoned for a private audience with his father, he didn't tell his wife. She found out quite by accident as she arrived in Pall Mall to visit the convalescing Princess Anne and spotted the prince as he departed the presence of the king. Despite her reservations, Caroline knew how important it was that the two men reconcile so when she was invited to her own private audience with George I, she was quick to attend.

---

39. Cowper, Mary (1865). *Diary of Mary, Countess Cowper, Lady of the Bedchamber to the Princess of Wales, 1714-1720*. London: J Murray, p.134.
40. Catherine, Lady Walpole, was married to Walpole from 1700 until her death in 1737. Among their six children was the famed diarist and courtier, Horace Walpole, 4th Earl of Orford, who was rumoured to have been fathered not by Sir Robert but by the waspish Lord Hervey.

Caroline said little about that meeting other than that it had been a pleasure to see her father-in-law so happy again. Walpole's version of events was somewhat different, and he claimed that the king had read the riot act to the princess. He had informed her in no uncertain terms that he knew how much influence she wielded over her husband and told her that, in future, she should exert it for good, not mischief.

In fact, the reconciliation was not a happy reunion between father and son, but a cynical arrangement borne out of financial need on the side of the Prince of Wales and public relations on the side of the king. The Jacobites, for so long agitating against the royal family, were now confronted with an apparently united front and the people of Great Britain likewise. Given free rein to see their children whenever they might wish, the Prince and Princess of Wales were allowed to return to court, though remained forbidden from using the royal residences as their own. As far as the world knew, all was happy at St James's Palace once more.

The Scourge of Smallpox

As Walpole had been working his charms on the warring father and son, Caroline had more medical matters on her mind. No stranger to the devastation wreaked by smallpox, she made it her mission to do all she could to spare anyone else the horrors she had known. She began to study the disease and its history, focusing on the treatments others had pioneered and eagerly devouring research on the subject.

It was during her studies that Caroline encountered the writings of Lady Mary Wortley Montagu, a courtier, lady of letters and traveller. Smallpox had claimed the life of Mary's brother and left Mary herself scarred for life, leaving her eyes without eyelashes and rendering them exceedingly prominent. Understandably, Lady Mary had quite an interest in smallpox so, when she heard of an ancient practice whilst living in the Ottoman Empire, she wanted to know more. Variolation, as the method was called, was barely known in the west yet widely practised in the east.

It involved introducing a very small amount of tissue infected with smallpox into a healthy patient, thus giving them permanent immunity. It was usually done by rubbing powdered smallpox scabs into scratches made on the skin of the recipient and though they should expect a mild infection to follow, once that had cleared up, they would be protected from the deadly disease for life. The practice had been documented in China since the fifteenth century though its origins are probably older than that, yet western physicians considered it to be superstitious folklore with no medical merit.

How wrong they were.

Lady Mary had seen firsthand how efficacious variolation could be during her travels in the Ottoman Empire. She was sure that if she could only get someone to take it seriously, it could revolutionize treatment in Europe. This was decades before Edward Jenner successfully pioneered his cowpox-derived smallpox vaccination and for hundreds of thousands of people, a diagnosis meant a death sentence.

In her letters, Lady Mary describes the practice, writing:

'[…] the old woman comes with a nut-shell full of the matter of the best sort of small-pox, and asks what vein you please to have opened. She immediately rips open that you offer to her with a large needle (which gives you no more pain than a common scratch), and puts into the vein as much matter as can lye upon the head of her needle, and after that binds up the little wound with a hollow bit of shell […] The children or young patients play together all the rest of the day and are in perfect health to the eighth. Then the fever begins to seize them and they keep their beds two days, very seldom three. […] There is no example of any one that has died in it and you may believe I am well satisfied of the safety of this experiment since I intend to try it on my dear little son.'[41]

In order to bring the treatment to Britain, however, she needed to find a champion who was respected amongst the medical establishment there. She found that champion in Charles Maitland, a Scottish surgeon who Lady Mary met in Turkey and who shared her enthusiasm for variolation.

Caroline, Maitland and Lady Mary shared a determination to battle the scourge of smallpox in Great Britain. With the Princess of Wales backing their cause things moved fast and Caroline established an experiment that may, to our modern eyes, appear just a little bit barbaric.

Six convicts from Newgate Prison were invited to serve as guinea pigs for the treatment, on the promise that they would receive their freedom in return for allowing Maitland to variolate them. Given the choice between Newgate and smallpox, it's hardly surprising that they all chose the latter and, in August 1721, the procedure took place.

> 'Yesterday morning they began the Experiment on Inoculating the Small-Pox upon the six Criminals in Newgate, […] Mr. Charles Maitland the Surgeon perform'd the Operation, who a few Years since hath practis'd it in Turkey, and has lately introduced it with Success into England.'[42]

The experiment was a success and all of the convicts survived to enjoy their newly-granted freedom. Though Caroline was satisfied that adults could survive variolation, it was her children that concerned her and she determined that there should be another experiment, this one on a handful of young orphans. The guinea pigs all lived and were shown off to the public, as the *London Gazette* testified:

> 'Since the Experiment made some time ago by Mr. Maitland of inoculating the Small-Pox upon several Criminals in Newgate, their Royal Highnesses the Prince and Princess of Wales being desirous for a Confirmation of the Safety and Ease of this Practice that a further Experiment should be made, six Persons more had the Small-Pox inoculated upon them […] which has succeeded very well […] and the Curious may be further satisfied by a Sight of those Persons at Mr Foster's House […] where attendance is given every Day from Ten till Twelve before Noon, and from Two till Four in the Afternoon.'[43]

Caroline was finally convinced, and allowed her children to be variolated, her name and patronage lending the process weight as over time, more and

---

42. *Daily Post* (London, England), Thursday, 10 August, 1721; Issue 581, p.1.
43. *London Gazette* (London, England), 6 March, 1722–10 March, 1722; Issue 6040, p.7.

more people underwent the procedure. Thanks to Caroline's involvement, variolation found a popularity it might otherwise not have known, and not one of those variolated royal children fell victim to smallpox.

A Happy Interlude

In the years that followed the reconciliation of the royal household, Caroline gave birth to three more children, William, Mary and Louisa,[44] yet without a doubt the favourite was William. He was the spare to the heir they had left behind in Hanover, Frederick morphing over the years from the child the Prince and Princess of Wales missed desperately into a puppet of George I, and a stranger to his parents. The couple's last child was born in 1724.

'ON Monday last, about Half an Hour past Four in the Afternoon, her Royal Highness the Princess of Wales was happily delivered of a Princess at Leicester House.'[45]

Years on, that pregnancy would be the death of Caroline. For now though, all was well; things were calm, the court was glittering and she was enjoying her life once more. Caroline's youngest children were born at Leicester House and remained in the custody of their parents, while the three older girls were all freely available to the princess whenever she wished to see them.

Casting about for something to do, Caroline adopted into her court a character known as Peter the Wild Boy, an apparently feral child who George I had brought back to England from a hunting trip in Hanover. With the boy treated as a pet, she saw to it that he received good care and an education, but this was little more than a diversion. Searching for a useful way to fill her days, she spent long hours improving her gardens and assembling an impressive cabinet of curiosities as well as an extensive library, but the politically engaged princess's life had certainly become a lot quieter.

Being unkind, one might suggest that Caroline rather enjoyed the drama of the separation. I don't necessarily agree with this, but I do wonder if she

---

44. William, Mary and Louisa were born in 1721, 1723 and 1724 respectively.
45. *London Journal (1720)* (London, England), Saturday, 12 December, 1724, p.2.

missed the intriguing and highhandedness of dealing with Walpole during those tumultuous years. Now Caroline contented herself with trouble of a more domestic sort, marshalling the increasingly wilful Anne, Princess Royal, pulling rank on Henrietta Howard and perhaps dreaming of the day when she would be queen.

That day came in 1727 when, on a visit to Hanover, King George I died. And all hell was about to break loose.

Hail to the Queen

On the day that George and Caroline heard from Robert Walpole that they were now the King and Queen of Great Britain and Ireland, they were together at Richmond Lodge. The news was momentous for any number of reasons, one of which was the realization that they would finally be reunited as a family. Once, long ago, Leibniz had likened Caroline to Elizabeth I and now she was determined to live up to that comparison. Later the couple would be mocked in the verse that follows but for now, the atmosphere was one of celebration:

> You may strut, dapper George, but 'twill all be in vain;
> We all know 'tis Queen Caroline, not you, that reign –
> You govern no more than Don Philip of Spain.
> Then if you would have us fall down and adore you,
> Lock up your fat spouse, as your dad did before you.[46]

When the family arrived at Leicester House, the court rushed out to greet them, bowing and scraping. One notable exception was Robert Walpole, who wasn't present to mark the arrival of the new king and queen. Indeed, it seemed as though his star had fallen at last when the monarch summoned Spencer Compton, and asked *him* to write an important speech. It was a clear signal to Walpole that he was yesterday's man and that the new king had already found his favourite.

---

46. Hervey, John and Croker, John Wilson (ed.). (1848). *Memoirs of the Reign of George the Second: Vol I*. London: John Murray, p.93.

In fact, Compton faltered, naively seeking assistance from Walpole. When George raised questions about the content of the speech, Caroline suggested that he call Walpole in to clarify matters, neatly undermining Compton and letting her favourite subtly claim credit for the work.

With Compton and Walpole still vying for the top job, Caroline then played her strongest card: *money*. She summoned Walpole and let him know that George needed cash. Compton, she confided, had promised him £60,000 per year; should Walpole be able to raise that to £100,000, it would go very well in his favour.

In that case, Walpole decided, £100,000 is exactly what he would offer.

The rest, as they say, is history. Walpole's feet were soon securely back under the royal table, and would remain there for years to come.

When Lady Walpole arrived at the drawing room that night she found herself shunned by courtiers who believed that her husband's power had evaporated. Caroline called out to Lady Walpole and summoned her forward, spending some considerable time chatting to her in full view of the other attendees. The message to the courtiers was clear: the Walpoles were a force to be reckoned with once more.

The coronation of George II and Caroline of Ansbach at Westminster Abbey was utterly magnificent. Although it took place in October, the weather was fine and the new queen was resplendent in her brand new state robes, proudly drenched in pearls, diamonds and the finest of everything. Sitting there at her side, observing the ceremony with great solemnity, George II must have blessed his good fortune. This was not another Sophia Dorothea, unhappy and desperate to escape, but the most loyal consort any king could wish for. Smart, shrewd and influential, Queen Caroline was more than a match for her husband.

Of course, she would never let George see that she was his superior in both intellect and politics. Far from it, in fact, as the new queen was quick to apparently defer to him in all things and in this deference, she gained even more influence. Her interjection in political meetings was always a little uncertain and she preferred to give the impression that she was reticent and reluctant to put her opinion forward, an approach that worked wonders. Employing secret signals with Walpole, Caroline was a past master at implanting her schemes in George's mind and letting him think that the ideas were his.

Alongside Walpole, the queen exercised immense influence over the nation yet George, shortsighted and self-important, saw none of it. He saw instead only what Caroline and Walpole wanted him to see.

Caroline the Illustrious

George I had not trusted his estranged son, George Augustus, to serve as Regent and he in turn had no intention of inviting his own son, Frederick, to take the role. Instead he selected his wife and, in 1729, Caroline ruled over Great Britain whilst George went home to Hanover. As apparently unassuming as ever, the queen meekly accepted the responsibility, even as in her heart she was no doubt rejoicing in having true power at last, the pinnacle of her ambitions realized with Walpole at her side.

No sooner had she dried her tears at her husband's departure than Queen Caroline was throwing herself into the job, holding her first Council less than a week after the king had departed. This was not ambition without ability though, because Caroline had both in spades. In fact, her husband could hardly have chosen a better candidate for the job.

The woman who had once been likened to Queen Elizabeth I proved herself a more than able regent, negotiating with foreign powers and even thrashing out the Treaty of Seville, which secured peace between Spain and England, restored English trade routes to America and passed responsibility for Gibraltar to the crown. Of course, she wasn't *solely* responsible for these discussions, but she had a confidence and lightness of touch that was welcome in negotiations. Caroline was given to listening to her own counsel over that of her ministers, enjoyed public popularity for her efforts to integrate into Britain and was a more valuable ally than any prime minister.

She was not, of course, infallible.

One of Queen Caroline's most serious brushes with unpopularity came in 1733 with the excise crisis. Walpole proposed a new Excise Bill that would bring tobacco and wine duty under the auspices of the excise, thinking it an uncontroversial move. In keeping with items such as tea and coffee, these goods would be subject to a duty not when they were imported into the country for storage, but only when they left storage to be sold. Should they never be sold in Great Britain and continue on from storage to another destination overseas, no levy would be due. By subjecting alcohol and tobacco to this duty, Walpole's Whigs envisioned a vastly increased amount of money pouring into government coffers; the Tories, however, saw things differently.

This was tantamount to handing the government the key to a man's home and inviting them in to rifle through his personal affairs, they argued. New officials would be appointed to oversee the system and, far from the relatively small number of agents that would actually be needed, the Tories stoked fears of a veritable army of government men rooting about in private business. Walpole's intention had actually been to lessen the burden on the weighty land tax; instead, his relatively unobtrusive ideas caused mayhem.

Wine and tobacco were, of course, two of the engines that drove Georgian society and they were indelibly linked with another: criminality. Everyone knew that booze and tobacco were popular commodities of smugglers and that the duties collected from both were far less than they should have been. Even the most innocuous, careful shopkeeper might not have been keeping the most up-to-date books, yet under Walpole's plan the gathering of these duties would be tightened considerably and those books might, just might, be looked at a little more closely. Soon the bill's opponents were fanning the flames of public concern and 'represented the excise as a monster feeding on its own vitals; and compared it to the Trojan horse, which contained an army in its belly.'[47]

The merchant classes were hugely powerful and pamphleteers swiftly took up the cause to warn of a few unexpected side effects of the new influx of excise men, as *A New Song* testifies!

YE Knaves and ye Fools, you Maids, Widows and Wives,
Come cast away Care and rejoice all your Lives;
For since *England* was *England*, I dare boldly say,

---

47. Coxe, William (1800). *Memoirs of the Life and Administration of Sir Robert Walpole, Earl of Orford: Vol II*. London: T Cadell, Jun and W Davies, p.198.

There ne'er was such Cause for a Thanksgiving Day:
For if we're but wise,
And vote for the Excise,
Sir Blue-String[48] declares (as you know he ne'er lies)
He'll dismiss the whole *Custom-House* rascally Crew,
And fix in each Town an *Exciseman* or two.

[…]

When we're *absent* they'll visit and look to our Houses,
Will tutor our Daughters, and comfort our Spouses;
Condescend, at our Cost, to eat and to drink,
That our Ale mayn't turn sour, or our Victuals mayn't stink.

[…]

An *Excise* that is *general* will set us quite free
From the Thraldom or Tryals by Judge and Ju-ry
And put us into a right *summary* Way
Of paying but what the Commissioners say:
And what need we fear
Their being severe,
Who for fining us have but a Thousand a Year;
'Tis better on such chosen Men to rely,
Than on Reason, or Law, or an honest Ju-ry.[49]

By whipping up fears of marital discord, the removal of trial by jury and the end of civil liberties, the bill's opponents successfully stoked the fires of dissent. The public listened in horror to the warnings of the Tories and Walpole's enemies saw this as a chance to finally move against the all-powerful prime minister. They approached Caroline with their concerns, mindful of

---

48. *Sir Blue-String* was a sly reference to Sir Robert Walpole, clad in the Garter blue riband.
49. Anonymous (1733). *A New Song: To the Tune of Packington's Pound*. London: F Giles, p.1.

her influence with Walpole and she sent them packing in no uncertain terms as, in the streets, demonstrations and dissent broke out. Across the land, the people united as one against the excise plans and effigies of Walpole and the queen were burned in the streets of London.

When Walpole tried to assuage fears that this was the first sign of a government intent on wringing every penny it could out of the public, he could hardly make himself heard over the furious demonstrations. Parliamentary support of the bill began to dwindle as politicians feared to be associated with the disastrous measures and Walpole, facing one of his rare failures, sought an audience with the royal couple.

The king, queen and prime minister agreed that the excise bill should be dropped yet, crucially, they decided that parliament shouldn't learn of this decision until *after* the vote. Having held such high hopes for the financial benefits of the bill this was a bitter blow to Walpole and Caroline, but worse was yet to come. At a private audience with the queen, Walpole offered his resignation. She rejected it, the thought of losing her closest political ally one she just couldn't countenance.

One day after that meeting the ballot was held and the government won by less than twenty votes, which essentially meant it wasn't really a victory at all. This was a humiliation that Walpole's enemies were sure he couldn't possibly survive, yet they didn't know that the king and queen had already rejected the possibility of his resignation. Walpole was safe as ever, even if he had to endure a little egg on his usually spotless face.

Amid scenes of utter chaos, Walpole stood before parliament and declared that the excise bill would go no further. He, however, wasn't going anywhere and those who had spoken against him in parliament now found that his revenge was swift and sure. Offices were revoked, dismissals were made and glittering careers ended in the blink of an eye.

It really didn't do to cross Walpole, let alone burn the queen in effigy, after all.

Farewell Henrietta, Hello Amalie

When Henrietta Howard became George's mistress, Caroline accepted the situation not with resignation, but readily. Ever the realist, she knew that court mistresses were a part of life and it was preferable that her husband took a lover whose ambition was only to escape her brutal spouse, rather than to wield any political power of her own. Henrietta was also a useful foil to absorb some of George's bad temper: far better he rant and tantrum in her chambers than Caroline's, after all!

Alongside Caroline's faithful confidante, Charlotte Clayton, later Baroness Sundon, Henrietta served as Lady of the Bedchamber to the queen. Mrs Clayton had gained her station through her friendship with the Duchess of Marlborough and was one of Caroline's most trusted confidantes. Likewise, Henrietta wisely chose to devote herself to Caroline's needs even as her husband was devoted to the service of the late George I so, when Caroline and George were banished from court all those years ago, it was to prove unexpectedly fortuitous for Mrs Howard.

When George I told his son to leave the palace and Caroline chose to go with him, it gave Henrietta a wonderful excuse to escape her husband. She flatly refused to abandon Caroline and, bound to George I, Charles Howard had no choice but to let her go. As time passed, he did all he could to win his wife back, including petitioning the Archbishop of Canterbury, but no matter what Charles did, Henrietta wouldn't budge. Things came to a head when the hot-headed courtier threatened to drag Henrietta bodily from the queen's carriage, causing Caroline to see him off in no uncertain terms. Although she sent him away with a flea in his ear, Caroline admitted to Hervey:

> 'I was horribly afraid of him (for we were tete-a-tete) all the while I was thus playing the bully. What added to my fear upon this occasion [...] was that, as I knew him to be so brutal, as well as a little mad, and seldom quite sober, so I did not think it impossible but that he might throw me out of that window...'[50]

Though she defended her servant vigorously, don't be fooled into thinking that Caroline and Henrietta shared any sisterly affection. Whether she was

---

50. Hervey, John and Croker, John Wilson (ed.) (1848). *Memoirs of the Reign of George the Second: From his Accession to the Death of Queen Caroline, Vol II*. London: John Murray, p.14.

an Electoral Princess of Hanover, Princess of Wales or Queen Consort of Great Britain, Caroline never lost sight of her exalted place, and she was certain that all the ladies who served beneath her would never have cause to forget it either.

Caroline always made Henrietta kneel when assisting with her toilet, holding the basin from which the queen would wash. Even when Henrietta's estranged husband became Earl of Suffolk in 1731 and she was elevated to the rank of countess, Caroline still insisted on having her kneel; queen trumps countess, after all. Finally the mild-mannered Henrietta enquired as to whether this was *strictly* protocol or simply intended to keep her in her place.

Lest we doubt that there was steel beneath Caroline's smile, Hervey was quick to relate a tale of the day that Henrietta went rogue. Far from indulge her friend or offer any comforting platitudes, the queen smacked her straight back down.

'But, after all this matter was settled,[51] the first thing this wise, prudent Lady Suffolk did was to pick a quarrel with me about holding a basin in the ceremony of my dressing, and to tell me, with her little fierce eyes, and cheeks as red as your coat, that positively she would not do it; to which I made her no answer then in anger, but calmly, as I would have said to a naughty child, "Yes, my dear Howard, I am sure you will; indeed you will. Go, go! Fa for shame! Go, my good Howard; we will talk of this another time."

'About a week after, when upon maturer deliberation she had done everything about the basin that I would have her, I told her I knew we should be good friends again; but could not help adding, in a little more serious voice, that I owned of all my servants I had least expected, as I had least deserved it, such treatment from her, when she knew I had held her up at a time when it was in my power, if I had pleased, any hour of the day, to let her drop through my fingers thus.'[52]

---

51. The matter of the earl's desire to regain control of his wife was settled once and for all by a legal separation and a pay-off from the king to Charles Howard.

52. Hervey, John and Croker, John Wilson (ed.) (1848). *Memoirs of the Reign of George the Second: From his Accession to the Death of Queen Caroline, Vol II.* London: John Murray, pp.16–17.

Hervey didn't quite agree with Caroline's accusations of Henrietta's grouchiness and was quick to point out that the lady from Ansbach was far from blameless. After all, he notes, the queen delighted in having Henrietta perform the most menial duties yet this was the only time Henrietta dared to complain. Perhaps it was just in time that Henrietta was promoted to Mistress of the Robes, a more senior role in keeping with her new rank that crucially meant there would be no more kneeling.

After so long in the royal household, Henrietta longed for a life of her own where she would be servant to nobody, would kneel before no peevish mistress and soothe the tantrums of no bad-tempered master. When the brutish Earl of Suffolk died, Henrietta no longer needed the care of the king and she determined to leave the royal household once and for all, dreaming of freedom and days in which she might finally please herself.

In 1734, Henrietta went to Caroline and asked if she could be relieved of her duties. The queen questioned her closely on why she would make such a request and Henrietta explained that she thought the king's affections had cooled. Caroline told her she was mistaken and was merely feeling emotional. Henrietta would not *want* to leave, she warned, if she realized how different life would be when she was no longer part of the court. In Henrietta, she had the perfect mistress for her husband; unpolitical, unassuming, popular and with no ambition beyond a quiet life. Should she go, who knows what upstart might take her place?

In the end, there was nothing Caroline could do but delay the inevitable. George was happy to bid goodbye to the companion who had lost her sparkle long ago. Henrietta's life after court was happy, fulfilled and peaceful. She took up residence at her beloved home of Marble Hill and married George Berkeley, a Member of Parliament who had been her friend and confidante for years.

This meant, of course, that there was a new opening in the bed of George II and nobody wondered more keenly than Caroline who would fill it. The answer was Amalie von Wallmoden, niece of George I's mistress, Melusine von der Schulenberg, and a woman who knew how to play the court game. Stunningly beautiful, cultured and twenty years younger than the king, she was everything Caroline feared in a mistress.

And George was besotted with her.

He came up with more and more excuses to visit Amalie in Hanover, and in 1736, she gave birth to his son, Johann Ludwig von Wallmoden.[53] This was unchartered territory for the queen yet she navigated it with her customary coolness, one unexpected side effect of George's absence being that the sympathetic public came to think ever more of her.

Her eldest son, however, was a very different matter.

Battling Wales

Years before Henrietta Howard departed the sociable, pompously ceremonial St James's court, trouble came calling in the shape of Frederick, that once seven-year-old son left behind so many years ago. Now a young man, it's fair to say that, as George I's influence over him increased, his place in the life of his parents diminished. They in turn had lavished adoration on their younger son, the Duke of Cumberland, and the stage was set for disaster.

Perhaps recalling the constant head butting with his father, George had no wish to summon Frederick, the new Prince of Wales, to join the family in England. In 1728, however, events rather overtook the king and queen and left them with no choice but to bring their errant son to Great Britain.

For many years, plans had been tentatively discussed to marry Fred off to his cousin, Wilhelmine of Prussia. This meant a long slog through protocol and negotiations, slowly and painfully chipping away at demand and counter-demand from both sides to try and reach an agreement that would suit both houses. Fred never had much time for painstaking negotiations and though he had never met Wilhelmine, he decided that he was madly, crazily in love and must have her as his own.

The young man drove a coach and horses through the marriage plans that had been started by his grandfather and inherited by George II. Unwilling to wait, Fred sent word to the Prussian court to tell them that he was ready to wed Wilhelmine whenever they said the word. This unforgivable breach of protocol put the final nail in the coffin of the marriage. Although the bride-to-be's mother quite liked Fred's chutzpah nobody else did, and when George heard what his son had done, he went through the roof. Without further ado, Fred was summoned directly to England.

---

53. Johann lived until 1811 and was a noted connoisseur of art.

No ceremony or celebration welcomed the Prince of Wales onto British shores and his first engagement was with his mother. Although she would later profess to hate him, Caroline welcomed Fred to the palace at the start, glad to see him after so long. The grumpy king was still furious though and received Frederick in one of his characteristic short tempers.

Caroline's rather tentative pleasure at her son's arrival didn't last long and her enthusiasm ebbed at precisely the rate his own popularity increased. Just as he was a stranger to Caroline and George, so too were they strangers to him, and the trio appeared to have nothing in common whatsoever. In fact, as the irritation deepened into a feud, they turned out to be far more alike than they might have expected…

Caroline, meanwhile, was dealing with not only a son who didn't want to be in England, but a daughter who fancied herself not just as the Princess Royal, but the Queen of Sheba too. Anne, Princess Royal, had become a right royal brat and had an ambition that would shame many a conqueror. She wanted to be a queen, to wield power and she wanted it now, yet no suitable husbands wanted *her*. At home she ruled her ladies with a rod of iron, making them stand beside her bed late into the night, reading until they dropped.

Intending to teach her daughter a lesson, Caroline summoned Anne to her own chamber to read. Rather than allow the young lady to sit, the queen kept her standing until she, like her own maid earlier, was ready to collapse. The point was made and the lesson, rather quickly, was learned.

Dealing with Frederick was considerably more difficult.

The Prince of Wales plunged headlong into London life, becoming part of a glittering social circle. He was always gambling, partying and wenching, and all of that cost money. As the months passed and the cash kept trickling though his fingers, both George and Caroline's indifference towards their son began to slowly be usurped by utter dislike.

The king and his son were politically poles apart and, just as George had in his day, Frederick made his opposing views loudly known. George blamed Fred for the collapsed marriage plans, Fred blamed George for his lack of funds and when the young prince started making eyes at a famed society beauty, things were bound to become even rockier.

The hugely influential society hostess, Sarah, Duchess of Marlborough, was on the lookout for an illustrious match for her granddaughter, Lady Diana Spencer. She let it be known that marriage to Diana would bring with it a dowry of £100,000 and Fred liked the sound of that even more than he liked the sound of the bride's beauty and grace.

Walpole wasn't about to let the Prince of Wales marry anyone less than a royal and, preferably, one who *he* could influence. He counted the Duchess of Marlborough as a longstanding political opponent and she wasn't someone he wanted to see so close to the heir of the throne, but how to stop the scheme before it started? How indeed. Walpole simply visited the queen and, accordingly, mentioned the Duchess of Marlborough's plans to her.

Accordingly, she torpedoed them.

In the end, it was George II who chose a bride for Frederick and she was Augusta of Saxe-Gotha, daughter of Frederick II, Duke of Saxe-Gotha-Altenburg and Magdalena Augusta of Anhalt-Zerbst. The king met Augusta during a trip to Hanover and when he presented Fred with the prospect of her wealthy hand in marriage, the Prince of Wales accepted.

This came as a great relief to Caroline, who had already found herself forced to dismiss a lady-in-waiting, Lady Anne Vane, once Fred fathered a child with her. In fact, Fred was at war with his former best friend, Lord Hervey, over who the child's father was and both were keen to claim credit. It ended their friendship, though the cunning Hervey remained close to Caroline for the rest of her life.

By this point, Caroline was suffering with poor health, her weight was ballooning and her gout worsening. With George pining for the distant Amalie, the relationship of king and queen grew ever more fractious and, without his regular evening appointments with Henrietta, George had taken to spending the time with his family instead. He was in a frequent bad temper and Caroline was on the receiving end of his cruel barbs all too often. Added to all this, that umbilical hernia of 1724 was beginning to make its presence painfully felt.

Clearly suffering with the effects of the neglected condition, the queen took to wearing her soft pregnancy stays permanently, relishing the comfort and respite they provided. Caroline would never accept her own weaknesses though, pushing on through pain and injury to continue with her duties no matter what.

Although the queen was keen to make a good start with the new Princess of Wales, Walpole counselled caution. He urged Caroline to let Augusta settle in and win the love and trust of the prince before she attempted to become a closer acquaintance. While the world saw Augusta as an innocent and indeed, when she arrived in England, she certainly was, Walpole had a suspicion that her innocence wouldn't last long.

History would prove him right.

Just like Caroline, Augusta was actually a shrewd and wily politician, and very quick to learn. She was also well-drilled, polite and unfailingly respectful to the king and queen, who soon came to adore her. Whatever she did, whatever she said, they contented themselves that she was the innocent puppet of her husband. Indeed, should Augusta ever go against the wishes of the king and queen, Caroline was quick to forgive and lamented, 'Poor creature, if she were to spit in my face I should only pity her for being under such a fool's direction, and wipe it off.'[54]

Things were about to get rather thorny and just as George William's birth split the royal family in two, the catalyst for trouble would, once again, be a baby.

First, however, it was time for a riot.

The Porteous Riots

For all his lobbying to get some real power, Fred had good reason to be glad that he was *not* regent when, in 1736, the Porteous Riots sent shockwaves through Edinburgh.

The riots occurred when disorder broke out during the hanging of Andrew Wilson, a smuggler, in the Grassmarket. In a fateful decision, John Porteous, Captain of the City Guard of Edinburgh, called out his men and issued orders for them to fire above the heads of the rioting mob. This they duly

---

54. Wilkins, William Henry (1901). *Caroline, the Illustrious Queen-Consort of George II and Sometime Queen-Regent: A Study of Her Life and Time, Volume II*. London: Longmans, Green and Co, p.295.

did, but their shots promptly hit some nosy neighbours who were watching the spectacle from windows high above the Grassmarket.

Now the crowd was not only angry but murderous, and Porteous gave the order to quell the unrest by shooting at will, resulting in the death of six people. At his subsequent trial, witnesses came forward to testify that he had *personally* fired on the people, not only given the order to his men to do so, and Porteous was found guilty of murder. Walpole, however, could hardly countenance the hanging of an official and soon he had a finger in a very problematic pie. His intervention took the form of a petition bearing the names of Scotland's most illustrious citizens and, with his *access all areas* pass to the queen, he knew that he would be listened to.

The result of his unwise intervention was a reprieve, granted on the grounds that Porteous had acted only under extreme provocation. Furious at this perceived royal arrogance and the outright and blatant dismissal of the decision of the jury, thousands of people poured into the streets and marched on the glowering edifice of the Tollbooth, the prison where Porteous was being held. With the guards easily overpowered by the sheer size of the crowd, the captain was dragged from his cell, and taken to the Grassmarket where the sorry story had begun. Here he was beaten mercilessly and strung up to die an agonizing death.

When news reached London of events in Edinburgh, the government was quick to put out the smouldering embers of revolution. Questions were raised as to why Porteous was not better protected, especially since he had almost been lynched when he was first brought to prison. The forces of law and order should have taken this as a warning and been prepared for such an incident, yet they were not. Caroline was furious with General Moyle, the man responsible for commanding the king's forces in Scotland, and wanted to know why more hadn't been done to keep Porteous safe from those who sought justice.

Caroline's initial hotheaded response was to hit Edinburgh with every force she had. Yet when she summoned an emergency council, good sense prevailed and a heavy fine was decided upon instead. Little by little Caroline's fury abated and from the enormous crowd that had marched on the Tollbooth, nobody was ever punished for the lynching of Captain Porteous.

It was to be Caroline's last regency.

A Flight by Moonlight

'There has been a very extraordinary quarrel at court, which, I believe, nobody will give you so exact an account of as myself.'[55]

And with those words, Horace Walpole plunged headlong into one of the most bizarre and damaging incidents of George II and Fred's fractious relationship.

Denied the chance to serve as regent in favour of his mother, Fred cast about for a purpose to his life, seeing precious little chance to acquire any practical experience in government. Caroline, meanwhile, had to face the bitter truth that her husband didn't merely have one more inconsequential mistress in Hanover, but was deeply in love with Amalie. She missed his presence, bad temper and all, and with no other course open to her, wrote to Hanover and invited George to bring Amalie to England. Walpole speculated that Amalie was too afraid of meeting Caroline to come and face her. He was right.

Left alone to weather the storm of the burgeoning feud whilst George lived it up in Hanover, the queen faced a new challenge when her husband's ship didn't make port as expected. Fred could hardly contain his excitement, believing that his father was dead and he was as good as king. No doubt he was plotting to make some big changes around the royal court but, unlike many of his fellow schemers, he made absolutely no secret of his delight.

Even as Caroline waited desperately for word of her husband's fate, she lamented, 'Fritz's popularity makes me vomit... [He] talked of the King's being cast away with the same sang-froid as you would talk of a coach being overturned, and that my good son strutted about as if he had been already King'.[56]

No doubt Caroline wondered what Fred had in store for her if his father was out of the way. Some thought that Fred loathed his mother so much that

---

55. Walpole, Horace (1842). *Letters of Horace Walpole, Earl of Orford, Vol I*. London: Lea and Blanchard, p.210.
56. Hervey, John and Croker, John Wilson (ed.) (1848). *Memoirs of the Reign of George the Second: Vol II*. London: John Murray, p.210.

he would cast her aside, others that he would tolerate her simply to benefit from her vast political experience. Hervey, meanwhile, was of the opinion that Caroline was far too precious a commodity to be anything but protected by her son. At the very thought of it, Caroline was bitterly amused, telling her friend that Fred hated her and would take advice from no woman, least of all *her*.

Happily for Caroline she would never need to find out, for the king was not drowned at all. For a desperate week she faced the uncertainty of her husband's fate and fell into a deep depression, praying for George and weeping at the very thought of him. When news reached Great Britain that the king was safe, an overjoyed Caroline put pen to paper and poured out the whole sorry story. She told her husband of her fear, of Fred's plotting, of the horror of believing herself a widow and the reply she received was loving, respectful and altogether unlike the usual bad-tempered king. It thrilled Caroline to realize how high she remained in George's estimation and when he returned in the flesh, suffering from a painful bout of piles but certainly nothing worse, his behaviour was just as kind as his words had been.

Fred, however, continued to be a thorn in his mother and father's sides. He wanted more cash and turned to his opposition friends to raise the matter in Parliament, banking on embarrassing them enough to be given a bit of hush money. With relations stretched taut, things reached breaking point in 1737 when Caroline learned that Augusta was pregnant. Rather than delight in the news, she was circumspect and, ironically given her own suspected phantom pregnancy years earlier, convinced herself that there was no baby on the way at all. No, she decided, far more likely that this was all a cunning subterfuge.

Fred's frail childhood had left his mother sure that he would not be able to conceive, which is why she believed Hervey to be the father to Anne Vane's child. Caroline and George knew that a baby for the Prince and Princess of Wales would make it highly unlikely that their beloved Cumberland would *ever* sit on the throne. The royal pair whipped up such a state of agitation that they came to suspect that the Prince and Princess of Wales might even try to pass off someone else's child as their own.

Augusta went into labour in July 1737 and, determined that the child would be born not in his father's Hampton Court home but in their own residence at St James's, Fred bundled her into a carriage and set off through the night. The princess howled in pain as, unaware of their departure, the party continued at Hampton Court. In fact, the king and queen were fast asleep when a messenger arrived at their chambers with word of the impending birth.

As the furious king railed at his wife, blaming her for the debacle, Caroline dressed quickly. She summoned Lord Hervey and her daughters, Amelia and Caroline, and set off in pursuit of her son. Her mind whirled with fears of the changeling the couple might force on the royal household and the possibility that Cumberland was about to lose his one and only chance at the throne.

When Caroline arrived at St James's Palace she found herself grandmother to a newborn baby girl. There could be no question of a changeling, with any number of eyewitnesses to the birth able to set fears of a substitution at ease. This was scant comfort to the queen and the final straw in a relationship that had gone off the rails years ago, when she was forced to leave her seven-year-old son in Hanover. Now, decades after that heartbreaking goodbye, she washed her hands of Fred once and for all, sending him a furious letter that included her honest opinion that, 'Your Royal Highness deserves to be hanged'.[57]

Fred and Augusta were banished and, just as George and Caroline had before them, they established an opposition court at Leicester House. Once again, the royal households were at war and for Caroline, there would be no white flag of peace. Instead she told Hervey, 'There he goes – that wretch – that villain! – I wish the ground would open this moment and sink the monster into the lowest hole in hell.'[58]

They would never reconcile.

57. Trench, Charles Chenevix (1973). *George II*. London: Allen Lane, p.194.
58. Chapman, Hester W (1971). *Caroline Matilda, Queen of Denmark, 1751–75*. London: Cape, p.22.

The Queen is Dead

> Last Sunday the 20th Instant, between the Hours of Eleven and Twelve at Night her most gracious Majesty WILHELMINA-DOROTHEA-CAROLINA, Queen Consort of *Great Britain*, departed this Life, after an Illness of Twelve Days, to the inexpressible Grief of his Majesty and the Royal Family. The many great and exemplary Virtues which so eminently distinguished her Majesty in every Character of Life and had long been the Object of universal Esteem and Admiration, render the Death of this most excellent Princess an unspeakable Loss to the whole Nation.
>
> Her Majesty was aged 55 Years, 8 Months, and 13 Days.[59]

Overweight, gouty and wracked with all manner of pains, Queen Caroline had come a long way since those heady days of the flaxen-haired eligible princess of Ansbach. She had gained influence, power, respect and enemies including her own son, but no one could accuse her of not having lived.

For many months, Caroline had been suffering from a litany of ailments yet still she soldiered on, refusing to admit that she was in pain. George hated any sign of weakness in the people who surrounded him and Caroline knew this all too well, so she had tried her best to keep her sickly state to herself. When her gout threatened to cripple her she took ice baths, freezing out the pain and forcing herself to go about her duties alongside her husband. When the pain became overwhelming, she gritted her teeth and took to a wheelchair, munching chocolate as she whizzed about the palace dispensing instructions.

In autumn 1737 Caroline was inspecting the new library she had commissioned from the legendary architect, William Kent, at St James's Palace. As fond of books as she was of gardening, she spent hours each day in the library, ensuring every tiny detail was exactly as she wished it. It seems appropriate, therefore, that the queen was in her beloved library when a violent pain tore through her abdomen, leaving her doubled over with agony.

---

59. *Weekly Miscellany (1732)* (London, England), Friday, 25 November, 1737; Issue CCLVII. p.3.

Although Caroline could barely stand she refused to cancel her planned drawing room and, determined to soldier on, dragged herself along to meet the attendees.

George knew nothing of how serious his wife's condition was and when Caroline finally retired to bed, the king went to a card game with friends. Attended by physicians and the ever-loyal Hervey, the queen's condition deteriorated as the night went on, little helped by the various potions that the court doctors plied her with.

With Caroline's convulsions swiftly followed by uncontrollable vomiting her physician, John Ranby, was summoned. He was at her bedside when George returned from his game, greeting the sight of his agonized wife with horrified concern. That night, George slept beside Caroline as Ranby bled her, desperate to bring down the queen's dreadful fever. She missed her engagements the following day and after another night of agony had passed, word began to leak out that Queen Caroline was desperately ill.

One of the people who heard the news was Fred, the troublesome Prince of Wales. Despite the bad blood between the prince and his parents he rushed to town only to find that the king had given orders that he should not be allowed into the palace. Undaunted, Fred sent a message in which he begged for permission to visit his mother. George II's reply was unequivocal: Fred was not to come, nor to send further word to or about the queen. His answer was full of rage and fury and he spat, 'I always hated the rascal, but now I hate him yet worse than ever. He wants to come and insult his poor dying mother; but she shall not see him.'[60]

Before we look too dimly on the king's reaction, it's worth noting that when Caroline found out that Fred had been to the palace, she was no less furious. She railed against the son she hated, claiming that he wished to see her only to take some morbid pleasure in watching her die, and told George that Fred must not be admitted to her rooms, no matter how he begged. Fred continued to come to Pall Mall and send couriers to the palace to ask for word of his mother but the moment for reconciliation, if there ever was one, was lost.

---

60. Hervey, John and Croker, John Wilson (ed.) (1848). *Memoirs of the Reign of George the Second: Vol II*. London: John Murray, p.500.

As the hours passed, the king and queen still said nothing of the hernia Caroline had suffered more than a decade earlier as a result of her last pregnancy, but why? Was it really because George or Caroline, or perhaps both, loathed ill health, perhaps fearing the all-too mortal flesh that was ageing more with every passing day? Maybe Caroline thought it was simply too intimate or that it meant she was somehow less of a woman, but every hour lost was another hour closer to the grave.

Only when the queen could barely move or speak did the king approach Ranby and mention the hernia. Yet even as the surgeon examined the queen, she tried to claim that there was no rupture, and that the pain did not originate from the site of the hernia. Eventually Ranby told Caroline that she could delay no longer; he must take action if there was to be any chance of saving her life.

Caroline wept bitterly as she submitted to Ranby's examinations and treatment, sure now that her days were drawing to a close. In fact, the operation she would undergo was to be more horrific than any of them could imagine.

There was no anaesthetic for the queen other than prayer when the surgeons made the first incisions into her abdomen and found, to the horror of all, that the herniated bowel within had already begun to decompose. The doctors cut out the decayed intestine yet this left them with no means to close it and join the bowel. The result was catastrophic and raw excrement seeped into Caroline's abdominal cavity until, with nowhere else to go, it began to ooze and drip from her surgical wounds. Writhing and crying in agony, Caroline passed a terrible night. The following morning, her doctors discovered that the fresh wound had already turned bad.

As the air of the palace filled with the scent of excrement and the odour of decomposition, Caroline summoned her family to her bedside and told them that she was dying. For each of those children present she had only kind words but for the absent Fred there was no such comfort. Instead she spoke only of his lack of worth, telling her other offspring that they should always endeavour to be better people than he was. She commended the care of her youngest children to Princess Caroline, asking that she guide them through the years to come. Finally, the dying queen placed her ruby coronation ring on her husband's finger and told him, 'Naked I came to you, and naked I go from you. I had everything I ever possessed from you, and to you whatever I have I return'.[61]

Overcome, the king broke down in tears as he faced life without the woman he loved. No matter what differences they had faced, nor what mistresses he had taken, Caroline's death would leave an immeasurable hole in George's life. The queen knew what a great loss she would be to her husband and, as he wept, she begged him to marry again once she was gone. In reply, George told her he would do no more than take mistresses, for no woman could ever match her as a wife. Indeed, George later told Walpole that he 'never yet saw a woman worthy to buckle her shoe'.[62]

The heartbroken monarch refused to leave his wife's side, clinging to her and kissing her as though that alone might somehow keep her alive. Sometimes sleeping, sometimes waking, always in agony, Caroline told her husband that she believed she would die on a Wednesday, the same day on which she had been born, married, gone into her first labour and been crowned queen. It was only right then that she would leave this world on the day that had always proved so eventful for her.

In fact she made it to Wednesday and beyond, and even seemed to rally a little, receiving Walpole for a visit at which she entrusted the royal family to his care. Yet it was to be a brief reprieve and when Thursday 17 November dawned, Caroline was as unwell as she had ever been. The wound still seeped so the doctors opened her abdomen and poked and probed again. Through it all, she actually apologized to the surgeons for making such a fuss, asking them to ignore her cries of pain.

On 20 November the king and Princess Amelia sat with the queen as the daylight faded into darkness. Caroline lay unmoving in bed, her breath audible and hoarse and her voice barely a whisper when she asked those present to pray for her. As Amelia complied, Caroline took George's hand in her own and told him, 'I am going.'

As the words left her lips, Queen Caroline closed her eyes and took her final breath, leaving the shattered King George II to kiss the face and hands of his dead queen one last time.

---

61. Ibid., p.513.
62. Coxe, William (1800). *Memoirs of the Life and Administration of Sir Robert Walpole, Earl of Orford: Vol II*. London: T Cadell, Jun and W Davies, p.510.

Caroline of Ansbach was a remarkable queen. History has judged her as the Georgian era's most formidable consort, a woman with a shrewd business brain and an understanding of politics that could put many of her contemporaries to shame. She was forged in the crucible of the Berlin court, introduced to intellectuals and nurtured by some of the finest philosophical minds of the generation. Those early years were to have an enormous impact on her life.

A woman of deep faith and enormous intellectual ability, Caroline was the first queen of Georgian Britain and, doubtlessly, one to be reckoned with. When she discovered that Lord Chesterfield had been mocking her behind her back she had him banished and after Lord Stair dared to answer back, he found his own career swiftly curtailed. She never forgave her son for his perceived slights, and so the family loathing dripped down from one generation to the next, infecting and poisoning the Hanover blood. Just as George II and his father went to war, so too did he, Caroline and Fred and, in a far less brutal manner, her successor would have troubles with her own son, yet another George.

We might theorize of course that George II was so devoted to his wife because he had wanted for a mother of his own. In Caroline, he found a loving female presence who would be there no matter what he did. She calmed his tantrums, soothed his troubled brow and always knew exactly what to say. Caroline was a strong yet affectionate woman, indulgent and adoring even as she made the best of her own influence, and she certainly knew how to flatter her bad-tempered husband. Yet let us not do George a disservice. Certainly she was a more than able regent, negotiating the gin riots, the Porteous catastrophe and all manner of other dramas, yet her husband was a far from weak man. She didn't totally dominate, no matter what the satirists claimed, but he certainly foundered a little without her.

It's hardly surprising that George mourned Caroline for the rest of his days, missing her good counsel and unflinching support no matter what wrongs he committed. In fact when the king died, he left instructions that their coffins be placed together and the sides removed, so that he might rest with Caroline for eternity.

Charlotte of Mecklenburg-Strelitz, Queen of the United Kingdom of Great Britain and Ireland

(Mirow, Holy Roman Empire, 19 May 1744 – Kew, England, 17 November 1818)

Once upon a time there lived a king who went quite mad and lost America. We all think we know his story, told in literature, film and theatre, but what of the queen who remained at his side through good and bad, exhausted, devoted, adoring?

She was Charlotte of Mecklenburg-Strelitz, Queen of the United Kingdom of Great Britain and Ireland and she could not have been more different to the woman who preceded her. Caroline was political, a game player, a woman with ambition, while Charlotte was none of those things. She wanted a quiet life, a happy family, and a settled, peaceful existence out of the limelight, with her beloved dogs at her side and no politicians beating a path to her door.

She *got* yet another feud and a husband who slowly and surely went utterly insane.

A Sheltered Childhood

Long ago, in the tiny land of Mirow, part of the Duchy of Mecklenburg-Strelitz, there was born a little princess. Baptized Sophia Charlotte, she was the eighth child and fifth daughter of Duke Charles Louis Frederick of Mecklenburg and his wife, Princess Elisabeth Albertine of Saxe-Hildburghausen. Unlike the queen who had preceded her in Great Britain, the young princess enjoyed a peaceful and sheltered childhood in the small land of her birth, spared the upheaval and sadness that had so blighted Caroline's younger years.

When she had a family of her own Charlotte did all she could to create a sanctuary for them away from the maelstrom of public life and press scrutiny, and perhaps, in her childhood, we see the genesis of that. Her mother and father were less concerned with territorial expansion and dynasty building than they were with hearth and home. The duke suffered from ill health and the duchess, who was Charlotte's match in terms of faith and temperament, focused her efforts on making her husband's life a comfortable and peaceful one. Charles and Elisabeth were very much a team, and they shared the same priorities, taking a particular interest in managing their estates and overseeing the education and religious development of their children.

Charlotte had a natural inquisitiveness and intelligence and, happily, it was not left to fester. Although she lacked the rich philosophical and literary influences that surrounded Caroline of Ansbach after her adoption by the court in Prussia, her education was not neglected. Instead she was placed under the tutelage of Reverend Genzmer, a Lutheran minister who was a long, long way from Father Orban, that Catholic priest who would reduce Caroline of Ansbach to tears during their audiences.

Still, Orban's impossible task was to convince Caroline to convert, whereas Genzmer's was to educate Charlotte and her siblings, and he did just that in fine style. His passion was for science and soon his young charges shared it too. From mathematics to botany, Genzmer's enthusiasm was infectious and the children grew closer than ever thanks to their shared lessons. The day to day care of the girls was entrusted to Mademoiselle Seltzer, a close friend of the duchess who viewed the children as an extension of her own family. She was devoted to them and they were to her in turn until 'the children almost regarded their amiable instructor in the light of a second parent'.[1]

Although the youngsters were tutored in languages and literature, Charlotte didn't learn English until she arrived in Great Britain, though no other 'ladylike' area of her education was neglected. Whether dance, theology, history or needlecraft, Charlotte was being moulded into the very model of a perfect young noble girl.

---

1. Watkins, John (1819). *Memoirs of Her Most Excellent Majesty Sophia-Charlotte, Queen of Great Britain*. London: Henry Colburn, p.33.

Real life intruded into this seemingly idyllic world in 1752 with the death of the sickly duke, an event that plunged the whole family into mourning. With her husband dead, the duchess and her children departed Mirow for Strelitz and a quieter life. For Elisabeth Albertine one thing was certain: *nothing* could be allowed to disturb the happy life of her youngsters. To this end, the beloved governess and trusted tutor went along too and on their arrival in Strelitz, the little household was joined by Madame de Grabow. She was to be a second governess to the children and this good friend of the admirable Mademoiselle Seltzer would one day exert great influence on her young charge.

So respected was Madame de Grabow as a poet that she was known by the soubriquet of *The German Sappho*, and Charlotte soon adored her. Grabow's fierce intelligence and love of teaching proved infectious and Charlotte flourished. She followed a strict timetable for lessons and years later, routine would dominate the court of George III, just as it did that of George II, with everything given its proper time and place. If it all seems too good to be true, the odd thing would seem to be that it *wasn't*. The family was far more united than those Hanoverians who sat on the British throne, with no hint of the feuds that fired the drama of St James's and Hampton Court.

Likewise, far from the marital scrums witnessed at courts across Europe, it seems as though the dowager duchess didn't entertain such lofty ambitions for her own children. She recognized that her family was far from a big court hitter, and had rather more serious worries as Frederick the Great's troops marched into Mecklenburg-Strelitz in 1760 and occupied the kingdom. War shattered the land, laying waste to it and leaving the people who lived there with nothing.

When she was just a teenager, Charlotte supposedly took up her pen and wrote directly to Frederick the Great. In her letter she sought to impress upon him how war had changed her country from a bountiful place of peace and friendship to a land in ruins, where men were forced to fight and once fruitful pastures were ruined by bloodshed and battle.

'I am at a loss whether I should congratulate or condole with you on your late victory, since the same success which has covered you with laurels, has overspread the country of Mecklenburg with desolation.

I know, Sire, that it seems unbecoming my sex, in this age of vicious refinement, to feel for one's country, to lament the horrors of war, or to wish for the return of peace. I know you may think it more properly my province to study the arts of pleasing, or to inspect subjects of a more domestic nature; but, however unbecoming it may be in me, I cannot resist the desire of interceding for this unhappy people.'[2]

The letter didn't emerge until Charlotte was queen and was probably a hoax inspired by her later dedication to her charitable causes, though there were certainly some who thought it genuine. After all, for a woman as steeped in philanthropy as Charlotte would become, there were those who believed that even at 16, her kind heart was more than a match for the mighty Frederick the Great.

Becoming a Bride

Hundreds of miles away, meanwhile, Great Britain was mourning the death of George II and celebrating the start of the reign of its new king, George III, who was 22. The late monarch died on 25 October 1760 whilst taking his toilet and, since the loathed Frederick, Prince of Wales, had predeceased him by nine years, it was left to Fred's son, George, to assume the throne. George III was a quiet young man, shy and timid, and with a temper as gentle as his predecessor's was fiery.

He was also single.

There had been several candidates for the role of George's wife. Some were his choice, some the favourites of his formidable mother, Augusta of Saxe-Gotha, but none had made it to the altar. Augusta was not the innocent that she had initially appeared to be, and she had instead proved herself to be every bit as shrewd as Caroline of Ansbach. It was she who oversaw the education of the prince after the death of his father, employing the future prime minister, John Stuart, 3rd Earl of Bute, as a companion and tutor to the young man.

---

2. Anonymous (1769). *Oxford Magazine, Or, University Museum, Vols 3–4*. London: S Bladon, p.219.

Bute and Augusta had met years earlier when a rainstorm at the races caused them to take shelter at the same card table. Unfounded allegations about the nature of their relationship and perceived nepotism would dog the pair to their respective graves. In George III, however, there was no denying that they had done a splendid job with their young charge.

Though Augusta and Bute had done their best to find George a bride when he was Prince of Wales, now he was king, things had to move a little more quickly. Envoys were dispatched in search of suitable candidates and one of these, Colonel Graeme, found his way to Strelitz. Here, in this tiny, unassuming land, he made the acquaintance of Charlotte and her mother. What he saw impressed him; she wasn't a beauty, he lamented, but nor was she ugly, and she was certainly an intelligent and well-made young lady. Crucially, she brought neither scandal nor ambition to the table, but *would* bring many years in which to bear her husband plenty of children.

Horace Walpole was, as ever, the go-to man for all the court gossip, and he wrote of Charlotte's appearance:

'She is not tall, nor a beauty; pale, and very thin; but looks sensible, and is genteel. Her hair is darkish and fine; her forehead low, her nose very well, except the nostrils spreading too wide; her mouth has the same fault, but her teeth are good. She talks a good deal and French tolerably; possesses herself, is frank, but with great respect to the King.'[3]

George wasn't at all sure. He had set his heart on the enchanting Lady Sarah Lennox but, under the gentle pressure of Augusta and Bute, he began to waver. Charlotte or Sarah, Sarah or Charlotte – which one would be his bride?

Finally, he caved in and told Bute, 'I own 'tis not in every particular as I could wish, but yet I am resolved to fix here'.[4] Before the king might have a chance to change his mind, Lord Harcourt was dispatched to Mecklenburg, 'if he can find it',[5] Walpole added waspishly in reference to the tiny court.

3. Walpole, Horace (1843). *Letters of Horace Walpole, Earl of Orford, to Sir Horace Mann, Vol I*. London: Richard Bentley, p.41.
4. Somerset, Anne (2004). *Ladies-in-Waiting: From the Tudors to the Present Day*. London: Castle Books, p.128.
5. Walpole, Horace (1843). *Letters of Horace Walpole, Earl of Orford, to Sir Horace Mann, Vol I*. London: Richard Bentley, p.33.

Charlotte was married to George by proxy, with her brother standing in for the absent groom whilst, for another sibling, it meant the end of a romantic dream. Charlotte's older sister, Christiane, had fallen in love with the Duke of Roxburghe, and he loved her in return. The royal wedding meant that Christiane and Roxburghe could never be together, because as the sister to a royal it was not deemed socially acceptable for Christiane to marry a mere noble. Forced to abandon their love, neither of them ever married.

And so it was decided. The sheltered, quiet girl from the tiny European duchy was about to become queen of a land she had never visited, whose language she didn't speak, alongside a man whom she had never met.

The signs weren't good.

The signs were, however, wrong.

To England

Though Charlotte was undoubtedly filled with anticipation and anxiety at what awaited her once the enormous celebrations in Mecklenburg-Strelitz were concluded, the impending departure weighed heavily on her shoulders. Her mother, Elisabeth Albertine, had done a marvellous job of ensuring that her family was devoted to one another and now, ready to depart, Charlotte felt the forthcoming separation keenly. The first parting was rather more permanent than anyone had anticipated, and came when Elisabeth died in June 1761, leaving her daughter an orphan.

In her own quiet way, Charlotte was shattered. It was a lonely princess who trod a path through the crowds gathered to see her off on her journey, rueful that her adored mother didn't live to see this moment. Opulent jewellery including a miniature of the king was provided by Lord Harcourt, so she knew what to expect, or at least, what the artists wanted her to expect, and she sent her own portrait and a lock of hair in return, yet this can't have done much to assuage her anxiety. Charlotte had to make it to England by 22 September 1761 as the date for the coronation was already set in stone, and by that point, the newly-orphaned queen must be in place and ready to face her public.

Charlotte took to the seas for a perilous voyage, the ship beset with storms and lashed with enormous waves. Through all of it, the young bride maintained her composure and, even more impressively, avoided seasickness. She contented herself with the company of the English ladies who had been sent to receive her, as well as the German attendants who were travelling with her, Johanna Louisa Hagedorn and Juliana Elizabeth Schwellenberg, and also, Frederick Albert, her hairdresser. In fact, George had been rather unsure about letting her bring *any* of the German household to England, fearing their influence might prove unwelcome but he eventually relented, allowing her this concession in view of the tragedy of her mother's death.

Charlotte had been given a harpsichord to while away the long hours and enjoyed playing and singing, charming everyone who shared the voyage, and keeping herself busy practising the national anthem of her new marital home. Her companions were not so fortunate as they were wracked with all manner of sickness, no doubt breathing a sigh of relief when the English coast finally came into view.

The procession from Harwich to St James's Palace made regular stops for Charlotte to meet various nobles and receive their gifts, whilst the roads were thronged with crowds desperate to get a look at her. By now attired in the English style, she peered back at them and this new land from the safety of her carriage. On the matter of her hair she was immovable though, saying she would change its style only if the king himself requested her to do so.

On 8 September 1761, Charlotte finally completed her journey to meet King George III. Now the 17-year-old princess's nerves threatened to consume her, and she stumbled as she stepped out of the carriage, glad for the steadying hand of the Duke of York, who accompanied her to the gate where her husband waited. Faced with the king, Charlotte faltered, about to throw herself at his feet, when George caught her before she could hit the ground and drew her into a welcoming embrace. One can only wonder what she made of this, so far from home and so recently bereaved, far from her friends and family and clinging to a man she had never met before yet was now joined to for life.

This was not, of course the bad-tempered George II, nor was it the stone-faced George I, and Charlotte was lucky in terms of her husband's temperament. She had nothing to fear from mistresses, for he had none, nor need she shrink from a violent nature, for he was placid, if occasionally obstinate. Of course, the future held some very unpleasant surprises for the newlywed king and queen but for now, all was going very well indeed. Perhaps in keeping with his own quiet nature, George didn't submit Charlotte to any great ceremony or public display. He was no doubt aware that she would have had quite enough of that on her journey from Harwich, and instead he welcomed her into the relative privacy of the palace.

There was, however, a rather serious bit of ceremony planned for later.

Marriage by Moonlight

Safely arrived in England and recovering from the arduous journey in the care of the king and his family, Charlotte was now given a few hours in which to relax and, hopefully, find her feet. This was not to be an evening of rest and recuperation though, and after an intimate dinner with George and other members of the royal family,[6] the moment of truth had arrived. Charlotte changed into her wedding finery and, beneath the late summer moon, the wedding ceremony began.

The dress, which Charlotte wore again two weeks later for the coronation, was heavy and hot. Exhausted, bewildered and thrust into the strange new world, Charlotte must have felt as though she was wearing someone else's skin, and the description of her gown is so opulent as to beggar belief.

'A silver tissue, stiffen bodied gown, embroidered & trimmed with silver. On her head a little Cap of purple Velvet quite covered with Diamonds, a Diamond Aigrette in the form of a Crown, 3 dropped Diamond Earrings, Diamond Necklace, Diamond Sprigs of Flowers on her Sleeves and to clasp back her Robe, a diamond Stomacher, her purple Velvet Mantle was laced with Gold and lined with Ermine.'[7]

Though this might summon images of finery and a resplendent, grand figure, Horace Walpole can be relied upon to paint a rather more earthy

---

6 Among those present was Princess Augusta, who would later marry Charles William Ferdinand, Duke of Brunswick-Wolfenbüttel, and give birth to Caroline of Brunswick, the ill-fated bride of George IV.

7. Ribeiro, Aileen (1984). *Dress in Eighteenth-century Europe.* London: BT Batsford, p.135.

description. Though Charlotte might have been dressed grandly, it seems that the logistics of such a slight young lady wearing such a grand assortment of heavy fabric and jewels were a little more challenging.

> 'The Queen was in white and silver; an endless mantle of violet-coloured velvet lined with ermine, and attempted to be fastened on her shoulder by a bunch of large pearls, dragged itself and almost the rest of her clothes halfway down her waist. On her head was a beautiful little tiara of diamonds; a diamond necklace, and a stomacher of diamonds, worth three score thousand pounds, which she is to wear at the coronation too. Her train was borne by the ten bridesmaids[8] [...]'[9]

On her finger Charlotte wore a diamond ring that George presented to her, inscribed with *Sept 8th 1761*. Along with the ring, he also gave his new bride an assortment of eye-wateringly expensive jewellery which was the perfect gift for Charlotte, who always had a weakness for opulent gems. As she struggled in her finery on what was the hottest night of the year, the wedding party did all they could to help her along, whispering supportive instructions when she appeared uncertain of what to do. When she gave her reply to the vows read by the Archbishop of Canterbury, she spoke in German.

> 'The Marriage Ceremony began at Nine at Night; at the Conclusion of which, the Guns at the Park and the Tower were fired, and the Cities of London and Westminster, &c, finely illuminated. The Rejoycings were universally expressed by the People, with that Chearfulness which true Loyalty inspires on the happy Occasion.'[10]

---

8. The ten bridesmaids included Lady Sarah Lennox, the girl who had so captured George's heart years before.
9. Walpole, Horace (1843). *Letters of Horace Walpole, Earl of Orford, to Sir Horace Mann, Vol I*. London: Richard Bentley, p.41.
10. *London Evening Post* (London, England), 8 September, 1761–10 September, 1761; Issue 5283, p.1.

Just as George was the first king of the House of Hanover to be born in England, so too was he the first to be married there, and the people took the couple to their bosom, celebrating them as Great Britain's royal family. George never visited his ancestral lands of Hanover and Charlotte never returned to her own homeland. Instead, she embraced life in this new country, making it her business to learn English as quickly as she possibly could after her arrival.

The celebrations and feasting went on into the early hours and the press published poetry[11] and comment to offer the heartfelt congratulations to the happy couple. In the hours before dawn broke the royal newlyweds eventually

---

11. One such poem, *An Ode on the Royal Nuptials*, was published in the *General Evening Post* and sets the tone admirably, as these choice extracts demonstrate!

> Haste ye Loves and gentle Graces,
> wait upon the Royal Pair,
> Bring your chaplets and your maces,
> Scatter odours thru' the air.
>
> [...]
>
> Amid' war, and hostile clamour,
> See our KING triumphant ride!
> Calmly he pursues his armour,
> Crowns his vict'ries with a Bride.
>
> [...]
>
> Neighbouring *States* send their blessing,
> Jarring Sects unite as one,
> All are eager for addressing,
> Proud to compliment the Throne.
>
> [...]
>
> May they share the same opinions,
> Still there mutual vows improve;
> Be allow'd in their dominions,
> Patters of conjugal love.
>
> May their reign be long and blessed,
> May their sons supply their room,
> Still approved and caressed,
> 'Till the universal doom

General Evening Post (London, England), 8 September, 1761–10 September, 1761; Issue 4354, p.3.

retired to bed together and, everyone hoped they would get on with the business of creating heirs. What transpired behind those closed doors we'll never know, though the fact that the couple eventually had fifteen children would seem to suggest that they got on rather well over the years!

The following morning, the royal couple held a drawing room (an event where senior courtiers would hobnob with the monarch) to introduce the queen to her court. It was here that the elderly Lord Westmorland, who wasn't in possession of the finest eyesight, knelt before Lady Sarah Lennox, mistaking George's earlier fancy for the queen. Happily this was the only occasion that day in which things threatened to go off the rails and the moment passed quickly enough. Those who saw the couple had high hopes, remarking that 'It does not promise as if they two would be the most unhappy persons in England, from this event.'[12]

That might not sound like a ringing endorsement but for a royal marriage it was practically the height of romance!

God Save the Queen!

Charlotte and George quickly discovered that they were the perfect match. With shared interests, shared ambitions and a shared love of the quiet life, their domestic existence was harmonious and, remarkably for a Hanoverian couple, uneventful. Although, Buckingham House was settled on as the queen's official residence there would be no question of it becoming a political maelstrom like the court of Queen Caroline had once been; for Charlotte, it was all about family.

Wherever the couple went, the public clamoured to catch a glimpse of them. It's little wonder that the forthcoming coronation was the hottest ticket in town.

Two weeks after their wedding, George and Charlotte attended Westminster Abbey to be ceremonially crowned as king and queen. Thousands lined the streets and those who lived along the procession route were quick to capitalize, charging a small fortune for a window seat from

12. Watkins, John (1819). *Memoirs of Her Most Excellent Majesty Sophia-Charlotte, Queen of Great Britain*. London: Henry Colburn, p.90.

which to watch the couple pass. The Georgians, always fond of any excuse for a bonfire, found that such demonstrations of joy were banned, with the fear of catastrophe rather occupying the minds of the authorities.[13]

On the evening before the coronation, thousands of people began to gather in London and by dawn on 22 September, the specially erected grandstands were already at capacity. Members of the public jostled with soldiers and gentry for the best view, with enterprising guards happily pocketing a few coins in return for letting determined spectators reach the front of the crowd.

Nothing was left to chance, with emergency hospital wards prepared in case of incident, streets closed and soldiers liberally scattered through the city. In fact, in spite of or perhaps because of these preparations, the happy day passed off entirely without incident. Look closely at those soldiers who guarded the route of the procession, however, and you might glimpse the occasional civilian. One or two opportunist officers loaned out military dress to friends so that they might masquerade as part of the official guard and watch the ceremony from the best seats in the house.

Wilting in the heat of the unseasonably warm autumn day, and suffering from such anxiety that she was experiencing pain in her face and teeth, there was no outward sign that Charlotte was anything other than a consummate professional. If the young queen had been tired, bewildered and a little unprepared for the finer points of protocol at her wedding ceremony, she apparently had no such concerns when it came to the coronation, as far as the spectators could see. This time she had been well-drilled and played her role to perfection, embodying poise, grace and a certain regal something that did her no harm at all in the eyes of the people.

Despite the heat Charlotte was in her full and finest regalia, wearing the dress she had first donned for her wedding of a 'stiffen body'd Robe silver embroidered [with gold] Tissue petticoat, Diamond Stomacher, Purple Velvet Sleeves Diamds, Pearls as big as Cherrys, Girdle, Petticoats Diamds, Purple Velvet Surcoat and Mantle with Ermine and Lace, Purple Velvet Cap, only one string of Diamds & Crown Aigrette, Fan Mother of Pearl, Emerald,

---

13. Years later, at a celebration given in honour of the marriage of Marie Antoinette and Louis XVI in 1770, fireworks were accidentally ignited. In the ensuing blaze, the crowd panicked and hundreds were killed or injured.

Plate 1: Sophia Dorothea of Celle. (*Courtesy of The British Library. Public domain*)

CAROLINE.
QUEEN. OF GREAT BRITAIN
FRANCE, AND IRELAND &c.

Plate 2: Caroline of Ansbach. Philip van Gunst. (*Courtesy of Rijksmuseum, under Creative Commons Public Domain Dedication CC0 1.0 Universal licence. http://creativecommons.org/publicdomain/zero/1.0/deed.en*)

Plate 3: Her Most Gracious Majesty Queen Charlotte. Thomas Ryder, after Sir William Beechey. (*Courtesy of The New York Public Library. Public domain*)

Plate 4: Caroline, Princess of Wales. John Murphy, after Thomas Stothard. 1795. (*Courtesy of The Yale Center for British Art. Public domain*)

Bartolomo Bergami.

Plate 7: The murder of Count von Königsmarck. (*Courtesy of The British Library. Public domain*)

Plate 8: Caroline of Ansbach. Alexander van Haecken, after Jacopo Amigoni, 1736. (*Courtesy of Rijksmuseum, under Creative Commons Public Domain Dedication CC0 1.0 Universal licence. http://creativecommons.org/publicdomain/zero/1.0/deed.en*)

Plate 9: Horace Walpole. Henry Hoppner Meyer, after Sir Thomas Lawrence. 1795. (*Courtesy of The Yale Center for British Art. Public domain*)

Her Royal Highness CAROLINE *Princess of Wales*
And the
PRINCESS CHARLOTTE.

London, Published June 25 1799 by Colnaghi, Sala & Co. late Torre / No 13, Cockspur Street

Plate 10: HRH Caroline, Princess of Wales and the Princess Charlotte. Francesco Bartolozzi, after Richard Cosway. 1799. (*Courtesy of The Yale Center for British Art. Public domain*)

Plate 11: George III and his Family. Richard Earlom, after Johann Zoffany. (*Courtesy of Rijksmuseum, under Creative Commons Public Domain Dedication CC0 1.0 Universal licence. http://creativecommons.org/publicdomain/zero/1.0/deed.en*)

Plate 12: His Majesty King George III returning to Town from Windsor with an Escort of 10th Prince of Wales' Own Light Dragoons. Charles Turner, after Richard Barret Davis. 1806. (*Courtesy of The Yale Center for British Art. Public domain*)

Plate 13: Robert Walpole, First Earl of Oxford. Jacobus Houbraken, after Arthur Pond. 1746. (*Courtesy of The Yale Center for British Art. Public domain*)

Plate 14: Henry Brougham, first Baron Brougham and Vaux. Charles Wagstaff, after Comte Alfred d'Orsay. (*Courtesy of The Yale Center for British Art. Public domain*)

Plate 17: Queen Caroline, wife of King George IV, is greeted by people from Marylebone. Theodore Edward Hook. 1820. (*Courtesy Wellcome Library, London, under Creative Commons Attribution only licence CC BY 4.0 http://creativecommons.org/licenses/by/4.0/*)

Plate 18: Caroline R (Queen of England). Abraham Wivell. 1820. (*Courtesy of The New York Public Library. Public domain*)

Plate 19: Her Majesty Queen Charlotte. Sir William Beechey. 1809. (*Courtesy of The New York Public Library. Public domain*)

Plate 20: The present royal family: George III, Queen Charlotte, Princess of Wales, Duchess of York. 1795. (*Courtesy of The New York Public Library. Public domain*)

Plate 21: Charlotte of Mecklenburg-Strelitz. Henrik Roosing. 1789. (*Courtesy of Rijksmuseum, under Creative Commons Public Domain Dedication CC0 1.0 Universal licence. http://creativecommons. org/publicdomain/zero/1.0/deed.en*)

Plate 22: Caroline of Ansbach. Leonard Schenk, after Adolf van der Laan. 1727. (*Courtesy of Rijksmuseum, under Creative Commons Public Domain Dedication CC0 1.0 Universal licence. http://creativecommons. org/publicdomain/zero/1.0/deed.en*)

Plate 23: The Prince and Princess of Wales.
Francesco Bartolozzi, after H de Janvry, 1797.
(*Courtesy of Rijksmuseum, under Creative*
Commons Public Domain Dedication CC0 1.0
Universal licence. http://creativecommons.org/
publicdomain/zero/1.0/deed.en)

Plate 24: Sophia Dorothea of Celle.
(*Courtesy of The British Library. Public*
domain)

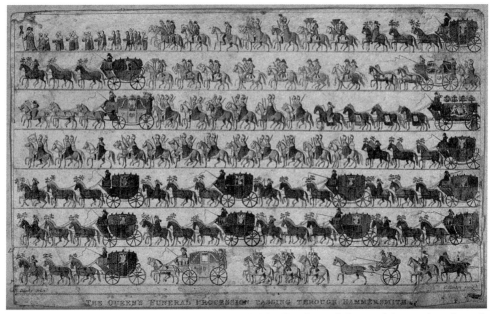

THE QUEEN'S FUNERAL PROCESSION PASSING THROUGH HAMMERSMITH

Plate 25: Funeral procession of a queen, probably Caroline of Brunswick, passing through Hammersmith in London. C Canton, after R. Banks. (*Courtesy Wellcome Library, London, under Creative Commons Attribution only licence CC BY 4.0 http://creativecommons.org/licenses/by/4.0/*)

CHARLOTTE, QUEEN OF GREAT BRITAIN, and the PRINCESS ROYAL.

Plate 26: Charlotte, Queen of Great Britain, and the Princess Royal. Valentine Green, after Benjamin West. (*Courtesy of Rijksmuseum, under Creative Commons Public Domain Dedication CC0 1.0 Universal licence. http://creativecommons. org/publicdomain/ zero/1.0/deed.en*)

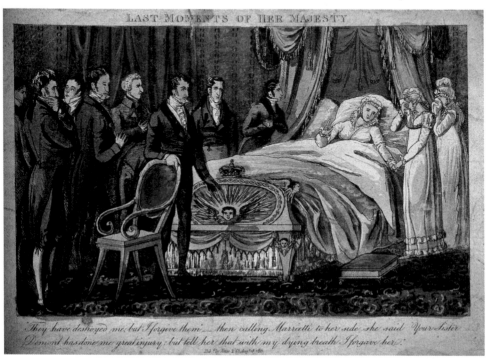

LAST MOMENTS OF HER MAJESTY

They have destroyed me but I forgive them — then calling Marrette to her side she said Your Sister Demont has done me great injury; but tell her that with my dying breath I forgave her.

The Royal Dozen; or the
King & Queen of Gr. Britain, with the 10 Royal Children

View of the Funeral Procession of Her late Majesty — taken on the Spot

London, Published by Jones & C.º Aug.¹ 1st 1821.

Plate 31: Queen Charlotte. Richard Houston, after Johann Zoffany. (*Courtesy of Rijksmuseum, under Creative Commons Public Domain Dedication CC0 1.0 Universal licence. http://creativecommons.org/publicdomain/zero/1.0/deed.en*)

Plate 32: The grossly agitated King and Queen seated in a latrine to receive a message from the emaciated Pitt; satirizing the Royal reaction to news of the King of Sweden's assassination. James Gillray. 1792. (*Courtesy Wellcome Library, London, under Creative Commons Attribution only licence CC BY 4.0 http://creativecommons.org/licenses/by/4.0/*)

Rubys and Diamd'.[14] The crown and fan were a gift from the besotted George and on her head she wore a set of 'coronation locks', better known today as hair extensions.

The banquet that followed was stage-managed to make Charlotte the undoubted star of the show. The guests sat in darkness awaiting the arrival of the royal couple and, when the queen stepped into Westminster Hall, a single candle illuminated the pitch black room. That candle was attached to a string and its flame travelled around the hall, eventually igniting a thousand wicks that lit the evening.

For Charlotte, this was the start of a new life and one that she was determined to enjoy. She spent hours studying English every day, with her husband encouraging her efforts. Musical parties and entertainments were commonplace, often with the queen singing and the king accompanying her on his violin. Famously, it was Queen Charlotte who commissioned an eight-year-old boy to compose six harpsichord sonatas in 1764. That boy was Wolfgang Amadeus Mozart, and the sonatas were *Opus 3*.

Although the couple shared a love of privacy, George was aware that their seclusion was attributed not to their own choice, but to the influence of Princess Augusta. She, meanwhile, was a far from effusive mother-in-law, holding Charlotte at arm's length. She kept a careful eye on the new arrival, determined that she would do nothing to lessen the influence the princess dowager enjoyed.

Both Caroline of Ansbach and Augusta of Saxe-Gotha, George III's mother, had been divisive figures. Indeed, Augusta would continue to be so until her death, when an out of control mob jeered and spat at her coffin, tearing the mourning cloth from the procession route at Westminster Abbey.

Charlotte's pious grace appealed to a nation that had grown tired of political interference and George delighted in her youth and immaturity, seizing the chance to mould an ideal queen for himself. He told Bute that 'every hour more & more convinces Me of the Treasure I have got',[15] especially as Charlotte appeared receptive to his warnings about becoming

---

14. Howard, Jean, Sinfield, Alan and Smith, Lindsay (2005). *Luxurious Sexualities: Textual Practice, Volume 11, Issue 3*. London: Routledge, p.65.

15. Hedley, Owen (1975). *Queen Charlotte*. London: J Murray, p.47.

involved in the political intrigues of court. It was a lesson well-learned, it seems, and Charlotte later admitted that she had no interest in 'medling in Politics which I abhor equal to sin'.[16]

All of this meant that Charlotte wasn't the most garrulous of queens. Although she agreed to hold drawing rooms at which the great and good could be presented to her, each attendee was vetted to ensure they were of suitable character and Charlotte maintained an aloof quality that she never really lost. It's only natural, however, that a young woman so utterly isolated from all that was familiar to her and plunged into the hothouse world of the Georgian court would struggle to know who was friend and who foe, who looked to her for personal advancement and who was truly trustworthy. Lacking in guile and guided by a husband who had been raised by his mother to be suspicious and watchful of those outside his most intimate circle, she was soon falling into George's own ways.

George III was far from a villain but his life had been one in which conflict was common and his father Fred had been bitterly estranged from his own parents. Upon the death of first Queen Caroline and then Fred, Augusta did reconcile with her father-in-law, George II, but by then young George wasn't a little boy and he must have been all-too aware of the divisions that had gone before. No doubt he discussed this with Charlotte in his quiet way and perhaps this only contributed to what became an insular relationship between the couple and their children. Pulled this way and that by courtiers, watched by her politically shrewd mother-in-law and keen to please all parties, Charlotte settled into placid obedience.

It meant, of course, that the queen was denied the opportunity to grow much beyond the seventeen years she had achieved when she arrived in England. This isn't to say she was immature, but rather that she was denied a chance to experience life beyond courts and family.

Though she stood squarely at George's side during feuds with politicians, brothers, sons and more, Charlotte's unwavering devotion to domestic routine would not be a positive thing for everyone. In time, it would have a rather negative impact on some of the many daughters she and George III would welcome to their family.

---

16. Ibid.

The Prince of Wales

'At seven this morning her Majesty was safely delivered of a Prince at the palace of St. James's to the great joy of his Majesty and of all his loyal subjects, who consider the birth of this heir to the crown as a pledge of the future felicity of their posterity under the happy auspice of his royal family.

[…]

Her Majesty and the new-born Prince of Wales are in perfect health, and nothing can surpass the testimonies of joy and affection expressed by all ranks and degrees of his Majesty's subjects for this great and desirable event.

It is worth observation, that her Majesty is brought to-bed of an heir to the crown on the same day that our most gracious Sovereign's great grand-father, King George the first, succeeded to the crown of these kingdoms by virtue of several acts of parliament for securing the Protestant succession in the illustrious house of Hanover.'[17]

Charlotte's primary duty as a queen consort was, of course, to provide her husband with that all important heir and, if possible, a spare too. This was something she had absolutely no problem in doing and within months of her marriage, she was pregnant. Cosseted in the calm atmosphere of Buckingham House, known as *the Queen's House*, Charlotte waited out the long months of pregnancy whilst her husband devoted himself both to her care and to building a library that would eventually number over 60,000 volumes. As the delivery day grew closer she was moved to St James's Palace, and began the traditional period of confinement.

All was peaceful and the household was slumbering when at 2.00 am on 12 August 1762, Charlotte began to experience labour pains. She called for assistance, and soon there was a veritable entourage gathering outside the

---

17. *London Evening Post* (London, England), 10 August, 1762 -12 August, 1762; Issue 5422. p.3.

queen's door, including the Archbishop of Canterbury, an assortment of court ladies, the great officers of state and the Dowager Princess, Charlotte's mother-in-law. Also present was Mrs Draper, the midwife who would have the honour of delivering the heir to the throne. A doctor, William Hunter, waited in case he was needed but Mrs Draper knew her business and, just after 7.00 am, Queen Charlotte gave birth to a son.

The labour was long and hard and, as the Tower cannon fired in celebration of the birth, the Earl of Huntingdon dashed off to beg an audience with George III and announce that he was now the proud father of a little *princess*.

Only a small mistake.

His error was no doubt soon put right and the earl was paid £500 for bringing such happy news. In what was seen as a wonderful omen for the years to come, as the queen settled back to catch her breath, a procession entered London carrying a fortune in treasure captured from the Spanish ship, *the Hermione*. It passed the palace where Charlotte and the baby were resting and the gathered nobles dashed to the windows to look out at the scene, as overhead, the cannon fire boomed in celebration.

Charlotte was utterly besotted with her son, who she named George Augustus, thinking him quite the most beautiful baby she had ever seen. He was settled in a grand cradle of crimson velvet and snow white satin, adorned with a coronet and gold Brussels lace. He wanted for nothing and was attended to by a retinue of help including a nurse and two attendants who were charged with gently rocking the new Prince of Wales in his slumber. Although she had hoped to breastfeed her son, Charlotte eventually had to hand him to a wet nurse, as she was unable to produce enough milk to satisfy the little boy's prodigious appetite.

He would *always* like his food.

The queen wasn't content to stop there and commissioned 'a whole length portrait of his Royal Highness modelled in wax. He was represented naked. The figure was half a span long, lying upon a crimson cushion, and it was covered by a bell-glass'.[18] As George Augustus grew from a newborn into a child and then a very troublesome man, she kept that wax figure in her private apartments, forever treasuring it.

---

18. Huish, Robert (1830). *Memoirs of George the Fourth: Vol I*. London: Thomas Kelly, p.34.

George Augustus was to be the first of fifteen children born to Charlotte and George over the next twenty-one years[19]. At his baptism there was no feuding, no threats and no drama, only celebration and two very proud, very happy parents who were already doting on their new arrival.

Although Charlotte couldn't breastfeed her children, she and the king always made time to play with their youngsters and, as the household grew with child after child, Lady Charlotte Finch was employed to act as governess. Lady Charlotte was to prove an inspired choice and she ensured that the young royals followed the routine set by their parents. Through all of this, the king grew closer than ever to his wife, sharing her joy at their children and taking refuge from the increasingly difficult strains of office in her gentle presence.

Charlotte, meanwhile, maintained her watchful silence. She was visited by family and, on occasion, ensured that they received titles or offices suited to their ability, but she was carefully to avoid accusations of nepotism. Mindful of warnings against politics, it was in Charlotte's domestic sphere that the drama could be found, with regular in-fighting amongst those attendants who had come from Germany and those who came from England. Through it all she remained serene, but that was set to change.

The Charitable Queen

In 1765, George III was at his wit's end. Assailed by battles in parliament and increasingly loud complaints from the colonists of North America, he hardly knew where to turn. He's now famous as the mad king yet then, at the height of his political troubles, nobody had any suspicion of just how bad things might become.

When the pressure that weighed on the king became too much to bear, he experienced his first bout of the mental illness that would later overwhelm him. A regency bill was introduced, yet with parliament fearing that the

---

19. The full roll-call of Charlotte and George's children and their birth years is George (1762), Frederick (1763), William (1765), Charlotte (1766), Edward (1767), Augusta (1768), Elizabeth (1770), Ernest (1771), Augustus (1773), Adolphus (1774), Mary (1776), Sophia (1777), Octavius (1779), Alfred (1780), and Amelia (1783). In addition, she suffered a miscarriage in 1764.

unpopular Augusta would be hungry for power, this most important matter could not be resolved easily. Although the queen might seem the obvious choice, those who *did* want Augusta raised all manner of questions over the decision.

Eventually it was decided that the queen *would* serve as regent should the king be indisposed, but Charlotte hardly took this as good news. For one who wanted no part in politics, she had been thrust into a role she hadn't sought, a victim of warring political factions. Although the king's recovery saved her from any further upset, Charlotte felt the strain of his illness keenly and things were only going to get worse.

Of course Charlotte had no crystal ball and instead channelled her efforts into her household and family. No matter what else was happening in her life, however, there was one other area to which the queen remained utterly devoted and that was charity and philanthropy.

What drove Charlotte into such a passionate championing of charitable causes we can never really know. Maybe it was a case of simply having a good heart, or perhaps, having seen the deprivations that war had brought to her homeland all those years earlier, she had a good understanding of suffering but, whatever her motivation, Charlotte could not resist a cry for help. Indeed, almost to her dying day, she was out and about patronizing charitable events whilst, behind the scenes, she did all she could to help those in need.

Charlotte even took a personal interest in the fate of a Mr Webb, one of the music masters to the royal children at Windsor. Mr Webb was disfigured by a large nose 'which spread over half his face', and Charlotte was most preoccupied by the thought that the children might laugh at him or simply stare; in fact, the outcome was rather more blatant.

'When first Mr Webb was to come to Sophia, I told her he had had some accident to disfigure his whole face, but I desired her to remember this was a misfortune for which he ought to be pitied, and she must be sure not to laugh at him, or stare at him. And she minded this very well, and behaved always very properly. [When] Mr. Webb was announced, Sophia coloured very red, and ran up to Lady Cremorne and said to her in a whisper, "Lady Cremorne, Mr Webb has got a very great nose, but that is only to be pitied – so mind you don't laugh." The little princess was only nine years old.'[20]

This is a credit to Charlotte's finer feelings, but she was equally as capable of distributing a rather more palpable charity to the causes or people that caught her attention. Her biographer related a tale that occurred early in the queen's reign when she heard of a Windsor clergyman whose health and finances were in a perilous state. Though Charlotte had no ready cash at her immediate disposal, she did have the jewels and treasures that brought her so much pleasure. Without paying it a second thought, she plucked out one of the diamonds that adorned her stomacher and told her attendant to take it to the unfortunate man. We aren't privy to what he did with it 'but the sick Clergyman went abroad, recovered, and lived long after his return to be a faithful leader of his parishioners. These are the bright jewels that make a Crown doubly splendid: the diamond taken from the stomacher was but representative of a more valuable treasure placed near it'.[21]

The queen grew so compassionate and so distressed at the sad tales of those who applied to her for help that she soon had a reputation for distributing aid *very* liberally. Indeed, Charlotte's biographer, William Marshall Craig tells us with what might be a *slight* touch of romance, 'the King was looked up to as the Fountain of mercy, and the Queen as the refreshing Source of tender charity and benevolence'.[22]

Pious, faithful and lucky to have a husband who adored her, Charlotte's heart went out to those women who were less fortunate, and she considered any charity case brought before her, including those of females who were once regarded as *fallen women*. The queen put her money where her mouth was too, funding housing and education for women who had been ill-used as well as orphan daughters of clergymen or military officers, who might otherwise be in danger of exploitation. Indeed, so generous was Charlotte that she was soon spending an eye-watering £5,000 per year on charity, far more than her

---

20. Fitzgerald, Percy (1899). *The Good Queen Charlotte*. London: Downey & Co, p.189.
21. Craig, William Marshall (1818). *Memoir of Her Majesty Sophia Charlotte, of Mecklenburg Strelitz, Queen of Great Britain*. London: Caxton Press, p.76.
22. Ibid., p.121.

budget could strictly afford. Still, this was hardly the wenching, boozing and gambling that other royals had wasted their money on in the past, and would do so again in the future, and Charlotte's reputation continued to blossom.

Her patronage brought publicity, money and prestige to any number of causes from the abolition of slavery to the education of the poor, yet she was particularly interested in the welfare of young ladies. Under her watchful care, the Magdalen Hospital achieved prominence and to this day she is memorialized in the very name of Queen Charlotte's Hospital.

Trouble at Home

In the years that followed the regency scare of 1765, Charlotte found her wish for an uneventful domestic life tested at every turn. Mother to an ever-growing brood of children, she and her husband took every opportunity to escape to their sanctuary of Kew as the world itself seemed to be railing against George III. He battled critics and enemies in Parliament, then there was the drama of the Seven Years' War and the fateful American fight for independence. Misery of a more personal sort found the family in 1767, when the Duke of York died at 28, swiftly followed one year later by his sister, Louisa.

This bereavement shook the royal household and it was rocked even further when, in 1769 another brother, Prince Henry, Duke of Cumberland and Strathearn, was successfully sued for adultery by Lord Grosvenor. Faced with a public scandal and the good name of the royal household being dragged into the mud, Charlotte and George became more insular than ever, yet Cumberland had an even bigger secret to share.

In 1771, he confessed that he had secretly married a widowed commoner named Mrs Anne Horton, and he hoped that his brother might accept the arrangement. George did not, and Cumberland and Anne were banished from court. Later that same fate would befall yet another brother, Prince William Henry, Duke of Gloucester and Edinburgh, when he confessed to his own clandestine marriage to Maria Walpole. The result was the Royal Marriages Act of 1772, which forbade any marriage without the express consent of monarch and Parliament, except in exceptional circumstances. The Act was, according to the press, evidence that 'there is something extremely tyrannical in the disposition of our Court',[23] and 'a most hateful, odious, and alarming bill; the principles of which will exceed even the despotism of the East'.[24]

Finally, to crown an almost perfect year, Charlotte was burgled, and *that* is a tale in itself!

The False Princess

Miss Sarah Wilson was a young lady of just 16 when she left her home in Staffordshire and travelled to London to find a respectable position. She landed on her feet almost immediately and was employed as a maid to Caroline Vernon, one of Charlotte's ladies-in-waiting.

The servant of a servant, no less!

Through her association with Caroline, Sarah enjoyed unfettered access to the queen's rooms and was left wide-eyed at the splendour and wealth that she found there. In 1771, Sarah could finally stand it no longer, and broke into a cabinet in the queen's private apartments. She stole some jewels, a dress and a miniature of George III, no doubt expecting that such items wouldn't be missed by one who had so much. She had reckoned without Charlotte's dedication to her jewels, and the queen noticed almost immediately that her belongings were missing. When Sarah returned to the scene of the crime later that week, she was caught red-handed and carted off to face trial.

In fact, though the queen loved jewellery, and delighted in examining and counting the pieces she owned, all that finery soon became a chore. Too many priceless jewels is a problem that many in any era would *love* to have, but for Charlotte, who was soon seen out and about without her glittering gemstones, they were just one more thing to fret about.

'Believe me', she told the estimable diarist and courtier, Fanny Burney, 'It is a pleasure of a week – a fortnight, at most – and to return no more! I thought at first I should always choose to wear them; but the fatigue and trouble of putting them on, and the care they required, and the fear of losing

---

23. *Bingley's Journal* (London, England), 8 February, 1772–15 February, 1772; Issue 89, p.4.
24. Ibid.

them – believe me ma'am, in a fortnight's time I longed again for my own earlier dress, and wished never to see them more!'[25]

Now the fear of losing them had almost come true and Sarah Wilson was about to face the full weight of Georgian law. Convicted of theft and violation of the royal privacy, the sentence was death. Shocked at her attendant's behaviour, but even more horrified by her fate, Caroline begged Charlotte to intervene on behalf of the girl. The queen relented and Sarah's sentence was commuted to transportation for life, with the young woman spirited off to Baltimore, Maryland.

Life in Baltimore looked like it would be hard and brutal for Sarah. She was purchased as a slave by plantation owner, William Devall, but she wasn't about to hang around. As soon as Devall's back was turned she fled and it soon became clear that this young lady wasn't an innocent abroad at *all*.

Sarah reinvented herself as Princess Susanna Caroline Matilda, Marchioness de Waldegrave. She claimed to be Queen Charlotte's sister who had been exiled due to an unspoken scandal that had led to a bitter estrangement. Her stories of drama and romance made Sarah a popular girl among the colonists. It seemed that she had a particular talent for winding gentlemen around her little finger and they offered her shelter, no doubt hoping that some rich rewards might one day come their way.

Sarah was audacious, shameless and skilled in the art of impersonation, but she couldn't keep it up forever. Devall had paid handsomely for his slave and he was determined to get her back, advertising in the *Pennsylvania Gazette* on 11 October 1771 for the return of a woman with 'a blemish in her right eye, black roll'd hair, stoops in her shoulders, makes a common practice of writing and marking her clothes with a crown and a B'.[26]

There are several versions of what happened to Sarah in the years following her escape from Devall, but it would appear that he recaptured her through the intervention of a lawyer, Michael Dalton, and for a time she was once again a slave. Of course, the *princess* wasn't a lady to be kept down and after some time on the plantation, she made good her escape. Devall,

25. Berkeley, Helen (ed) (1844). *Memoirs of Madame D'Arblay*. London: James Mowatt & Co, p.98.
26. *The Pennsylvania Gazette*, 11 October 1771.

away from home and fighting for independence, had more important things on his mind and this time, he let her go.

Sarah found some measure of respectability eventually when she married an English soldier, Captain William Talbot. Sadly, the scandalous Sarah's ultimate fate is lost to history so we shall never know what became of 'the most surprising genius of the female sex that was ever obliged to visit America. What an improvement on Moll Flanders!'[27]

This wasn't the only incident of drama among Charlotte's ladies-in-waiting, who seemed to be constantly jostling for prestige and influence. In fact, they even went on strike in 1775, complaining that they were kept too busy to eat the free supper that they were entitled to. The king was sympathetic and agreed to pay each of the ladies £70, to compensate for their empty bellies!

Goodbye Augusta

'This morning between the hours of six and seven, her Royal Highness the Princess Dowager of Wales departed this life to the great grief of their Majesties and all the Royal Family, after a very long and painful illness, which she bore with the greatest fortitude and resignation.'[28]

Ever since Charlotte arrived in England, it would be fair to say that she and Augusta, her mother-in-law, had felt no great affection for one another. Used to influence and quite settled as the number one woman in the life of George III, Augusta had no intention of surrendering her position to Charlotte.

Augusta installed a Miss Dashwood in Charlotte's household and received regular reports from her spy on the comings and goings of the queen's circle, yet she can have found little to concern her. After all, Charlotte was focused on family and philanthropy, and what political interests she did have were limited, posing no threat to the canny dowager.

---

27. *Rhode Island Gazette & Country Journal*, January 1774.
28. *Middlesex Journal or Chronicle of Liberty* (London, England), 8 February, 1772–11 February, 1772; Issue 447, p.1.

By now, riddled with throat cancer, the Dowager Princess of Wales attempted to soldier on. George was beside himself with worry at his mother's condition and he and Charlotte spent long hours at Augusta's bedside as she grew more and more frail, battling desperately to cling onto life.

She might have been dying, but Augusta managed to snatch at the threads of influence to the last and when she passed away on 8 February 1772, there were few among the public who mourned her loss, thanks to her insistent meddling in government affairs and her alleged relationship with Lord Bute. Augusta's popular sheen had long since worn off and her funeral provided bitter evidence of this.

The badly-behaved audience spat on Augusta's coffin and 'the mob huzzaed for joy'.[29] As the crowd grew more restless, it turned into a free-for-all, tearing the platform cloth at Westminster Abbey clean away. Rather than assert their authority to bring the spectators back into line, 'the soldiers on guard, fearful of losing their share, began to help themselves'.[30]

So it was that Charlotte finally became the one and only senior royal lady in George III's life. Had she shared the ambition of Augusta of Saxe-Gotha or Caroline of Ansbach then this would be the moment to assert it, to swing into action and begin consolidating her position. In fact, she didn't have any ambition other than to continue her patronage of her chosen charities, share in the upbringing of her adored children, and to soothe her husband's troubled brow.

However, if the saintly Charlotte appears a little *too* good to be true, the ever-reliable Walpole can be relied upon to lend a little shade to her halo.

In 1764, George's sister, Princess Augusta, and husband, Charles William Ferdinand, Duke of Brunswick-Wolfenbüttel, visited England and set about immediately endearing themselves to the people. Augusta, of course, would later become mother-in-law to Charlotte's son, George IV, but for now, that was far into the future.

The Duke and Duchess of Brunswick knew how to play the crowd and appeared regularly in public, enjoying the approbation of George and Charlotte's

---

29. Walpole, Horace (1910). *The Last Journals of Horace Walpole During the Reign of George III from 1771–1783*. London: John Lane, p.17.
30. Ibid., p.18.

subjects. The king and queen, just a little suspicious, began to wonder if they were intending some mischief or intrigue and decided that they would treat the Brunswick couple civilly, but keep them decidedly at arm's length.

Augusta returned to England at the invitation of her mother, the dying Princess Dowager of Wales, and once again found herself in hostile waters. She wasn't given a residence in one of the royal palaces, but instead squirrelled away in a private house on Pall Mall even though St James's Palace was empty at the time. She was in constant attendance on her mother during the visit yet Charlotte forbade George from seeing his sister alone, and insisted on being present at all their meetings.

Horace Walpole attributes this entirely to jealousy on the part of the queen and details another incident in which Charlotte publicly reprimanded one of her household for a slip in protocol. This time Charlotte took the opportunity to hurl an altogether too innocent insult in the direction of the unwelcome Duchess of Brunswick.

'Lady Gower, having formerly been Lady of the Bedchamber to the Princess, and now civilly waiting on her, followed her into the ball-room, and by sufferance of the Duchess of Argyle, her great friend, sat next to her, who was in waiting on the Queen. Her Majesty was exceedingly angry, and in a day or two afterwards, all her ladies being present, said aloud to the Duchess, "Duchess I must *reprimand* you for letting Lady Gower take place of you, as Lady to the Princess of Brunswick. I had a mind to speak to you on the spot, but would not for, fear of saying anything I should repent of, *though I should have thought it*. The Princess of Brunswick has nothing to do here, and I insist on your recovering the precedence you gave up. One day or other my son will be married, and then I shall have his wife's ladies pretending to take place in my palace, which they shall not do.'[31]

Of course, given her rather insular life, it's hardly surprising that the queen became embroiled in such domestic sniping. It was she who urged George

---

31. Walpole, Horace (1859). *Journal of the Reign of King George II from the Year 1771 to 1783, Volume 1*. London: Bentley, p.18.

to come down hard on his erring brothers, no doubt driven by her passion for faith and fidelity and her husband's desire to safeguard the moral and spiritual wellbeing of the monarchy at all costs. In this quiet, pleasant and good-humoured woman there lurked, one suspects, something of a tiger. She was plunged into a close-knit court with a husband whose life had been sheltered and ruled by a strong mother and Charlotte, torn from all that was familiar at home, would let nothing shatter this new idyll that she had built.

Fate, however, had other ideas.

The Lost Sons

The years that followed the death of Augusta were politically tumultuous, with the American War of Independence eventually resulting in a decisive victory for the colonists. In Denmark, barely weeks before the death of the dowager, George's sister, Caroline Matilda, had been embroiled in a scandal of epic proportions, having indulged in an affair with the doctor responsible for treating her husband's mental illness. When that same doctor, Johann Friedrich Struensee, became virtual regent of the nation with Caroline Matilda at his side, the stage was set for tragedy. Their affair ended when a coup engineered by her stepmother-in-law sent Caroline Matilda into exile and Struensee to the executioner.

This was all small beer compared to events in the colonies, of course, and when the smoke of battle cleared and the king and queen surveyed the remains of their empire and the shattered public, exhausted by war and taxes, they must have wondered what had happened to their green and pleasant land.

Through all of the drama and upheaval, Charlotte continued her routine of childbirth and the youngest of the brood were two infant sons, Octavius, born in 1779, and Alfred, born in 1780. There can be little doubt of how much affection was lavished on these children but Charlotte found the pregnancies exhausting, her body tired by nearly two decades of almost constant childbearing. Just as they had with their older children, the king and queen elected to have their youngest sons vaccinated against smallpox, mindful that the risks of the procedure were slight.

The royal couple was undertaking a tour to visit various nobles when Prince Alfred fell ill. At first, there was little suggestion that this was anything other than a routine indisposition and it was agreed that the best thing for the little boy was a trip away. So it was that 'his Royal Highness Prince Alfred, attended by Lady Charlotte Finch, and others of his Majesty's household, set out from the Queen's Palace for Deal Castle, to make use of the salt waters for the recovery of his health'.[32]

His face marked by the unmistakable signs of smallpox, Alfred remained at Windsor for six weeks as his condition grew steadily worse until, with the little boy struggling to breathe, he and Lady Charlotte returned to the royal household at Windsor. Concern about his condition reached the press who were soon reporting that 'Prince Alfred [...] was so dangerously ill [...] but we have the satisfaction to find that he is now quite out of danger'.[33]

One can actually track the decline of the cheery little boy over the summer, the false hope and heartbreaking chinks of light in what was already a fatal condition. He took trips into the countryside with Lady Charlotte and, as summer wore on, appeared to be rallying. Suddenly though, his condition worsened and, on 20 August 1782, the youngest son of George III and Charlotte died.

> 'Yesterday morning died at the Royal Palace, Windsor, his Royal Highness Prince Alfred, their Majesties youngest son. The Queen is much affected at this domestic calamity, probably more so on account of its being the only one she has experienced after a marriage of 20 years and having been the mother of fourteen children.'[34]

Of course, to have more than a dozen children survive infancy in the eighteenth century was no mean feat but that shouldn't be allowed to obscure or cloud the tragedy of Alfred's death. In fact, we might speculate

---

32. *Whitehall Evening Post (1770)* (London, England), 11 May, 1782–14 May, 1782; Issue 5639, p.3.
33. *London Chronicle* (London, England), 13 August, 1782–15 August, 1782; Issue 4011, p.154.
34. *London Chronicle* (London, England), 20 August, 1782–22 August, 1782; issue 4014, p.1.

that the extraordinary good fortune of the family made the tragedy even harder to bear and every member of the household was shattered by the death of its youngest member. Now, in the parlance of the time, Charlotte could be considered a *proper mother*, having finally endured the loss of one of her children.

The death of Alfred was, one might hope, somewhat ameliorated by those children who still lived and the king and queen threw themselves into the company of their other offspring. Little Octavius, now the youngest member of the family, was doted on by his mother and father and, just as Alfred had been, he too was inoculated against smallpox.

And history repeated itself.

Charlotte was pregnant with her fifteenth and last child when, in April 1783, Octavius fell ill. If Alfred's had been a steady decline, Octavius seemed to reach death's door at a shocking speed. This time there was no trip to the coast, no jaunts to the countryside, just a swift decline followed by the inevitable.

> 'On Saturday, on the Majesties arriving at Kew, in their way to Windsor, and finding Prince Octavius in a dangerous Way, they determined to stay there all Night and sent an Express to Windsor to acquaint the Attendants of the Reason of their continuing there.
>
> The same Night died at Kew, his Royal Highness Prince Octavius, his Majesty's youngest Son, in the fifth Year of his Age.'[35]

It was a devastating blow to a family already struggling to cope with the loss of a child and, heavily pregnant, Charlotte was at an incredibly low ebb. No doubt concerns for her husband, who felt the death of his sons with an extraordinary keenness, weighed equally on her mind, and it was with a sigh of relief that the court greeted the news that Charlotte had delivered a healthy baby girl. When that baby was born on 7 August 1783, Charlotte must have worried for the fate of this new arrival, fearing that a third child might be in the grave before infancy had passed.

---

35. *Daily Advertiser* (London, England), Monday, 5 May, 1783; issue 17249, p.1.

Princess Amelia would become the family's pride and joy, known by the diminutive nickname, *Emily*. It was, the court believed, the start of happier times.

Or so they hoped.

The Regency Crisis

Although Charlotte had successfully weathered the earlier storms of the prospective Regency Bill, her respite was to be a temporary one and, in 1788, life for the royal couple changed forever. Shattered by political feuding, conflict overseas and the misery he still felt over the death of his sons, the king was in dire straits.

In the summer of that year, George complained of a stomach pain and from this unremarkable beginning, there came a crisis. That abdominal pain was merely the physical manifestation of the madness that would later claim him and by autumn, he was raving. Sleepless and violent, he began making lurid accusations of adultery against the queen. Charlotte was at her wit's end. It seemed as though the court physicians could do nothing. The king's condition grew worse by the day and the queen had no alternative but to call in further assistance.

That help came in the shape of Francis Willis, a Lincolnshire physician and clergyman who had been credited with curing the madness of Lady Harcourt. He also had the blessing of the Lord Chancellor, and when Charlotte agreed to let him see her husband, it must have seemed as though she had no other alternative. She tried to maintain their domestic routine and slept beside George until his ravings became so severe that there were fears for her safety. When the devoted couple finally had to sleep in separate rooms, Charlotte missed George so much that rest eluded her.

Eventually the *patient* was removed to the serenity of Kew, where it was hoped he might benefit from the more bucolic surroundings. The palace had once been George's sanctuary and he had made a wedding gift to Charlotte of a small cottage in the grounds, where she hosted family picnics and intimate gatherings. The elder royal boys had been educated at Dutch House whilst the family spent summers in the quiet surroundings of the White House, far removed from the problems of London.

Now, however, Kew became George's prison. Just as the king was isolated and subjected to the treatment of Doctor Willis, so too was Charlotte to become a captive, though in a less literal sense. Foaming at the mouth and jabbering incoherently, for George, the tranquil sanctuary of Kew had become a place of brutal punishment and coercive correction. Plunged into ice cold baths and force fed purging potions intended to bring on vomiting and diarrhoea, the king suffered through a brutal and agonizing regime. Leeches fed from his forehead, his scalp was shaved bare and hot vinegar and mustard was spread on his skin until the monarch howled in agony and fought as though his very life was at stake.

Gagged with a handkerchief and forcibly restrained in a straitjacket, George III was ruled with a mixture of fear and coercion as, in the lonely halls of the palace, the queen fretted and worried. As the king's condition worsened and he fancied himself in love with Lady Pembroke, one of Charlotte's circle, the queen's hair began to turn grey and weight fell from her. Kept from her husband, she was allowed to see him only when Willis decreed that his behaviour had been good enough to be rewarded with a visit. Fanny Burney writes of Charlotte during this period as a woman who was by turns stoic and heartbroken, weeping in private for the husband she adored.

Privy to the doctor's findings and those occasional audiences with her husband, Charlotte's nerves grew ever more frayed. She alone was left as sole parent to her children, to the Prince of Wales who grew more belligerent every day, as well as the youngsters who wondered what had become of their cheerful, playful father. She was also entirely at the mercy of those who would use the king's indisposition to feather their own nests.

> 'The Queen is almost overpowered with some secret terror. I am affected beyond all expression in her presence, to see what struggles she makes to support serenity. To-day she gave up the conflict when I was alone with her, and burst into a violent fit of tears. It was very, very terrible to see! [...] Sometimes she walks up and down the room without uttering a word, but shaking her head frequently, and in evident distress and irresolution.'[36]

---

36. Burney, Frances (1910). *The Diary and Letters of Frances Burney, Madame D'Arblay, Vol II*. Boston: Little, Brown and Company, p.27.

As Fanny Burney's writings show, the queen was suffering as much as any spouse dealing with an ill loved one, perhaps more so, since her husband had been at the centre of her rather secluded life. Charlotte took comfort and refuge in religion, barely leaving the house as she devoured reports of George's condition in the press, her distress only increasing at what she saw in newsprint.

Charlotte was bewildered and confused by her husband's fate and had little choice but to submit to the decisions made by Willis. She had no experience of dealing with mental illness and could only sit by whilst the learned Lincolnshire gentleman gagged the king with a handkerchief, fastened him into a restraining device nicknamed *the coronation chair* and plunged him into ice-cold baths. In his delirium, the king ranted and raved at Charlotte for bringing Willis into his life, believing in his madness that the queen and the doctor were somehow ranked again him in a dark and cruel conspiracy.

Although the Prince of Wales had become a thorn in the side of his parents, with his womanizing, gambling and constant demands for money, it would be wrong to think that he didn't care for his father. He and his brother, the Duke of York, became regular visitors to Kew and it soon became apparent that, if the king were not about to recover, then difficult decisions had to be made. In Parliament, the question of a regent once again reared its head, and the obvious candidate was none other than the Prince of Wales.

As an avowed Whig, Wales would make a potentially troublesome regent and though William Pitt the Younger agreed that he was the *obvious* candidate when it came to drafting the bill, he didn't agree that he was the *only* candidate. Charles James Fox, the Whig leader and close friend of the prince, lobbied hard for Wales to be awarded the role, dreaming of the glittering prizes that might come to his party if he could only oust the Tory-loving king.

In fact, Pitt's bill proved that he was indeed a loyal friend to George III and included tight restrictions on the power of the regent, who wouldn't be able to dismiss the sitting government, nor have any power over the king's estates. Crucially, responsibility for the monarch's wellbeing and care would remain in the hands of Charlotte, a sure signal to her opponents that her political ambitions were finally making themselves known. The Prince of

Wales was particularly stung by the fact that he wouldn't have custody of the king's belongings, no doubt wringing his hands at the rather valuable goodies contained therein.

Charlotte wasn't driven by political nor financial interests, but by care for her husband. She prayed that his swift recovery would render a regency unnecessary, and intended to ensure that things remained as unchanged as possible even *if* a regent was appointed. Deeply loyal to Pitt, the Tories and George, she had always loved routine and calm and now, in her darkest hour, she was not about to let the world change any more than it already had. The Prince of Wales, though concerned for his father, was a man who loved to spend money that he didn't have, and his mother knew that giving him authority over the royal estates might prove financially catastrophic. There was no way that Charlotte was about to sit by and let Wales throw out the king's government, install his favourites, and spend the crown's money on wine, women and song. This, of course, led some to speculate, 'whether he or the Queen is really *King*'.[37]

It was during this period that the queen really began to consolidate what her daughters would later refer to as 'the Windsor nunnery'. Lonely, unhappy and lost, the girls became Charlotte's closest companions, forming a secretive circle into which no outsider would be admitted. In the years to come many of those daughters would be kept as virtual children, denied the chance to flourish. It's telling that, of those six girls, only three would marry and only one of those before 1816.

Slowly, surely, it began to seem as though the queen's faith in her husband was to be rewarded as his health recovered. Public celebrations were ordered, charity and mementoes distributed to the poor at the queen's direction, and a general sense of relief fell over the country. By early 1789, George was once again well enough to govern and the Regency Bill, much to the relief of the government and queen, became a moot point. Her relationship with the Prince of Wales had been strained by those past few months, with each suspecting the other of political intrigue, and when a concert and even a trip abroad was discussed to celebrate the monarch's return to health, it made an already bad situation far, far worse.

37. Minto, Emma Eleanor Elizabeth (ed.) (1874). *Life and Letters of Sir Gilbert Elliot First Earl of Minto from 1751 to 1806*. London: Longmans, p.292.

As George recovered he began to discuss in some seriousness the possibility of going to Hanover. The rather absurd idea was likely just a hangover from his illness, but the Prince of Wales decided that such talk had to be addressed. He set out his thoughts on paper and gave them to the queen, asking her to discuss his concerns with her husband. She refused to do any such thing, sure that the king was in too delicate a state to discuss matters of business and travel.

Never one for finer feelings, Wales summoned the Duke of York, and the two men combined forces to lean on their mother. Eventually the princes received a letter from the king in which he explained that he wasn't yet well enough for an official audience with them. Wales and York were furious, certain that this was a transparent effort by Pitt and Charlotte to keep them away from their father. Thinking only of her husband's wellbeing, Charlotte hardly cared if her sons were about to throw a tantrum, and throw a tantrum is exactly what Wales did.

Sir Gilbert Elliot, 1st Earl of Minto, a Whig and friend of Wales, rarely found fault with the young man's conduct. After all, it doesn't do to criticize the future king when he also *happens* to be a rather senior supporter of your own opposition party. However, even *he* winced when he recalled the eventual fallout between queen and prince, the ongoing war for the king's attention eventually exploding into an ugly altercation.

'The Prince of Wales has had a smart little tussle with the Queen, in which they came to strong and open declarations of hostility. He told her that she had connected herself with his enemies, and had entered into plans for destroying and disgracing him and all her children, and that she countenanced misrepresentations of his conduct to the King, and prevented the explanations he wished to give. She was violent and lost her temper; and the conversation ended, I believe, by her saying that she would not be the channel of anything that either he or the Duke of York had to say to the King, and that the King did not mind what either he or the Duke of York either did or said or thought. I do not think such a conversation well judged on the part of the Prince.'[38]

---

38. Ibid., p.287.

Indeed it was not. This was a prince already at odds with his family, a prince forced to beg his supporters to deny rumours of an illegal marriage in Parliament, a prince who seemed to always be coming, cap in hand, for money. This was also the man who, in the event of a regency, would do all he could to wield power, and Charlotte knew it. When a concert was planned to celebrate George's return to health and neither Wales nor York were *formally* invited, both took this as a slight. They received a letter from the queen explaining that they could attend if they really wanted to but, since the event was intended as a thank you to the Tories, who had supported the monarchy, the Whig princes may prefer *not* to be in the audience.

When York attempted a little damage limitation and suggested that the whole nation had supported the king, regardless of political opinion, Charlotte was having none of it. The event was for *supporters*, she told him plainly, and neither he nor Wales fitted that description. To make matters worse, among the invitees was Princess Sophia, the daughter of the scandalous Prince William Henry and Maria Walpole, aka the Duke and Duchess of Gloucester. The king had banished Gloucester when he learned of his secret marriage to Maria, so to have the daughter of this marriage invited and the eldest sons of the king and queen excluded was just another insult. Needless to say, this went down as well as you might expect and York declared that he wouldn't be seen dead there!

York and Wales took their lack of a formal invitation not just as an offence against them, but as an out and out declaration of war. Charlotte had as good as accused them of being against the king though as unabashed Whigs, they really shouldn't have been surprised if she took issue with that. Perhaps she could have handled it differently, but Charlotte's only thought was for preserving the status quo and for ensuring that her husband's recovery went as smoothly as possible.

Mindful of the damage that a public rift might do to all parties concerned, advisers on both sides suggested that everyone take a moment to let things cool down a little. Eventually the Duke of York did send a letter of conciliation but the damage to the family was done; it would not recover for a long time.

Marie Antoinette

Though Great Britain had lost the North American colonies, the fires of revolution never, thankfully, spread as far as her shores. Under the reign of the Prince Regent, radicals rattled their sabres but in the end things remained *relatively* under control.

In France life was considerably harder for those who wore the crown and by 1793, things had reached an endgame. It is outside the scope of this book to dissect the events of the French Revolution, and there are many excellent volumes that do so. Suffice to say that in 1793, things were dire indeed. The last hope of escape or exile had long since gone and the dethroned king and queen of France were due to face a gruesome end.

Charlotte and Marie Antoinette had long been what we might have termed, before the days of mass social media, *pen pals*. Their lives had run along parallel lines to some degree, and it's likely that each welcomed the friendship of the other, happy to know that they weren't alone in their transition from wide-eyed girl to queen of a major power.

Although eleven years separated the birth of the women they had lived similar lives. Neither was considered a particularly great marriage prospect, the looks of each were questioned and dissected and, eventually, each was declared a suitable bride. Though Marie Antoinette underwent an extreme makeover that even included cosmetic dentistry *without* anaesthetic, Charlotte was, at least, accepted as she was.

Charlotte and Marie Antoinette each found themselves bewildered by the world they were plunged into, with Charlotte watched by Augusta just as Marie Antoinette was spied upon by gossiping courtiers who reported her every move to her hawkish mother. Both queens had an eye for bling, and built themselves idyllic homes in which to hide away; with Charlotte never happier than roaming the grounds at Kew and Frogmore, while Marie Antoinette constructed her very own pastoral idyll at the Petit Trianon.

The two queens kept up an intermittent correspondence throughout Marie Antoinette's life and even when France allied with the American revolutionary cause, there was no change in their friendship. One can only imagine Charlotte's increasing horror as she learned of events across the English Channel and she sent gifts of clothes to the royal family, no doubt hoping that this might offer them at least some comfort in their moments of need. In fact, the British queen did wonder whether there might be an opportunity for her French counterpart to flee the continent and join her in England, but it was not to be. Powerless to help her friend, she wrote that, 'ancient history can hardly produce anything more barbarous and cruel than our neighbours in France.'[39]

When Marie Antoinette went to her death, plans for an anniversary celebration to mark Charlotte and George's coronation were cancelled. The queen, once so vibrant and cheery, and always so busy in her garden or her library, playing with her children and keeping well away from politics, had been changed forever by these tumultuous years. Now grey-haired, drawn and pale, the young lady who had so charmed those who journeyed with her to England was long gone. In her place, was a woman who had by necessity grown harder, who had been forced into the politics she had sought to avoid, and had been mocked and jeered by her opponents and her sons. Her temper had frayed and her moods had become dark, especially with the daughters who were forced to serve as her constant companions. Of course, one can only speculate that her husband's lewd and cruel comments at the height of his illness must have hurt Charlotte deeply too. He raved about his attraction to Lady Pembroke, told the queen that she was loathed, that her children feared her, that even her dog was more loved and loving than she was.

George had been the cause, it would seem, of both Charlotte's greatest happiness and her greatest despair. Her daughters, however, would have to wait a very, very long time to have husbands of their own.

The Madness Returns

If the queen had dared to hope that life would now be uneventful, she was to be sorely mistaken. At the dawn of the nineteenth century, her husband was once again embroiled in political challenges, ill health and familial disputes, as the Prince of Wales embarked on a messy and very public war of attrition with his estranged wife, Caroline of Brunswick. Although things were back on an even keel with the Duke of York, this lapse in George's health sent the entire family a sudden and unwelcome reminder of what had once been, and what might one day be again.

---

39. Levey, Michael (2005). *Sir Thomas Lawrence.* New Haven: Yale University Press, p.20.

Nobody felt this more keenly than Charlotte, who was torn between wanting to care for the man she loved and living in fear of the episodes that seized him at every moment of emotional trauma. She no longer liked to be alone with her husband, keeping her girls with her at all times and locking her bedroom door at night. This, of course, intensified George's own anxiety and Charlotte became ever more agitated in turn, completing the unhappy circle. So it went on and on, illness alternating with good health until everyone was exhausted by the sheer emotional strain of it all.

By 1804 George was once again insane, yet this time, the feared Doctor Willis was not summoned. The king was so terrorized by memories of his time in the doctor's custody at Kew that he had the White House torn down, making his family promise *never* to let Willis near him again. This time he was attended by Doctor Samuel Simmons yet once again the queen was forced to endure his ravings, to listen to his cruelty, the crude talk and bad language that so distressed her. In Parliament, the Whig opposition was once again gaining ground, but all of this was of no concern to the queen, who cared only for her children and spouse.

Together the family struggled on and the queen occupied herself with the gentle company of Princess Charlotte of Wales, her only legitimate grandchild and the daughter of the bitterly estranged Prince and Princess of Wales. Over the years that followed, George shifted violently and suddenly from madness to sanity and back again yet it wasn't only his mental state that was growing more troubling. His eyesight was failing at a terrifying rate, his rheumatism was crippling him and, bit by bit, the years began to close in on George III and Queen Charlotte.

The Nunnery

Of the fifteen children of George III and Charlotte, two, Alfred and Octavius, did not survive to adulthood. Although the couple's other sons would all eventually marry, sometimes unwillingly, for the six daughters of the king and queen, things were to be very different.

As the oldest daughters of the House of Hanover, the first girls to enter the marriage market *should* have been Charlotte, Princess Royal, and Princess Augusta Sophia. They would have made highly eligible candidates for any would-be groom in search of a royal bride, but their parents had very different plans.

As early as 1785, Frederick, the Danish Prince Royal and son of George's ill-fated sister, Caroline Matilda, had approached the king and indicated that he would be interested in pursuing a marriage to his cousin, Augusta. The king remembered all too well the way in which Caroline Matilda had been cruelly used by her husband, Christian VII, who had left her isolated and alone until she had begun her fateful affair with Struensee. Because of that affair she had been imprisoned, her tattered reputation following her to an early grave and George would not, could not, agree to send one of his daughters to Denmark to face what might turn out to be the same fate. The next proposal for Augusta came in 1791, courtesy of Duke Ferdinand of Württemberg, a soldier noted for his good character and handsome looks.

Naturally Augusta had high hopes for this possible betrothal and the court waited with baited breath, fully expecting a happy announcement. Off hunting with the Prince of Wales, Ferdinand was ready to return for an audience with the king and queen at a moment's notice, yet the summons never came. Augusta's hopes were dashed when her father decided to reject the proposal, citing the fact that she couldn't marry before her older sister, Charlotte, Princess Royal.

Other proposals followed and were swiftly rejected, usually as soon as the king heard of them. Whilst Charlotte must have initially been sympathetic to her daughters, one wonders whether she didn't eventually come to bless her husband's reticence as she came to rely on the girls for comfort and support. Fanny Burney remembered finding the queen and princesses working at their spinning wheels together, silent and apparently content in their secluded family unit, drawn tightly together by their shared suffering and secrets.

When the king's mania grew so violent that he was put in isolation by his doctors, it was Augusta who moved into the queen's chambers to comfort her mother and this, perhaps more than anything, sealed her fate. Along with her sisters she became Charlotte's rock, her company in times of lonely need and a gentle, soothing presence when York and Wales were raging. Less soothing, perhaps, was the formidable Princess Royal and tellingly, she was also the first princess to make a match.

The Princess Royal found her escape in the shape of a proposal from the Hereditary Prince Frederick of Württemberg, a widowed father of three whose late wife[40] had accused him of brutal behaviour. Initially Charlotte and George refused the suit yet the princess was no accepting Augusta, and she was determined to be married. She cajoled and niggled at her parents until they could stand it no more and it was George who caved in first, leaving his spouse with no choice but to give her blessing to the proposed marriage, possibly much to the chagrin of Viscount Brome and Lady Gordon:

'The marriage of Lord Viscount BROME to Lady L. Gordon is postponed to next week; probably the same day that joins the PRINCESS ROYAL to the Duke of WIRTEMBERG.'[41]

The wedding was held on 18 May 1797 at the Chapel Royal of St James's Palace, amid enormous rejoicing. What the Princess Royal's sisters might make of this we can only guess but *she* was delighted and, most remarkable of all, she was *free*.

The Princess Royal was the last princess to marry until 1816,[42] although Elizabeth did receive an offer from the Duke of Orléans and future King of the French, Louis Philippe, in 1808. As a Catholic, he was considered entirely unsuitable and Charlotte vetoed the proposal. With the king's health suffering, George was in no fit state to travel abroad to negotiate marriages and he was hardly well enough to do so from home, whilst the memory of his sister's unhappy fate constantly haunted him.

---

40. His first wife was Augusta, sister of Caroline of Brunswick, the wife of George IV and daughter of Princess Augusta of Great Britain. Princess Augusta was, of course, George III's sister: royal courts were nothing if not tangled!
41. *True Briton (1793)* (London, England), Friday, 14 April, 1797; Issue 1343, p.6.
42. Whilst rumours flew that Augusta secretly married Sir Brent Spencer, the next *official* marriage came when Princess Mary wed her cousin, Prince William Frederick, Duke of Gloucester and Edinburgh, in 1816; Princess Elizabeth later married Prince Frederick of Hesse-Homburg in 1818, after falling for him in his uniform! Princess Sophia, rather more scandalously, adored Thomas Garth, an equerry to whom she *may* have been illegally married. Indeed, rumour has it that she was the mother of a mysterious child he cared for in Weymouth!

As the king grew sicker and Charlotte became the first port of call for suitors, none of them ever really stood a chance. Here we might see the true impact of her husband's madness on the queen who had been forever hardened by the pain of caring for him. She created a secretive, secluded circle into which outsiders rarely if ever strayed, the same secluded circle that bid an almost ceremonial farewell to Fanny Burney in 1791.

'They all were now going — I took, for the last time, the cloak of the Queen, and, putting it over her shoulders, slightly ventured to press them, earnestly, though in a low voice, saying, "God Almighty bless your Majesty!"

She turned round, and, putting her hand upon my ungloved arm, pressed it with the greatest kindness, and said, "May you be happy!"

She left me overwhelmed with tender gratitude. The three eldest Princesses were in the next room; they ran in to me the moment the Queen went onward. Princess Augusta and Princess Elizabeth each took a hand, and the Princess Royal put hers over them. I could speak to none of them; but they repeated "I wish you happy! — I wish you health!" again and again, with the sweetest eagerness.

They then set off for Kew.'[43]

To me, the image of the three girls and their mother, each bound tightly to the other, is evocative and haunting. It's hardly surprising that when Charlotte's companion, Juliana Elizabeth Schwellenberg, died in 1797, she clung to the girls more firmly than ever. Of course, we know now that those daughters sought no such bond. They longed to be allowed to grow into women, to escape the family bosom and find their own way in the world, yet instead they were forced to sit obediently at home as, little by little, the youthful sun set.

George's own favourite and the youngest family member, Amelia, would make her own spirited bid for love with the Honourable Charles FitzRoy, an equerry more than two decades her senior. He chaperoned the sickly young

---

43. Burney, Frances (1843). *The Diary and Letters of Madame D'Arblay, Vol V.* London: Henry Colburn, p.226.

lady to the coast in the early years of the nineteenth century and, during the trip, the pair fell in love. That the couple might have allowed themselves to hope that the king and queen would give the union their blessing is, it must be said, surprising, but Charles and Amelia really did dream of a life together.

Amelia approached her mother and told her of the relationship, begging for Charlotte's approval and asking if she might speak to the king and seek his blessing. Instead the queen refused to even *mention* it to her husband. She feared what impact such news might have on his health and instead forbade Amelia from pursuing the affair, leaving her in no doubt that there could be no hope for the couple, no matter how much they adored one another.

For years, Amelia clung to the hope that her mother might change her mind, even signing her letters as *AFR*, Amelia FitzRoy. The hope was, of course, a false one and when Amelia died in 1810, her last words were, 'Tell Charles I die blessing him'.[44]

It was Amelia's death that eventually pitched her father over the precipice and into irretrievable madness, the queen's best efforts to save him from that fate having, in the final analysis, failed.

Although her daughter had died heartbroken, Charlotte didn't waver and when Augusta's own hopes of marriage were dashed she, Elizabeth, Mary and Sophia wrote letters to their mother begging her to give them some freedom. Charlotte's unequivocal reply stated coldly, 'in your Sex, and under the present Melancholy Situation of your father the going to Public Amusements [...] would be the highest mark of indecency possible'.[45]

There was to be no freedom for the princesses for now, and though the Prince of Wales did what he could to smooth the path with his mother, Charlotte was not to be swayed. She needed her girls and wouldn't let them go, no matter what the cost to them.

Years later the newly-installed Prince Regent granted his unmarried sisters increased allowances and official residences in the hope that they might be able to see something of the world they had been so sheltered from.

---

44. Childe-Pemberton, William Shakespear (1911). *The Romance of Princess Amelia*. London: John Lane Company, p.227.
45. Smith, EA (1999). *George IV*. New Haven: Yale University Press, p.126.

For the residents of the *Windsor nunnery*, life would only really change with the advent of Queen Charlotte's death and then the closed palace doors were flung wide, allowing them to emerge into a nation ruled by the flamboyant, fabulous Prince Regent.

Breaking Hearts

When Princess Amelia, *Emily*, died in 1810, the last strands of George III's sanity snapped forever. Blind, immobile and so lost in his own fantasies that he conversed for hours on end with the dead, nothing remained of the man who had welcomed Charlotte to St James's, the caring, gentle, unassuming king with whom she had, for a time, been so content.

He was confined at Windsor Castle, leaving Charlotte in the position of widow to a man who still lived. The Prince of Wales was made Regent in 1811 and, to everyone's surprise and Charlotte's great relief, elected *not* to oust the Tory government in favour of the Whigs. He recognized, just as his mother did, that maintaining some sort of status quo was key at such a tumultuous time.

For all the bad blood and harsh words that had passed between them, Charlotte and her eldest son now came together in a new understanding, united by a distrust and dislike of his estranged wife, Caroline of Brunswick. He needed her gentle guidance to navigate these new waters and she, more than ever, needed her family around her. In fact, even when the new regent bestowed households and allowances on his unmarried sisters Charlotte bore this with stoicism, though no doubt she wondered what would become of her now as she faced the uncertain twilight. Still, she was more than occupied with overseeing the care of the king, and the ongoing charitable interests which never failed to engage her attention.

As the years flew by, Charlotte watched her husband fade away, torn between missing his familiar face and hardly recognizing the blind, insane figure who no longer knew her. Charlotte found her grip on the family growing ever looser with each passing day and at the death of her brother, Charles II, Grand Duke of Mecklenburg, she no doubt felt the years keenly, growing more secluded than ever in her isolated sanctuary at Kew.

For decades, Charlotte had been strong for her family, the custodian of her husband's health and the daughters she could not let go. Now, in her final years, that strength began to crumble into frailty. As we shall see when we meet Caroline of Brunswick, the Prince Regent was a deeply unpopular man and Charlotte's alliance with her son saw some of that unpopularity rub off on her. She was heckled and jeered at in the streets, just as Augusta had been and, whilst she had endured assassination attempts on her husband stoically, when stones and insults were hurled at the ageing Charlotte, she felt the humiliation like a knife in her breast. Life seemed determined to batter her and she had barely recovered from mourning Charles when a second, more brutal death shattered the uneasy peace at the heart of the House of Hanover.

The final straw for Queen Charlotte's morale came in November 1817 with the death of her granddaughter, Princess Charlotte of Wales, the only child of the Prince Regent and Caroline of Brunswick. The darling of the people, she was smart, sassy and married to her adored Leopold. In fact, it seemed as though she was actually headed for a happy ending. The two Charlottes had not always seen eye to eye, with the young lady a loud and proud Whig as well as an opinionated and outspoken champion of her mother, Caroline. When Caroline left England for the continent, however, Charlotte and the princess grew closer and the queen took pains to get to know Leopold, and to ensure that the Prince Regent recognized what a good son-in-law he had. It's only natural then that, when Princess Charlotte fell pregnant, her grandmother joined in with the national celebrations.

The pregnancy ended in tragedy when Charlotte died shortly after giving birth to a stillborn baby boy who was large enough to have 'the size and appearance of a child of ten days old'.[46] Across Great Britain people mourned, with the succession suddenly in crisis and the woman everyone adored lost before her life had really begun. When her granddaughter died the queen was at Bath seeking a water cure for her own ailments, where she had been greeted warmly by the people of the city.

---

46. *The Morning Chronicle* (London, England), Saturday, 8 November, 1817; Issue 15139, p.3.

This welcoming celebration was forgotten as soon as news of the death of the princess reached the queen's ears and she left Bath to join her family with haste. Behind closed doors, the Prince Regent mourned deeply for his lost child, and he turned to his mother for support, with their two hearts breaking as one.

Even in the depths of their grief, Charlotte and her regent son were afforded no compassion by their subjects who so loathed the prince. Why, they asked, were no members of the royal family present at the birth? Who held the princess's hand as she laboured and died, did none of them even *care*?

'We deplore only that she was not supported in the hour of trial by the tender relatives whom she was known to love.'[47]

In fact, Queen Charlotte cared deeply and the tragedy of her granddaughter's death was one from which she did not recover. Though she returned to Bath and made a round of visits intended to buoy her fading spirits, Charlotte's life was approaching its final curtain.

Fading Away

Queen Charlotte's last public appearance came in April 1818 when she made a visit to the Mansion House to attend a prize giving in honour of the National Society for Promoting the Education of the Poor. Here she found herself once again received warmly, with no trace of the unpleasant scenes that had followed the death of Princess Charlotte. Having presented a donation of £500, the queen spent happy hours among the children who benefited from the charity, as well as those who ran it.

Though Charlotte took great comfort in philanthropy, her faith and family, she took none from the state of the king. Perhaps in her darkest hours she might have found herself wishing him dead. At least then he would be at peace and she would be able to grieve properly for the man she loved. Instead, George lived a half-life, blind, raving, chatting to the dead and inspecting

---

47. Ibid.

invisible soldiers. His was a pitiful existence and yet he didn't know it; for the wife who loved him though, there was no such respite. Still she longed to be with him, and having completed her final engagement, Charlotte became seized by the desire to be at George's side once more.

Nothing could deter Charlotte from this fervent wish and it's tempting and perhaps a little romantic to wonder if she knew that she was entering the final months of her life. She wasn't fated to see her final wish come true and before the queen's party could set out for Windsor, she fell ill.

Confined at Kew and attended by Princess Mary and Princess Augusta, Charlotte fought a losing battle against the agonies of dropsy. The Prince Regent was never far away, whether making regular visits or communicating with the physicians charged with her care. Known by modern medics as *oedema*, dropsy causes the soft tissue to swell thanks to the accumulation of excess water. Most common in the feet and legs, dropsy is often the result of a more serious disorder of one of the major organs and brings with it agonizing pains.

'DRO'PSY [hydrops, Lat.] A collection of water in the body.'[48]

For a woman who had so delighted in the outdoors, even going as far as to assemble a menagerie of exotic beasts at Kew, dropsy was a particularly cruel condition for Charlotte to suffer from. It robbed her of the ability to do anything physical, so she couldn't enjoy the walks that had brought her so much simple joy, nor stroll in the gardens she had helped to cultivate, or even visit the animals in her menagerie. Instead she could only wait for death, undergoing treatments that did nothing to ease her suffering.

Dropsy was merely the first of many ailments that crowded in on Charlotte, and by November 1818, she was gripped by pneumonia. The regent visited every day, sitting for hours beside his mother and bringing her comfort just as he had brought her headaches in the years gone by. He was attentive and loving, ensuring that Charlotte was given the very best care that money could buy. The press followed events at Kew closely, with everyone in the

---

48. Johnson, Samuel (1828). *A Dictionary of the English Language: Vol I*. Heidelberg: Joseph Engelmann, p.335.

country suffering alongside the woman they had loved, loathed and then, somehow, loved again.

'HER MAJESTY. – The following Bulletins have been issued since
our last:-

KEW, Nov. 8. – The Queen passed the evening of yesterday very uncomfortably, and has had a restless night; but there is no material alteration in her Majesty's symptoms.

[The queen's condition on each intervening day is summarized in one line]

KEW, Nov. 13. – The Queen had some sleep in the night, and her Majesty appears to suffer less to-day than she did yesterday.

Towards noon yesterday the Queen was more composed but her exhaustion was so great, that she continued throughout the remainder of the day, to all appearance totally unconscious. Her Majesty declines rapidly.'[49]

As the evening of 16 November 1818 drew on, Charlotte seemed to suddenly decline, yet even in her discomfort she remained serene. She made no complaint throughout the long night and the following morning, the Prince Regent and Duke of York were called to their mother's side. Also summoned were various doctors, notables and the Archbishop of Canterbury, a sure sign that the queen's life was entering its final hours.

At just after 1.00 pm, in the tranquil solitude of Dutch House, the queen rested in an armchair. Although barely conscious, when the Prince Regent approached, she held out her hand to him and he took it in a gentle grip as her other children gathered around. There, in the home that had been her

---

49. *Hampshire Telegraph and Sussex Chronicle etc* (Portsmouth, England), Monday, 16 November, 1818; Issue 997, p.3.

sanctuary through the decades, with her hand protectively held by her eldest son and a peaceful smile on her lips, Queen Charlotte died.

Only now did the much-mourned queen make the longed-for trip to Windsor, where she was laid to rest. King George III never understood that his wife was dead, and little more than a year later he was interred beside her, the devoted couple united once more.

Queen Charlotte was unique among the Georgian queens. Her marriage was happy, devoted and faithful until the king's illness claimed his wits and her family life was, until the Prince of Wales discovered the joys of gambling and girls, a relatively settled one. We might look rather critically on the actions that kept her daughters cosseted in the Windsor nunnery and might question the judgement that kept them as girls, but this was a woman who had been plunged into one of the most closed, domestic courts in the Georgian era. With little interest in politics, family was all she knew and when her husband fell victim to madness, Charlotte turned to that which was most familiar, gathering her daughters to her.

When Charlotte had first come to England, leaving her sheltered life behind her, she could not have imagined what awaited her in the decades to follow, nor how she would be forced to navigate the choppy waters of regency, family feud and illness. She handled it all with a grace and dignity that would have made her adoring mother and loving husband proud. From that shy and nervous girl, she became a most admirable queen indeed.

Act IV

Caroline of Brunswick, Queen of the United Kingdom

(Brunswick, Holy Roman Empire, 17 May 1768 – London, England, 7 August 1821)

A nd so we come to the last but by no means least of our illustrious Georgian women. The original Queen of Hearts, the Princess of Wales who won and lost the love of the people and the woman who wasn't just estranged from her husband, she *hated* him.

Step forward, Caroline of Brunswick, the queen without a crown, the woman who found herself the target of gossip, rumour and scandal. Accused of adultery, of birthing a bastard, and of shared baths with her household help, she became the pretender to her husband's throne.

For the queen who ended up on trial for her crown, life was never dull and she lived every moment as though it was her last.

A Shuttlecock at Court

Caroline Amelia Elizabeth of Brunswick-Wolfenbüttel was a woman of illustrious stock. She was the second daughter of Charles William Ferdinand, later Duke of Brunswick-Wolfenbüttel and Princess Augusta of Great Britain, the sister of King George III. Her childhood was far from settled, with an unhappy mother and a rather *laddish* father to contend with.

Born in 1768, Caroline was entrusted to the care of an English wet nurse named Mrs Ward. Augusta took a great interest in the education of her new daughter and did her best to make sure that Caroline's inquisitive, bright nature was kept stimulated and entertained. She knew that the day would come when Caroline would be looked upon as a possible candidate for marriage, and she was determined to ensure that her daughter would have every opportunity of making a good match.

The feisty Caroline, however, didn't find her interests particularly excited by the gentle pursuits of needlework and any of the other suitably feminine pastimes that had so enthralled Queen Charlotte. She adored handicrafts and had a passion for music, devoting hours to mastering the harpsichord.

The Brunswick court was, to put it mildly, *ribald*. Robert Huish, never one to spare the more melodramatic details, sums it up in typically colourful style.

'[…] where the warrior rests, there rests also "Heaven's masterpiece"; he forgets the toils of war in the glance of the lustful eye, and the remembrance of its dangers vanish when the midnight kiss is stolen. It must, however, be properly considered that the licentiousness which distinguished the court of Brunswick was not confined to it alone. A general laxity of morals pervaded the whole country, and if the fountain head was impure, it was not to be expected that the minor channels were to be uncontaminated.'[1]

One person who didn't enjoy the licentious court of Brunswick was Caroline's mother, Augusta. In the early years of her marriage she had been happy, as taken with her husband's good looks as he had been with her enormous dowry; yet as the years had passed, her enthusiasm had waned as his flirtations grew. She found the Brunswick court baffling and at times ridiculous, utterly refusing to amend her own Hanoverian and British methods of doing things. Instead Augusta remained a detached observer throughout the years, frequently complaining of her husband's behaviour and his penny-pinching ways, though strangely, he was nowhere near as frugal when it came to splashing about Augusta's dowry on his *own* interests.

Perhaps inevitably, Augusta eventually lost her appetite for court life altogether and turned to religious seclusion, effectively separating from her husband for a period. In fact as Caroline grew into her teens she too was

---

1. Huish, Robert (1821). *Memoirs of Her Late Majesty Caroline, Queen of Great Britain.* London: T Kelly, p.7.

similarly secluded. She was kept isolated with her governess and away from society as much as possible. Forbidden to appear at the window or to dance at the rare court functions that she was allowed to attend, Caroline's circle was small and was made up of ladies several years her senior. She entertained herself by tying her tutors up in knots and embroiling them in discussions about fate, free will and metaphysics!

Unlike his pious wife, the duke preferred the company of his mistress, Luise von Hertefeld, to the solitude of prayer. Luise was a regular fixture at court and one of the main reasons for Augusta's dissatisfaction with her lot. Though her husband had always been a flirt, the presence of his official mistress proved rather stinging and as Caroline grew up her parents became ever more distant. As is so often the case the children of the unhappy couple felt the split, unofficial though it was, more keenly than anyone. Years later Caroline's lady-in-waiting, Lady Charlotte Campbell Bury, recounted her mistress's unhappy recollections.

The faux-German accent is, I hasten to mention, Lady Charlotte's own affectation!

'My fader was most entirely attached to a lady for thirty years, who in fact was his mistress; she was the beautifullest creature, and the cleverest; but though my father continued to pay my moder all possible respect, my poor moder could not suffer this attachment, and de consequence was, I did not know what to do between them; when I was civil to the one, I was scolded by the other, and was very tired of being shuttlecock between them.'[2]

Years later Caroline's own daughter would suffer a similar fate of her own.

The Mad Princess?

Perhaps it was the unhappy atmosphere at home that led the adolescent Caroline to fall ill with a condition that worryingly resembled that of her

---

2. Bury, Lady Charlotte Campbell (1838). *Diary Illustrative of the Times of George the Fourth: Vol I*. London: Carey, Lea and Blanchard, p.19.

uncle, George III. Initially complaining of physical pains, these gave way to hysteria until she couldn't appear at court for more than the shortest possible periods.

Although both the duke and duchess were concerned for their daughter, the illness also had the unfortunate side effect of putting Caroline out of action when Prince Frederick, Duke of York and Albany, and son of George III and Charlotte of Mecklenburg-Strelitz, paid a visit to Brunswick. Augusta was keen to marry her daughter off to one of George's sons so she must have been sorely disappointed that Caroline was indisposed. Had she been well enough to attend court and be presented to her cousin the future might have changed forever but instead she missed York's visit, leaving her still single when the Prince of Wales needed (though far from *wanted*) a bride.

Was there, however, more to Caroline's teenage malady than mere adolescent angst?

'[…] a landsman or magistrate, formerly an officer in the Duke of Brunswick's Guards [maintained] that it was the general opinion that in early youth the Princess had shown strong symptoms of insanity.'[3]

Common thinking now is that George III's madness was the result of porphyria and that illness is, of course, hereditary. Although there is no concrete evidence of the kind of repeat episodes experienced by the monarch, those who witnessed Caroline's teenage illness had their own thoughts on the matter. In her darkest moments, even the duchess told her friends that Caroline was not right in the head!

At 16, when she was forbidden to attend a ball, Caroline took to her room. She was soon screaming in agony, and her face, apparently, took on a very odd, dark pallor. When her terrified parents asked her what the matter was, Caroline exclaimed that she was in labour and must receive medical attention as a matter of urgency. She howled and shrieked, writhed and convulsed, with all those in earshot having heard the shocking announcement of her

---

3. Haywaed, A (ed.) (1864). *Diaries of a Lady of Quality from 1797 to 1844*. London: Longman, Green, Longman, Egberts & Green, p.186.

unexpected pregnancy. Of course, as soon as the midwife arrived Caroline mysteriously recovered from her pain, wiped away the make-up that she had used to colour her face and burst into hysterical laughter. Let that be a lesson well-learned, she told her horrified and no doubt rather disgusted parents. Whether they ever dared to ban the precocious princess from another ball again, we are not told!

Does this really suggest madness or was it simply an act of teenage rebellion?

Far from an example of insanity, the entire charade is nothing more than a rather extreme prank intended to cause as much embarrassment and upset to her parents as possible. Caroline was smart, wilful and, crucially, *bored*, often a heady and dangerous mix. Perhaps she had something of her father's wanderlust, his need for flirtation and entertainment, for she certainly had *very* little of her mother's thin-lipped piety. Not for *this* princess religious seclusion and study.

Where Caroline showed her softer side, however, was in her compassion for poor or orphaned children. From early childhood she had played with local youngsters when out on her rides and as she grew older, these visits grew more frequent and charitable. Of course, there was plenty of gossip about what the princess was *really* getting up to when she popped into local cottages, but that does a disservice to her. Caroline couldn't pass by a child without speaking kindly and she became the patron of many youngsters in her homeland, taking delight in showing them compassion. Years later, that kindness would lead to an embarrassing and very public scandal.

A Lonely Princess

As Caroline grew, word began to circulate of the pretty princess kept secluded from society far away in Brunswick. One of her admirers, Sir John Stanley, remembers her as a 'lively, pretty child with light-coloured hair hanging in curls on her neck, with rosebud lips' and lamented that she was sadly out of his reach. Of course, this piqued the interest of a few would-be suitors and in 1783, the Margrave of Baden came knocking at the door of Brunswick.

Though Augusta would have preferred a marriage among her brother's sons, she knew that the second son of Baden would be a reasonable catch and did all she could to aid negotiations along. She decided that the margrave had settled on Caroline *because* of her secluded upbringing, telling George III, 'not being a coquette […] has, I think, decided the Margrave of Baden to take my daughter. […] If this does not come off, I know of no more husbands for her'.[4]

It did not come off.

Nor did the princes of Orange or Hesse-Darmstadt, not to mention the Duke of Mecklenburg-Strelitz and one can imagine the increasing frustrations of Augusta as they rattled through the swiftly diminishing list of candidates.

It would seem that something in Caroline's character was putting potential suitors off.

What though of a forbidden love, a tantalizing glimpse of lost romance lurking in the story of the young, isolated lady?

Locked away, kept in the company of her accomplished and hardworking governess, Countess Eleonore von Münster, and instructed to remain seated and silent during her appearances at court, one so hungry for life as Caroline of Brunswick was bound to rebel. She had a romantic and some might say rather flighty manner, and in adulthood, nostalgically remembered the love she had lost in her teens. Forbidden to marry by her mother, the romance foundered yet who was this mysterious suitor, and what became of him?

The sad truth is that we simply don't know anything beyond the barest details and for these we're indebted to one of Caroline's more sympathetic nineteenth century biographers.

When Caroline was in her mid-teens and her mother was busy writing letters to George III intended to drop *enormous* hints about the marital promise of her daughter, the young princess happened to catch sight of a visitor to the court who she later remembered as 'the handsome Irishman'. He was an Irish soldier who fought for Brunswick with distinction and, tall, handsome and immaculate in his Hussar uniform, he cut a rather dashing figure. Indeed, he would hardly have been out of place in romantic fiction, all snowy plumes, dashing jet black chargers and lusty cries of 'Victory'!

---

4. Fraser, Flora (2012). *The Unruly Queen: The Life of Queen Caroline*. Edinburgh: A&C Black, p.20.

In the showy Brunswick court, handsome, young Hussars found themselves with plenty of admirers, and among them was Caroline. The ladies trailed after the unnamed soldier offering their breathless compliments on his valiant courage and he responded with perfectly judged self-deprecation, sure it was really *nothing*. Caroline, however, somehow managed to evade her keepers for just long enough to add her own voice to his fan club and to her, some said, he gave far more than kind words.

Of course there was no hope for Caroline and her soldier, no matter how gallant and brave. Socially they were from different worlds, and when the princess and her admirer grew too close, too *keen*, Caroline was taken on a trip into the countryside and away from temptation.

Caroline was always a slightly unreliable narrator and, one suspects, was given to over-romanticizing, never more so than reminiscing over matters of the heart. Perhaps this is why rumours later whispered through the courts that she had fallen pregnant at just 15, and *that* was why she whizzed off to the countryside: to give birth. Even better, the rumour-mongers whispered, what if those young peasant children were not merely subject to her charity, what if one of them was the fruit of her labour?

There's no evidence whatsoever to support this gossip yet Caroline seemed to attract rumour throughout her life. After all, let's not forget that it was only one year after this supposed pregnancy that some were declaring the princess mad.

Mad and, it must be said, worryingly single.

The (Not Quite) Princess of Wales

Caroline of Brunswick would not be single forever, of course, and the ambitious Augusta was about to hit the jackpot. Not only would she secure her daughter *a* husband from the House of Hanover, but *the* husband from the House of Hanover.

The heir to the throne.

Just one problem… the heir in question was already married.

Mrs Maria Fitzherbert was neither a legitimate royal bride nor a queen of Georgian Britain and so, sadly, she is relegated to a supporting character here in Caroline's story. In order to understand the circumstances into which Caroline was destined to marry, it is necessary to take a trip back to Park Street, Mayfair, in December 1785, and meet the prince and the widow, otherwise known as the happy bride and groom.

'When Mrs. Fitzherbert was young, people talked of her as a White Rose. And even when she was old my mother said that her cheeks felt as smooth as petals when you kissed her.

[…]

Her hair was of a pale gold, her eyes hazel-brown, her complexion of the wild rose and hawthorne.'[5]

Quite something.

Born a Shropshire Catholic, Maria Ann Smythe's romantic history was littered with heartbreak. Her first marriage ended just three months after her wedding when an equestrian accident left her a widow with only an unsigned will to remember her late husband by. Maria then had nothing but was soon fortunate enough to catch another wealthy husband, Thomas Fitzherbert.

In fact Thomas fared little better, managing less than three years before he too was in the grave. This time he had at least signed the will, and Maria was set up for life. Still young, beautiful and now the proud owner of a home in Mayfair and a valuable nestegg, Maria was about to make quite a splash. With the patronage of her half-uncle, Lord Sefton, she was soon a familiar sight in the most fashionable London venues, including the theater and the salons, and was often seen riding out in her carriage on a fine afternoon. It was Lord Sefton who introduced her to the pretty, profligate Prince of Wales in 1784, and from that first moment, he was smitten.

George pursued Maria endlessly and she avoided him just as surely until the wily prince put into action a scheme as cunning as it was cruel.

George sent word to Maria that he had attempted suicide by stabbing himself and had only hours left to live. His last wish on this earth was that she would come to his bedside. The horrified lady agreed on condition that

---

5. Leslie, Anita (1960). *Mrs Fitzherbert: a Biography*. York: Scribner, p.16.

she would be chaperoned by their mutual friend, Georgiana, Duchess of Devonshire. Maria and Georgiana dashed to the side of the stricken prince who lay in bed at Carlton House, pale and bandaged.

On Maria's arrival George fixed her with a tired, and one can imagine *poetic* gaze and asked if she would consent to take a ring from him, as one last gesture of friendship. Maria, fatefully and foolishly, agreed to take a loaned ring from Georgiana, who we must imagine was a little sceptical about all this. She was right to be, for no sooner was the ring on Maria's finger than the prince was suddenly feeling *much* better. The ring, he declared, constituted a betrothal and Maria was now *his*.

Maria's response was to flee, return Georgiana's ring and sign a statement declaring that she was not betrothed to *anyone*. Georgiana drafted the document and no doubt felt a sense of relief as she waved Maria off from English shores, the Catholic widow determined to avoid the prince until his ardour cooled. For the Prince of Wales, however, this just made the game more delicious and as he ranted and raved, tore at his hair and threatened suicide, his agents made petitions to Maria on his behalf, passing on lovelorn notes and heartfelt letters.

She caved in, of course, and on that December day in 1785, George and Maria were married. The union was secret and illegal under the strict terms of the Royal Marriages Act, forbidding as it did the heir to the throne from marrying into or converting to Catholicism, on the penalty of losing the crown. The marriage would be tumultuous throughout the years and marked by periods of contentment and estrangement. Such a union did nothing to help the Prince of Wales refill the coffers he had emptied with his love for gambling, partying, girls and a hugely expensive lifestyle. He wanted the best of everything, from houses to horses and for that, he needed money. His parents and Parliament were unequivocal; if he wanted cash, he had to compromise.

He had to marry.

Marrying for Money

Just when the duke and duchess, not to mention the bored Caroline, must have utterly given up on all hopes of a wedding, marriage is precisely what happened.

In 1793, the Prince of Wales was buried under his debts, arguing with Maria and desperate for cash. He approached his father and Parliament for funds and they responded with a chorus of refusal unless he would agree to a rather stern condition. Should he consent to marry a respectable German princess and get on with producing an heir, his debts would be settled.

By now George was sharing his bed with the infamous and scheming Frances Villiers, Countess of Jersey, and she convinced him that marriage might actually be a rather wise move. Lady Jersey was a smart woman, more than a match for her lover. She knew that Maria, who George had married for love, was a threat to her place as mistress whereas an *official* wife, one married only for money, would pose no challenge to her position. George merely shrugged and decided that he may as well go along with it, deciding that 'one damned german frau is as good as another'.

By this point Caroline was a girl no longer but a woman in her mid-twenties. 'She had "a look of great good nature and affability; expressive eyes, flaxen hair, teeth as white as ivory, a good complexion, beautiful hand and arm, and may certainly be deemed a very pretty woman". So far, so good, but might we raise an eyebrow to learn that "she bears something of HIS MAJESTY'S resemblance, particularly in her upper lip, which rather projects."'[6]

Quite a heady mix, and one further enhanced by the *St James's Chronicle*'s confirmation of that resemblance, not to mention what must have been striking eyelashes!

'The Princess of Wales bears an agreeable feminine resemblance of his Majesty. […] Her Eye-lashes are white.'[7]

---

6. *Oracle and Public Advertiser* (London, England), Tuesday, 7 April, 1795; Issue 18 973, p.3.
7. *St. James's Chronicle or the British Evening Post* (London, England), 7 April, 1795–9 April, 1795; Issue 5818, p.5.

So it was that James Harris, Lord Malmesbury, was sent to Brunswick in 1794, with the task of bringing Caroline safely back to England. One has to feel for her, for she must surely have given up all hope of ever escaping the stifling world into which she had been born. Suddenly not only was she escaping, she was going to marry the heir to the British throne. She was, Malmesbury recorded, 'vastly happy with her future expectations'[8]. As far as Caroline knew from his portraits, the Prince of Wales was still as pretty as he had ever been, with no hint of his already growing waistline and she couldn't *wait* to be shot of Brunswick.

Malmesbury was not a romantic but a man of business. He noted Augusta's rather self-satisfied observation that 'all the young German princesses had learnt English, in hopes of being Princess of Wales'.[9] It is left to the waspish editor of *Littell's Living Age* to note that, 'all, of course, *but one*, had a lucky escape'.[10]

During what must have been a very businesslike meeting with Caroline and her parents, Malmesbury gave them a full appraisal of the Prince of Wales's character, sparing nothing. Of course, Augusta was far too taken with the victory of the marriage to worry about what might lie ahead, but Caroline's father was a little more circumspect and asked Malmesbury to be a friend to his daughter once she arrived in England; he had heard all about the Prince of Wales, it seems!

He wasn't the only one.

Some anonymous well-wisher had already warned the bride about Lady Jersey and when a concerned Caroline asked after her, Malmesbury smoothly responded that *she* would be the Princess of Wales and her ladies would conduct themselves accordingly. He warned her not to show any jealousy to the prince, nor to allow herself to be drawn into intrigues designed to drive a wedge between her and her husband. She appeared to take this on board but with each meeting, Malmesbury's worries about the impending nuptials grew.

---

8. Littell, E (1845). *Littell's Living Age, Volume IV*. Boston: TH Carter and Company, p.631.
9. Ibid.
10. Ibid.

Far from the poised, thoughtful Queen Charlotte, Caroline appeared to Lord Malmesbury to be vulgar and thoughtless. George was a dandy; immaculate, a leader of fashion, a lover of cultured, older women, and now here was his bride to be. She was dishevelled, childish, and represented everything he loathed in a woman. Not only that, both were flighty, and Malmesbury had a feeling that this wasn't going to end well.

'We [Malmesbury and Sir Boothby] regret the apparent facility of the Princess Caroline's character – her want of reflection and *substance* agree that with a *steady* man she would do vastly well, but with one of a different description, there are great risks.'[11]

Malmesbury thought her much-vaunted charity was more like someone mindlessly throwing money this way and that regardless of merit, whilst the rather delicate matter of her hygiene gave him more than a little cause for concern. This was one thing on which George placed great importance and Malmesbury did all he could to press the point home. Caroline was so neglectful of her personal hygiene, the Whig sniffily wrote, as to be offensive. Her language and speech was equally off-putting and time and again, he raised the matter with Caroline and her attendants, utterly baffled as to how she could have reached her mid-twenties without this ever becoming an issue.

Let us spare a thought for Caroline though.

Vulgar, dirty and childish?

Perhaps.

Malmesbury wasn't a cruel man but he *was* worldly. She, however, was anything *but* worldly and had been kept closely watched in a court famed for its licentiousness. Perhaps if Caroline had her mother's pious, watchful demeanour this would have suited her but she didn't. If anything, her character matched that of her pleasure-loving, *live for the moment* father. Her academic education hadn't been extensive and any reaction to perceived bad behaviour had simply been to further restrict her horizons until Caroline

---

11. Harris, James (1844). *Diaries and Correspondence of James Harris, First Earl of Malmesbury: Vol III*. London: Richard Bentley, p.182.

seemed destined to remain not only unmarried but forgotten in the court she longed to escape. To us, the thought of an unwed woman is hardly and rightly the end of the world but for Caroline no husband meant no freedom, no escape, no *life*.

Is there any wonder she was excited?

Caroline had every hope for this new life and every intention of being a good wife. She couldn't know what she was going into, or that Lady Jersey, far from being someone who would know her place and do her duty, was determined to make as much mischief as possible. Instead Caroline was set on making the most of this exciting new opportunity and flourishing in the land she longed to see.

'The Princess of Wales has ever been known to entertain a strong partiality for England, and frequently to express that she considered herself more of an English woman than a German, her mother being of this country. When she landed at Greenwich, she pleasantly observed, "I am now perfectly happy, for I have reached my country at last."'[12]

Finally, much to Malmesbury's relief, he set off for England with Caroline in tow. On parting from her homeland, Caroline was overcome with emotion, whilst the duke once again implored Malmesbury to look after her and ensure that she wasn't thrown to the gossip-hungry wolves of the British court. Over the course of their journey, the Whig's doubts about the suitability of the marriage only grew, yet there was nothing he could do to prevent it. Still, as the days wore on he began to admire a few of Caroline's qualities, especially her cheery nature and bravery. What he didn't admire, however, was the way she was often short-tempered with her mother and when the princess sent Malmesbury a tooth that had been extracted he was disgusted, calling the act, 'nasty and indelicate'.[13]

---

12. *London Packet or New Lloyd's Evening Post* (London, England), 6 April, 1795–8 April, 1795; Issue 4001, p.1.
13. Harris, James (1844). *Diaries and Correspondence of James Harris, First Earl of Malmesbury: Vol III*. London: Richard Bentley, p.201.

In England, meanwhile, everything was in place for a wedding and when George III made the following announcement in Parliament, there was no going back.

'I have the greatest satisfaction in announcing to you the happy event of the conclusion of a treaty for the marriage of my son the Prince of Wales with the Princess Caroline, daughter of the Duke of Brunswick.'[14]

Meeting the Husband

It took a long time for the party to finally reach England and after delays caused by troop movements on the continent, the journey fell badly behind schedule. With each passing day they were forced to delay in Hanover, Caroline's enthusiasm waned and Malmesbury soon grew fatigued with this singular princess.

'The COUNTESS of JERSEY and some other Ladies of distinction, set off last night, in order to meet her Royal Highness [...] The PRINCESS is hourly expected in this Metropolis.'[15]

They couldn't tarry forever though and on 4 April 1795, the mismatched travellers anchored off Gravesend. They slept on board that night before proceeding to Greenwich the following day, where Caroline finally set foot on English soil. Here she was *supposed* to be met by a party that would include the scheming Lady Jersey, who had, rather awfully for the newly-arrived princess, been appointed as her Lady of the Bedchamber. The high-handed Lady Jersey arrived an hour late to that most important meeting and one can only feel for Caroline at being finally faced with the woman that she already *knew* to be trouble. In her new role, the scheming lady would be able to intrigue as much as she wished, safe in the knowledge that the Prince of Wales was wrapped around her little finger.

---

14. Fox, Charles James (1845). *Speeches of the Right Honourable Charles James Fox, Vol V*. London: Longman, p.325.
15. *St. James's Chronicle or the British Evening Post* (London, England), 31 March, 1795–2 April, 1795; Issue 5815, p.4.

Led by Lady Jersey, the women who received Caroline declared themselves dismayed at her dress and pulled her this way and that until she was squeezed into a fashionable outfit of white satin that had been sent by the prince. The garment was unlike anything Caroline had worn before and was as ill-fitting as it was ill-suited, so no doubt Lady Jersey *loved* to see her hopelessly outmatched rival looking so uncomfortable. The cunning countess, however, was about to find that she was no match for the worldly-wise Malmesbury and when she refused to take her place in the lead carriage opposite Caroline, he finally reached the end of his tether.

As they prepared to depart, Lady Jersey made a great production of being forced to sit backwards in the carriage, declaring that she would certainly be sick. It was left to the unflappable Malmesbury to observe dryly that perhaps she shouldn't be a Lady of the Bedchamber if she was so very particular. Rather guessing that she wouldn't want to be removed from the heart of the action, when he offered to let Lady Jersey ride in *his* carriage and sit anywhere she might wish, her nausea was soon mended.

> 'A little after two o'clock, her Serene Highness left the Governor's house and got into one of the KING's coaches, drawn by six horses. In this coach were also MRS. HARCOURT and Lady JERSEY. Another of his MAJESTY's coaches and six preceded it, in which were seated MRS. HARVEY ASTON, LORD MALMESBURY, LORD CLERMONT, and COLONEL GREVILLE. In a third coach with four horses, were two women servants, whom the Princess brought from Germany, and are her only German attendants from thence.'[16]

In the midst of so many illustrious ladies and gentlemen, Caroline couldn't have been more alone. She had just two attendants from Brunswick to accompany her to England but unlike her predecessor, there was no warm family welcome waiting for her, which was typical of George's III's low-key court.

The party passed along a well-lined procession route towards the city and Caroline peered from the window as the vehicles carried her into her new life.

---

16. *Star* (London, England), Monday, 6 April, 1795; Issue 2068, p.4.

The people of Britain were tired of the unpopular Prince of Wales and his profligate ways. Rumours of his romance with Maria were commonplace and nothing seemed likely to raise his popularity, so a new princess was a much needed dose of good press, not to mention the cash he had been promised if he went through with the wedding. Perhaps George thought Caroline was as cynical about the marriage as he was and that she knew *exactly* what she was getting into, but she really didn't. Despite Malmesbury's attempts to warn the young woman of the prince's ways and temperament, Caroline's spirits were high; she really thought this might be her moment.

> 'Westminster Bridge, and all the avenues leading to the Park and Palace were crowded with spectators and carriages; but the greatest order was preserved. The people cheared [sic] the lovely stranger with loud expressions of love and loyalty; and she in return, very graciously, and with the utmost good nature, bowed and smiled at them as she passed along. Both the carriage windows were down. At three o'clock her Serene Highness alighted at St James's, and was introduced into the apartments prepared for her reception, which look into Cleveland Row.'[17]

No doubt Caroline's heart was racing when they arrived at the appointed meeting place and she was ushered inside to meet her betrothed. The crowd roared for the princess to appear and Caroline briefly came to the window of the palace. She soaked up the atmosphere and, as she did *all* her life, gave the audience exactly what they had come to see. It was a heady first encounter with the British people.

> 'After a short time, the PRINCESS appeared at the windows, which were thrown up, that the people might have a sight of her charming person. The people huzzaed her, and she curtsied; and this continued some minutes, until the PRINCE arrived from Carlton House.'[18]

---

17. Ibid.
18. *Sun* (London, England), Monday, 6 April, 1795; Issue 787, p.1.

With the arrival of the apparently somewhat agitated (at least if the *Oracle and Public Advertiser* of 7 April 1795 is to be believed) Prince of Wales, the show was over.

And the trouble began.

Swallowing what must have been quite a surprise at the corpulent, grandly overdone figure dressed in a full Hussar uniform before her, Caroline knelt at the feet of the Prince of Wales. He raised her gently to stand, offered a slight and, one suspects, somewhat reticent embrace and scurried into a corner to call for brandy. He then hurried away to seek out the queen and, I imagine, make his complaints loudly known.

Caroline was mortified and no amount of excuses for the prince's indisposition would calm her. Never one to hold her tongue, she asked where the handsome man of the portraits was, wondering who this fat fellow could be that had taken his place. Later in the evening the couple met again over dinner with that same party who had travelled from Greenwich as outside, the crowd called for Caroline. It was a lesson the unpopular George would learn all too well over the years to come. Caroline had that certain something that appealed to the public, that indefinable x-factor that he could never quite capture. She would, in time, turn it to her own devastating advantage.

> 'The people continuing to huzza before the Palace, His Royal Highness, after dinner, appeared at the window, and thanked them for this mark of their loyalty and attention to the PRINCESS; but he hoped they would excuse her appearance then, as it might give her cold. This completely satisfied the crowd, who gave the PRINCE three cheers. [...]'[19]

What, one wonders, did the prince make of this turn of events? If he thought some of his bride's popularity might rub off on him permanently, he was to be sorely mistaken. Caroline, after all, already knew her fiancé wasn't impressed by her and the feeling was more than mutual. Yet marriages have survived and even flourished from such inauspicious starts and besides, George had those debts to think about.

---

19. *Star* (London, England), Monday, 6 April, 1795; Issue 2068, p.4.

By now it was too late to turn back for on 8 April 1795, Caroline of Brunswick and the Prince of Wales would be joined in holy, hellish matrimony.

A Wedding to Remember

'Yesterday being appointed for the solemn celebration of the nuptials of his Royal Highness the Prince of Wales and the Princess Caroline of Brunswick [...] all the avenues to the palace were crowded with spectators and [...] the Prince, on leaving the Queen's House, had a hearty shake of the hand from the King.'[20]

We shall come back to this shortly and examine whether the prince was *able* to share a hearty handshake at *all*.

Caroline was now, for better or worse, embarked on a new life for which she can hardly have felt prepared. Luckily she always looked on the bright side, and one imagines that she was determined to do just that when it came to marriage too. Although the Prince of Wales might not have been her handsome Irishman, he *was* her betrothed and after waiting for more than two decades to escape Brunswick and grab at a chance of happiness, she wasn't about to let it slip through her fingers.

On the evening of 8 April 1795 the appointed moment arrived and with Lady Jersey in constant attendance, Caroline prepared to become the Princess of Wales. She swept into the Chapel Royal of St James's Palace in a gown that was possibly more elaborate than any she had worn before. Draped in silver tissue, taffeta and lace with a crimson velvet mantle that sported an ermine trim, the whole look was set off by jewels including a diamond coronet set upon her head.

Gone were the coarse petticoats, shifts and stockings that Malmesbury complained were never 'well washed, or changed often enough'.[21] Gone, on the outside a least, was the vulgar, young woman from Brunswick and in her

---

20. *London Packet or New Lloyd's Evening Post* (London, England), 8 April, 1795–10 April, 1795; Issue 4002, p.1.

21. Harris, James (1844). *Diaries and Correspondence of James Harris, First Earl of Malmesbury: Vol III*. London: Richard Bentley, p.211.

place stood a lady fit to be called Princess of Wales. Those present on the day commented on how bright and optimistic Caroline appeared to be as she stood before the Archbishop of Canterbury and awaited her moment.

Her groom was a little less radiant than his bride and had good reason to be glad for the presence of his groomsmen, the Dukes of Bedford and Roxburghe. Bedford's brother recorded the rather embarrassing scene of the prince's inebriation; perhaps he had downed a few glasses between that handshake with his father and his arrival at the chapel!

'The Prince was so drunk that he could scarcely support him from falling. He told my brother that he had drunk several glasses of brandy to enable him to go through the ceremony. There is no doubt that it was a compulsory marriage.'[22]

Staggering and clearly the worse for wear, George didn't speak to Caroline and appeared to be on the verge of tears throughout. When the archbishop asked those present if anyone knew of any just cause that might prevent the marriage from taking place, he looked pointedly at the king and then the prince. Of course, the gossip of his relationship with Mrs Fitzherbert would be all too well known to the cleric yet nobody spoke. Suddenly the prince began to sob and with his gaze fixed on Lady Jersey, the ceremony rolled on to its inevitable conclusion.

What must Caroline have thought and, more importantly, did she know of the rumours of an illegal marriage? It's unlikely given that her concerns when she spoke to Malmesbury were all of Lady Jersey's place in George's life, but surely she can't have believed all was well? Given her own happy demeanour, the excited chatter she shared with the Duke of Clarence as she made her way to the chapel and what appears to be a self-possessed performance at the ceremony, perhaps she suspected her new husband was merely overcome by the occasion. She knew there were other women and that this wasn't a love match, so it's not unthinkable that she assumed his reaction was that of a confirmed bachelor and good time guy waving farewell

22. Greenwood, William de Redman (1910). *Love and Intrigues of Royal Courts*. London: T Werner Laurie, p.334.

to his single days. Whatever she thought, by the close of the ceremony she was a wife, the Princess of Wales.

At the reception in the Queen's House, George barely spoke to Caroline and for this, we can hardly forgive him. His argument wasn't with her after all, for she was as much an innocent victim as he was. She hadn't petitioned for an arranged marriage or cajoled to get her hands on the prize and to make her the villain of the peace shows his capricious nature in all its unpleasant glory. Indeed, as Caroline later sighed, 'the moment one is obliged to marry any person, it is enough to render them hateful'.[23] She never clarified if the feeling was mutual.

When the reception ended the newlyweds travelled to Carlton House and were left alone to start work on that heir and spare. What happened that night must remain between the far from happy couple, but Caroline summed it up succinctly when she sniffed, 'Judge what it was to have a drunken husband on one's wedding-day, and one who passed the greater part of his bridal-night under the grate, where he fell, and where I left him!'.[24]

Into the Bridal Bed

The couple lived together for a few scant weeks yet, at some point during that period of domestic disharmony, they managed to conceive their only child. Don't be fooled into thinking that this was a happy event or a turning point in the unhappy marriage, for it was nothing of the sort.

Just as Caroline had been dogged by tales of a secret pregnancy in her teens, she was to be the subject of rumours regarding her sexual escapades once more. This time, the man spreading them was her husband. Sex was just one of his many complaints and as George cast about for someone to hit out at, his first target was Malmesbury.

Why, he asked Malmesbury, did he do nothing to prevent the wedding once he had met Caroline? Could he not see how rotten she was, how ugly, how unhygienic, how utterly unsuitable she was for a gentleman of *his* standing?

---

23. Bury, Lady Charlotte Campbell (1838). *Diary Illustrative of the Times of George the Fourth: Vol I*. London: Carey, Lea and Blanchard, p.17.
24. Ibid., p.25.

Malmesbury replied with studied care, explaining that his mission had not been to vet the princess's suitability as a bride, but merely to issue to an invitation of marriage. This he had done and, furthermore, he had gone out of his way to school Caroline and advise her of what to expect before she arrived in England.

With this avenue closed to him, George fixed his spite on Caroline's virginity, or supposed lack of it. She couldn't be a virgin, he claimed, for she had complimented him on the size of his manhood, exclaiming, '*Ah mon dieu, qu'il est gros!*'.[25] How could she possibly know such a thing if she hadn't seen others to compare it against? It never entered his head that it might have been an effort to curry favour with a husband who clearly disliked her. After all, this was an intimate encounter so it's perfectly natural to imagine the anxious princess summoning all her bravado whilst at the same time, massaging her husband's massive ego.

George, however, was never so charitable.

When their first sexual encounter left no blood on the bedsheets, he accused Caroline of conspiring to mix up a potion that she could pour onto her linens, thus misleading him into believing that she was indeed a virgin.

'I have every reason to believe [that I was not the first], for not only on the first night was there no appearance of blood [...] Finding that I had suspicions of her not being *new*, she the next night mixed up some tooth powder and water, coloured her shift with it...'[26]

He claimed that they had intercourse three times in total, twice during that drunken bridal night and once the following evening. However, Caroline had 'such marks of filth both in the fore and *hind* part of her... that she turned my stomach and [...] it required no small [effort] to conquer my aversion and overcome the disgust of her person.'[27]

This, it must be said, is the part of the story that might actually be true. We know from Malmesbury's constant nudging of the princess and her

25. Robins, Jane (2006). *The Trial of Queen Caroline: The Scandalous Affair that Nearly Ended a Monarchy*. New York: Simon and Schuster, pp.17–8.
26. Ibid.
27. Ibid.

attendants that she wasn't a fan of taking a long toilette and, indeed, prided herself on how quickly she could wash and be ready. By contrast, George was fastidious in his personal preparations and always powdered and preened to perfection so if anything was going to upset him, it would be this.

Even worse for the prince, his hated wife got on splendidly with George III and had done a fabulous job of endearing herself to the royal family and people of Britain. In response, he merely treated her more shabbily than ever, bestowing expensive gifts, (including the pearls he had given Caroline as a wedding present) on Lady Jersey and leaving his wife in no doubt as to her place at the bottom of the romantic pecking order. Still, when Caroline fell pregnant as a result of one of those three encounters, her place in the hearts of those who loved her was secured.

The Heir to the Throne

'Yesterday morning, a few minutes after 9 o'clock, her Royal Highness the princess of WALES was safely delivered of a PRINCESS at Carlton House [...] The Princess was delivered near a month before her expected time. She has only been married nine months this day [...] The PRINCE of WALES is much recovered; but we believe all parties are a little disappointed that the child is not a Boy.'[28]

Caroline later commented that she was surprised to discover that she was pregnant, this wide-eyed suggestion of innocence casting some serious shade on the prince's reputation as a lady's man. She was undoubtedly with child and on 7 January 1796, Princess Charlotte of Wales was born. When the birth was reported, the press couldn't resist mentioning the fact that just nine months had elapsed since the wedding night.

Caroline's labour was long and hard and when she delivered the apparently immense baby, the country rang with celebration. No doubt George had cause to rejoice too, because it meant his duty was done. Never again would he have to take his hated wife to bed and never again would she have to submit to the man who made no secret of his loathing for her. Just days after

---

28. *Evening Mail* (London, England), 6 January, 1796–8 January, 1796, p.4.

the birth of their child he wrote out his will, leaving everything to Maria Fitzherbert. To Caroline, he bequeathed a single shilling.

The king was delighted to welcome a new baby girl to the family but if Caroline thought this might be the start of a new chapter in her marriage, she was badly mistaken. With the baby cared for by a handpicked team of loyal retainers led by Lady Dashwood, George went off to Parliament intending to use the birth of his daughter to increase the size of his coffers yet again.

Denied a further payment, the prince lashed out at his wife, imposing strict rules on the time she would be allowed to spend with her daughter. Charlotte's whole life would be spent witnessing the war of attrition between her estranged parents and it began in the cradle, with her mother given a single, supervised visit to the nursery each day. Children were always weapons in the House of Hanover and little Charlotte was no different but Caroline was not about to be silenced.

She was determined not to let the little girl be taken from her life. Befriending members of the nursery staff, she made secret trips to see her daughter. Unlike his father, the Prince of Wales wasn't a particularly hands-on dad and was hardly ever in the nursery himself, hence he didn't notice that his wife was becoming a regular fixture.

In the years to come, Caroline must have looked back and blessed these clandestine days because she and Charlotte were never to be as close again.

The Lady from Blackheath

In the end, for all the claims and counter claims, for all the hygiene concerns and mutual loathing, it was Lady Jersey who struck the death blow to the marriage of the Prince and Princess of Wales.

In early summer of 1796, letters from Caroline to her home in Brunswick fell into the hands of the royal family. In them, she was less than complimentary about her mother-in-law, Queen Charlotte, but if the party who leaked the letters expected this to end Caroline's reign as the Queen of Hearts, they were wrong. Instead, the press rounded on Lady Jersey for it was she, they claimed, who had taken the private correspondence and made it public.

Under the headline *Domestic Fracas*, *The Oracle and Public Advertiser* perfectly summed up the mood of the moment. For that boisterous girl from

Brunswick, the moment had come and she was the people's favourite, her husband foundering in her wake.

'The DOMESTIC ANECDOTES of any PRIVATE FAMILY can be of little consequence to the Public; but where the future happiness and honour of a nation are concerned, it behoves all parties to be candid, and it is but right that the COUNTRY AT LARGE should know the real state of facts.

That the Gentleman, whose MATRIMONIAL REPOSE has been unquestionably Interrupted, has neglected his fair BRIDE, and estranged himself from her, is a matter well known, and we believe, not to be contradicted. IF that coolness and contempt proceeded from any trifling misunderstanding, such as will sometimes arise in even the happiest connections, let him prove to the Nation that it was a temporary resentment, that harmony AGAIN pervades the mansion of honourable attachment.

Let him REMOVE from the presence of his lovely BRIDE the OBJECT of ABHORRENCE. Let HIM be the COMPANION IN PUBLIC, and the avowed PROTECTOR of the WOMAN who is united to him by the sacred bonds of wedlock. Let him contradict the TALES now in circulation, and PROVE that they are GROUNDLESS. Let him prevail on his parent to espouse the cause of the INNOCENT and LOVELY STRANGER; and to discard from protection the WOMAN who has excited the INDIGNATION of all HONOURABLE BRITONS.

The neglected and amiable female has proved, that Englishmen have not wholly relinquished the spirit of chivalry: Her sorrows are thrown upon a nation who will examine their source and soften their severity. The love of the PEOPLE will sustain HER fortitude; and their penetration will not fail to point out her ENEMIES. In a few words – Let the illustrious HUSBAND awake from his dream by banishing the EVIL GENIUS which haunts him, once more prove that he values DOMESTIC VIRTUE and PUBLIC CHARACTER.'[29]

---

29. *Oracle and Public Advertiser* (London, England), Thursday, 2 June, 1796; Issue 19 336, p.2.

Things got so heated for Lord and Lady Jersey that they eventually confronted the matter head on with a pamphlet intended to quash suggestions that the countess was responsible for the leak. The earl himself penned the introduction in which he assured the reader that his wife was indignant and outraged at the falsehoods attached to her character and that this, he hoped, would be an end to the matter.

Instead it was the touch paper that set off the final estrangement of the Prince and Princess of Wales. Usually reduced to happy tears by the cheers of the opera audience when she attended, Caroline's seat was suddenly, inexplicably empty. Dropping a hint heavier than an anvil, the press furrowed its brow and wondered why she would not be present, commenting that it 'must be an idle rumour that we asserted we should see her *there* no more. Her reception must have given the highest pleasure to herself, and to WHOM ought it to give pain?'[30]

George wrote to his wife and father requesting a separation and in the interim did all he could to keep Caroline from enjoying her popularity or gathering more supporters to her cause. Eventually she decided to leave Carlton House to set up a new residence at Montague House in Blackheath where George could no longer control her movements. Even better, Lady Jersey was far, far away.

The Delicate Investigation

And what would a lady like Caroline of Brunswick get up to in Blackheath?

Needlepoint… bible study… botany?

Not a bit of it.

Caroline hadn't come all this way and left behind everything that she had known to sit quietly. She was going to live, and live she did. Caroline's social circle widened greatly and much to her husband's annoyance, was peopled by plenty of his Tory opponents. Soon it was whispered that any number of illustrious gentlemen were keeping her bed warm, among them, the future prime minister, George Canning, and, fatefully, the naval hero, Sir Sidney Smith.

---

30. *Oracle and Public Advertiser* (London, England), Wednesday, 8 June, 1796; Issue 19 341, p.31.

Smith was lodging with Lord and Lady Douglas, the princess's Blackheath neighbours, and for a time all was rosy. Caroline and Smith flirted heavily, the Douglases enjoyed the show and then, quite out of nowhere, everything turned very sour indeed.

Having tired of Smith's attentions, Caroline threw herself wholeheartedly into a new flirtation with another naval man, Captain Thomas Manby. In the unseemly spat that followed there isn't one single reliable narrator, so let's try to piece together what caused Lady Douglas to make the *very* audacious claim in the early years of the nineteenth century, that Caroline, Princess of Wales, had given birth to an illegitimate child.

Smith was a guest of the Douglases and when we learn that Lady Douglas often took him his breakfast in bed and remained in his room whilst he ate it, I think it's fairly easy to see what motivated her dislike of Caroline: good, old-fashioned jealousy. Tellingly, Lady Douglas's household claimed that she became agitated whenever Smith paid his frequent and prolonged visits to Caroline, so it really does sound as though the two ladies had formed an attachment to the same man.

Caroline's attraction to Smith was strong and appeared to be mutual, with the couple most likely becoming far more than friends. Having already endured Lady Jersey's attentions to her husband, there was no way that Caroline was going to stand by and play second fiddle again. When someone, heaven knows *who*, sent Lord Douglas a letter alleging that his wife and Smith were lovers, including a rather indelicate illustration, Lady Douglas assumed the author was her former friend, and rounded on her. How dare Caroline besmirch her reputation, asked Lady Douglas, when she herself had shared her bed with Smith, Manby, Canning and a whole host of other men?

On and on went the gossip and the sniping between the two women until Lady Douglas made her move. When she did, Caroline's compassion for charity children was about to land her in *very* hot water.

In 1802 Caroline welcomed into her household a child named William Austin, nicknamed *Willikin*, an infant from Deptford. There was nothing strange about that for Caroline, and mindful of her separation from her only child, she fairly threw herself into caring for him. He would be at her side until the day she died and she would brook no criticism of him, nor sanction any attempt to discipline the boy. Yet Lady Douglas suddenly remembered how fat her friend had become before the child arrived and recalled, worse still, that Caroline had jokingly suggested that she might decide to pass off another man's child as the offspring of the Prince of Wales. Those words spoken in jest in 1802 had by 1806 become a weapon. After all, Lady Douglas now posited, what if Austin was Caroline's son by some stranger; why, it was treason!

When word of this reached the Prince of Wales courtesy of Lady Douglas, he saw his chance to finally get rid of the troublesome princess once and for all. He dragged her reputation into the court of public opinion, calling for the *Delicate Investigation* to be convened under the stewardship of Prime Minister, William Grenville.

Things would never be the same again.

The intention of the investigation was determine whether William was Caroline's boy and, if he was, then to decide on a suitable punishment for the princess. Ready to face her accusers, Caroline chose her friend, Spencer Perceval,[31] to defend her, and he would do so with some considerable success!

Lady Douglas was the star witness and in her hands those innocent jokes between two friends became something far darker. Assuring the investigation that she was motivated entirely by concern for the future of the crown, Lady Douglas carefully distanced herself from Smith, whilst at the same time crediting the princess with false flattery, manipulation and a level of scheming that Machiavelli would have been proud of. The Caroline that emerged during the investigation is certainly recognizable in her excitable nature and refusal to stand on protocol, and one wonders whether some of her immature behaviour was not the result of false flattery, but of that childish wish to please. She had been denied friends in childhood, might she now be trying to make up for it by coming on a *little* strongly to her new BFF?

'Leaving her attendants below, she would push past my servant, and run upstairs into my bedchamber, kiss me, take me in her arms, and

---

31. Perceval is, of course, the only Prime Minister of the United Kingdom to date to die at the hands of an assassin. He was shot dead on 11 May 1812 by John Bellingham.

tell me I was beautiful, saying she had never loved any woman so much […] We soon saw that her Royal Highness was a very singular and very indiscreet woman, and we resolved to always be very careful and guarded with her.'[32]

Alas, Lady Douglas stated, she soon became aware that Caroline was so vulgar that she was *not* suitable company for a respectable, married woman, and she determined to end the friendship. When Caroline offered to arrange an assignation between Lady Douglas and the Duke of Gloucester, that was the final straw, and she disengaged herself from the friendship. Either way, she just happened to stay friends long enough for the princess to drop the bombshell that she was with child.

Members of Caroline's household were questioned and, piece by piece, the evidence didn't so much as stack up but crumble away. Many of the names linked to Caroline were senior Tories, natural enemies of her estranged husband and everyone knew that George was casting about for a divorce, something his father was bitterly opposed to. Whatever we may think of Caroline's bizarre behaviour, this was a bitter attack from the Prince of Wales and if the intention was to publicly savage her reputation, he couldn't have chosen a more blunt instrument than illegitimate children.

Caroline, however, had a trump card.

Two, in fact.

Joining the growing cast of the Delicate Investigation were Sophia and Samuel Austin, William's *legitimate* parents.

Mrs Austin had met Caroline way back in 1802 when she had travelled from Deptford to Blackheath seeking work or a crust of bread, her infant bundled in her arms. Instead she found the Princess of Wales and, as she did so many times in her life, Caroline took one look at the little boy and fell in love. Recently laid off from his job on the docks, Samuel suggested that Sophia and their brood of children commit themselves to the care of the parish yet surely the care of the Princess of Wales would be a far better option? The couple grabbed the opportunity with both hands and gave their

---

32. Nightingale, Joseph (1821). *Memoirs of Her Late Majesty Queen Caroline*. London: J Robins and Company, p.167.

son up to Caroline, sure she would give him a life that they could only dream of. Faced with this irrefutable evidence, the commission quickly reached its conclusion, and it was the last thing George wanted to hear.

> 'We are happy to declare our perfect conviction, that there is no foundation whatever for believing that the child now with the Princess of Wales is the child of her Royal Highness, or that she was delivered of any child in the year 1802; nor has any thing appeared to us which would warrant the belief that she was pregnant in that year, or at any other period within the compass of our inquiries.'[33]

Although she was cleared of giving birth to the little boy, Caroline was not declared innocent of adultery and as a result found her access to her daughter restricted even further. The press rallied behind her, portraying the princess as the wronged party and turning their venom on the prince, whilst Caroline sallied forth with her popularity intact.

> 'We are now informed, that, on an inquiry instituted by authority, and conducted by individuals among the most respectable in character and highest in station, there has not been found any ground for the slightest imputation on the character of the beautiful and distinguished personage thus cruelly aspersed.'[34]

Spencer Perceval had another trick up his sleeve. Not content with supporting Caroline in her hour of need, he wrote down all that had transpired at the Delicate Investigation in what the Prince of Wales must have considered to be the most eloquent and lengthy blackmail note in the history of Britain. *The Book* would lift the lid on everything that had happened in lurid detail, proving that Caroline was cruelly used, that her husband was selfish and her friends were false and, unless she was received at court once more, then it would be published for all to enjoy.

---

33. Urban, Sylvanus (1813). *The Gentleman's Magazine: Volume LXXXIII*. London: Nichols, Son, and Bentley, p.260.
34. *Caledonian Mercury* (Edinburgh, Scotland), Thursday, 26 June, 1806; Issue 13179, p.3.

George III dragged his heels on making a decision as the letters Caroline sent him grew increasingly agitated. She had been cleared of the serious charges against her, she pointed out, and it was wrong to continue to deny her the opportunity to appear at court. Wisely Caroline never actually criticized or blamed the king, but played on his own dislike of the Prince of Wales, making it clear that she knew who was really behind the delay in the king's decision. She wasn't all sweetness and light either, and she warned the monarch that her only recourse was to appeal to the court of public opinion. After all, Caroline said, the people would no doubt be wondering what was causing the delay in her return to the royal presence, so perhaps it was time that they knew exactly what was really going on behind the scenes.

'This revocation of your Majesty's gracious purpose has flung an additional cloud about the whole proceeding, and the inferences drawn in the public mind from this circumstance, so mysterious, and so perfectly inexplicable, upon any grounds which are open to their knowledge, has made, and will leave so deep an impression to my prejudice, as scarce anything short of a public exposure of all that has passed, can possibly efface.'[35]

The shadow of Perceval's book now loomed larger than ever, with copies printed ready to tell the whole sorry story. In what can only be called the nick of time, the Grenville ministry fell and Caroline's Tory friends found themselves occupying the seat of power. This meant that the new administration could formally clear the princess and the king could welcome her back to court, even putting apartments in Kensington Palace at her disposal. George III was happy to agree, spared the agony of making a decision that might upset his son or further inflame his daughter-in-law.

'[…] there is no longer any necessity for your Majesty being advised to decline receiving the princess into your royal presence, [I] humbly submit to your Majesty, that it is essentially necessary, in justice to

---

35. Melville, Lewis (1912). *An Injured Queen, Caroline of Brunswick: Vol I*. London: Hutchinson & Co, p.156.

her royal highness, and for the honour and interests of your Majesty's illustrious family, that her Royal Highness the Princess of Wales should be admitted, with as little delay as possible, into your Majesty's royal presence, and that she should be received in a manner due to her rank and station, in your Majesty's court and family.'[36]

In the change of government, Perceval gained office as Chancellor of the Exchequer and when he made his maiden speech in the House of Commons, Caroline was there to cheer him on, swept along on a wave of triumph.

Into the Public Eye

In the years that followed Caroline's life was nothing short of a whirlwind. She carried on with her philanthropic activities, went to every party she could wedge into her diary and continued to receive those movers and shakers who had proved so useful to her in the past. One thing she couldn't do, however, was to enjoy unrestricted visits to her daughter as Charlotte remained in the custody of her father or, more correctly, the ladies appointed to oversee her. George still firmly believed that his estranged wife was unfit to be a mother, fearing her influence over the child who was increasingly coming to display the same rambunctious, opinionated manner.

With the advent of George III's last, terrible and prolonged illness, the Prince of Wales became Prince Regent and was forced to watch as his wife and daughter's popularity far outgrew his own. By now no longer a child, the cosseted Charlotte was desperate for a taste of freedom and she fled her father's custody, hurrying to her mother's side. Although there's no doubt that Caroline loved Charlotte, she also knew that any effort to keep her daughter was pointless and instead called on influential friends to persuade the girl to go home.

Like her parents, Charlotte was a keen follower of politics and when her father abandoned his Whig principles in favour of Tory values, she declared her fellowship with the Whigs. It was one of these, Henry Brougham, 1st Baron Brougham and Vaux, who sought an audience with her. Brougham had become one of Caroline's most valued advisors and it was he who convinced

---

36. Ibid., p.166.

Charlotte to return, thus saving Caroline from any claims of conspiracy to keep her child!

Caroline, however, had had enough with her fortnightly visitations, and was determined to make her complaints known. When George didn't respond, Brougham leaked the letter to the newspapers so the public might see how the princess was bring wronged. It's a long letter and, famously, inspired the legendary Jane Austen to comment on how much she loathed the prince. No wonder, really, when we consider some choice lines from the missive that represent not only Caroline's own distress, but the possible cost to the nation itself.

'There is a point beyond which a guiltless woman cannot with safety carry her forbearance. [...] the separation, which every succeeding month is making wider, of the Mother and the Daughter, is equally injurious to my character and to her education. [...]

The plan of excluding my Daughter from all intercourse with the world appears to my humble judgement peculiarly unfortunate. She who is destined to be the Sovereign of this great country, enjoys none of those advantages of society which are deemed necessary for imparting a knowledge of mankind to persons who have infinitely less occasion to learn that important lesson; and it may so happen, by a chance which I trust is very remote, that she should be called upon to exercise the powers of the Crown, with an experience of the world more confined than that of the most private individual.

[...]

The pain with which I have at length formed the resolution of addressing myself to Your Royal Highness is such as I should in vain attempt to express. If I could adequately describe it, you might be enabled, Sir, to estimate the strength of the motives which have made me submit to it. They are the most powerful feelings of affection, and the deepest impressions of duty towards Your Royal Highness, my beloved Child, and the Country, which I devoutly hope she may be preserved to govern, and to shew by a new example the liberal affection of a free and generous people to a virtuous and constitutional monarch.'[37]

Did Caroline write this letter though, or does it bear the hallmark of Brougham or even a committee of authors? Whoever was responsible, Caroline's signature is the one at the bottom of the page and her advisors *must* have known that the prince wouldn't reply. They must have known too that the intelligent young Princess Charlotte of Wales would see that the intention of the letter wasn't so much her wellbeing as someone taking the chance to make a very public point against her father.

The Prince Regent's revenge was wreaked anonymously as quite out of nowhere, Lady Douglas's accusations from the Delicate Investigation suddenly appeared in the press. If he had hoped to horrify the people into turning their backs on Caroline, however, it did quite the opposite. She was now a wronged woman and though Charlotte was furious at Brougham for having leaked her mother's letter, she too stood firmly beside the Princess of Wales.

The Princess of Orange

As Prince Regent, George could wield his full power against his estranged wife and she was once again banished from court, her access to Charlotte reduced more than ever. The young princess's life was about to become even more dramatic too, because her father had decided that the time had come for marriage. Though he knew too well the agony of an arranged match, the choice was not to be left to his daughter and George selected the Prince of Orange. But Charlotte was having none of it.

When Caroline told Charlotte that such a marriage would mean she couldn't make her home in Britain, Charlotte was horrified and asked her father to reconsider. When he wouldn't, she turned to her mother, sure that she of all people might intervene. After all, Caroline seemed to understand her daughter's wish to be happy, and had even encouraged a romance years earlier.

---

37. Flower, Benjamin (ed.) (1813). *Flower's Political Review and Monthly Register, Vol III*. London: M Jones, p.23.

That odd interlude took place in 1811, when Charlotte fell for Captain Charles Hesse who was rumoured to be the illegitimate son of the Duke of York. Caroline had been quick to give the relationship her blessing, delighted to see her daughter dewy-eyed over the dashing soldier. She carried notes for the couple, arranged secret meetings, scandalously left them alone in her own bedroom, and generally played at being Charlotte's best friend. Of course, this could have ruined Charlotte's reputation but, happily, it would appear that nothing transpired during that lock in or, if it *did*, that there was no permanent reminder! When George discovered the attachment, the fallout for the young princess wasn't pleasant. Her attendants were told never to let her out of their sight again and to keep her closely watched. Surely though, Charlotte thought, no mother who would carry love letters for her would force her to submit to an arranged marriage, even if she *couldn't* have Hesse.[38]

Caroline would take any opportunity to oppose George and she threw her weight behind Charlotte's desire to be free of the betrothal, no doubt utterly unsurprised when the British people did the same. Despite his initial refusals to countenance any change to the planned marriage, the Prince Regent couldn't fight against the tide and eventually, amid much grumbling, he grudgingly agreed to call off the wedding.

'The Treaty of Marriage between the Princess Charlotte and the Prince of Orange has been broken off – on what account has not been officially stated. […] It is not improbable that some personal considerations may have been the real motives with the Princess to declining this union. She has had too many opportunities of witnessing the miseries which result from state marriages, to render her indifferent to the consequences of an union, in which the heart has no share.'[39]

In time, of course, Charlotte would make a love match, marrying Prince Leopold of Saxe-Coburg-Saalfeld. Her happy ending was to be short-lived, though.

---

38. When Caroline left for her continental travels in 1814, Hesse visited her in Brunswick.
39. *The Leeds Mercury* (Leeds, England), Saturday, 2 July, 1814; Issue 2558, p.3.

To the Continent

Caroline might have won the battle over marriage, but on what seemed like all other matters, she was in her husband's thrall. Even though he made it clear that he would *never* meet her again, Caroline remained all too *present* for George, if not physically, then mentally. She was always just on the periphery of his existence, entertaining his political enemies and enjoying a public popularity that served only to remind the prince how much his own subjects disliked him.

Caroline also longed for something more, dreaming of the freedom she thought her money might give her that she could never enjoy in England. She eventually fixed on a return to Europe and when she made her feelings known, her husband was all too happy to agree. She explained that she had wished to quit England for some years but hadn't wanted to leave her daughter. Now, with the matter of Orange settled, she was ready to travel. Caroline wrote a letter to the Prime Minister, Lord Liverpool, in which she railed against the wrong the Prince Regent had done to her. Whilst the king still reigned, she wrote, she might have some hope of a happy life but now his son was regent that had been crushed.

When Parliament voted to give Caroline an annual income of £50,000, she instead insisted that she would take only £35,000 in order to lessen the burden on the public purse. Not only that, but when Caroline finally left the country, it was reported that she ensured, 'all those domestics of her household who might be discharged should receive one year's wages, and board until they should procure another situation; and to those faithful domestics who had been some years in her service, her Royal Highness granted annuities for their lives'.[40]

Such PR was cheap at the price.

George might have been delighted to see the back of Caroline, but Charlotte was devastated and felt as though she was losing her only champion. Mother and daughter met one last time at Connaught House in July 1814 and said

---

40. *The Bury and Norwich Post: Or, Suffolk, Norfolk, Essex, Cambridge, and Ely Advertiser* (Bury Saint Edmunds, England), Wednesday, 14 September, 1814; Issue 1681, p.4.

their goodbyes. They would never see each other again and within the decade, both, tragically, would be dead.

Caroline sailed from Worthing on 9 August 1814 and who should be by her side but Willikin, that boy who had been the subject of such drama more than a decade earlier. A great crowd followed her to her vessel, keen to wish their princess well as she embarked on her adventure. With her she carried a large box in which she kept her memoirs, pages that the prince would no doubt give *anything* to get his hands on

When the princess finally arrived in Brunswick she found her wounded spirits buoyed by the heroine's welcome that was paid to her. Initially Caroline planned to make her home there, but wanderlust got the better of her, and instead she toured the continent. Freed from the censure of the prince, she dressed as she wished, behaved as she wished and painted Europe red. Her escapades were all reported back to her husband and wherever she went, she was the centre of inquisitive attention.

And she *loved* it.

Caroline was finally free of the restrictions of the regent yet her daughter felt her loss keenly, so how should one look on her decision to leave? It's easy to take a dim view of Caroline's departure but might it also be fair to consider that she had never really been allowed to know Charlotte as a mother should? Immature, excitable and full of the need to shock, when Caroline *did* have time with Charlotte, she behaved more as a friend than parent, never more so than when locking that door behind her daughter and Captain Hesse. She didn't leave England with the intention of abandoning her child, but to escape the constant watch and endless judgment of her husband and his peers. After all those years in a place she had learned to loath, can we really blame her? From the night of her marriage to the day she left England almost two decades later, Caroline had never really settled and had remained, as she once memorably complained, a *shuttlecock*.

Recalling her wedding years later she declared that, given the choice to marry George knowing what she then knew, she would have rather died.

'If anybody say to me at this moment — "Will you pass your life over again, or be killed?" I would choose death […] for, you know, a little sooner or later we must all die; but to live a life of wretchedness twice over — oh! mine God, no!' [41]

How must Caroline have felt as she travelled Europe, the wind in her hair once more, no ladies of the bedchamber to make her life miserable and her husband so far away that he might as well be on another planet? What must have been going through her head, this woman so full of wanderlust, as she crisscrossed the roads of the continent indulging her every whim? Was freedom everything she had imagined it to be?

Absolutely.

In her last meeting with Charlotte, Caroline told her to put her faith not in men, but in God; the Princess of Wales, however, would put *her* faith in a rather strapping Italian soldier...

An Italian Caller

'The first person who opened the door [...] was the one whom it was impossible to mistake, hearing what is reported; six feet high, a magnificent head of black hair, pale complexion, mustachios which reach from *here to London*.'[42]

And who was this fine figure of Italian manhood?

None other than Bartolomeo Pergami, a married father and a former soldier who Caroline had met during her travels in Italy. Cultured, charming, handsome and *strapping*, he was just what she was looking for in a travelling companion and the princess employed him at first sight.

Their initial meeting in Milan reads like something out of a romance novel, as Pergami, hearing that there might be an opening for a courier in the princess's staff, arrived at the Royal Hotel in Milan to seek an audience. Resplendent in the uniform of the Italian Hussars, he strode into the lobby

---

41. Melville, Lewis (1912). *An Injured Queen, Caroline of Brunswick: Vol I*. London: Hutchinson & Co, p.60.
42. Bury, Lady Charlotte Campbell (1838). *Diary Illustrative of the Times of George the Fourth: Vol II*. London: Carey, Lea and Blanchard, p.116.

to discover a lady who had caught the train of her gown in a piece of saloon furniture. The gallant Pergami freed the damsel from her entanglement and politely asked where the princess might be found. The woman replied that she *was* the princess and her hero went down on one knee, at which point she employed him more or less on the spot!

Led by Baron Ompteda, George's spies wrote to the Prince Regent to inform him that Pergami was a good looking man, though they did mention that local gossip seemed to suggest he was not able to perform sexually. Whether that is true we cannot know, but since Pergami was to be central in the prince's efforts to gain a divorce, he wasn't about to probe too deeply. In all honesty though, that gossip seems a little far-fetched. Far be it from me to impugn Caroline's character, but I'm not entirely convinced that she was fond of Pergami for his whiskers.

In fact, Caroline was lucky to have met Pergami abroad because, when accusations of adultery began to fly around, overseas was the best place to be. Had she been accused and found guilty of adultery against the regent in England, Caroline might have found herself facing the death penalty.

Now more than ever Caroline embraced her scandalous lifestyle, with this nineteenth century biographer perfectly summing up the sniffy attitude which her behaviour occasionally attracted:

> 'The Princess danced there with indescribable abandon. Her dress consisted of a single embroidered garment, fastened beneath the bosom, without the shadow of a corset and without sleeves. A shawl floating in the air did not succeed in making the costume decent even to the eyes of the Roman ladies, who were themselves not particularly scrupulous in the matter of dress.'[43]

Ompteda and his agents constantly shadowed Caroline yet this did nothing to slow her down. The Baron's efforts to win her servants to his side were generally unsuccessful until he met Maurice Credé, a member of the princess's household who didn't share the scruples of his fellows.

---

43. Chapman, Frederic (trans.) (1897). *A Queen of Indiscretions, The Tragedy of Caroline of Brunswick, Queen of England*. London: John Lane, pp.55–56.

He admitted Ompteda to Caroline's private rooms and, unfortunately for Credé, was discovered; unsurprisingly, she swiftly dismissed him from her service. Credé confessed to the whole sorry affair in a letter. He begged unsuccessfully to be readmitted to the household, painting himself as a man who had a moment of madness and was now struggling under the weight of his own guilty conscience.

> 'I persisted for some time in refusing to have any concern in this plot; but at length the Baron's threats, who told me I was a ruined man if I did not listen to him, together with the money he offered me from time to time, corrupted me, and I was weak enough to accept the commission, although fully persuaded that there was no foundation whatever for the Baron's infamous suspicions.'[44]

Naturally Ompteda denied all the allegations against him but this must have left Caroline shaken and suspicious of those in her household. Perhaps this is one of the reasons why she was so generous in giving positions to the family of Pergami, a man she was sure she could trust. She rewarded him too, elevating him to the station of Baron of Francina and Knight of Malta!

Although it would be naive to suggest that Caroline wasn't attracted to Pergami, there might have been more to him than good looks and charm. His daughter, Victorine, appealed to the princess's well-documented need to look after other people's children. Indeed, she eventually came to call Caroline *mamma* and regularly shared her quarters. Pergami's wife, however, remained safely at home and was nowhere to be seen as the happy household made its way around Europe and into Greece and the Middle East. Finally the roaming drew to an end and the party settled in Italy at Pesaro, safe from the spies of the Crown.

For a time Caroline seemed to settle into a happy domestic life here in Pesaro, living as a family with Pergami, whose rooms at the very least *adjoined* her own. She spent happy hours with the gentleman and his daughter, punctuating the tranquillity with occasional travels. Indeed, as the princess

---

44. Nightingale, Joseph (1820). *Memoirs of the Public and Private Life of Her Most Gracious Majesty Caroline, Queen of Great Britain.* London: J Robins & Co, p.516.

wrote to her *own* daughter, her contentment was worth the travails she had suffered to achieve it.

'But my fatigues are now drawing to a close; and although if I could have foreseen all that I have had to meet with I might not have undertaken so distant and dangerous a journey, I am far, very far from repenting it; I have gleaned so much real knowledge, and been gratified with such long-anticipated sights, that I feel well repaid for the trouble, and I shall be the more disposed hereafter to sit down contentedly wherever my destiny may fix me.' [45]

In England, meanwhile, *another* happy home was about to be shattered by tragedy.

The Death of a Princess

On 2 May 1816, Princess Charlotte of Wales and Prince Leopold of Saxe-Coburg-Saalfeld were married in London. They were deeply in love and with the Prince Regent giving the match his blessing, it seemed as though Charlotte was about to get her fairytale ending.

'The marriage of the Princess Charlotte of Wales and Prince Leopold of Saxe Cobourg was solemnized yesterday evening at Carlton House [...]

A great concourse of persons were attracted yesterday in consequence of the Royal Marriage. The crowd was particularly great from Charing-cross to the neighbourhood of Carlton House and the Queen's Palace. The open space opposite to Clarence House more thronged with spectators than upon any former occasion.'[46]

---

45. Princess Charlotte of Wales and Caroline, Princess of Wales (1820). *Royal Correspondence, or, Letters between Her Late Royal Highness the Princess Charlotte, and Her Royal Mother, Queen Caroline*. London: Jones and Company, p.118.
46. *Jackson's Oxford Journal* (Oxford, England), Saturday, 4 May, 1816; issue 3289, p.3.

Although Charlotte and Caroline hadn't seen one another since the Princess of Wales had left for the continent, they had exchanged letters. No doubt Caroline understood the importance of this match, and felt pleased that her daughter had married for love. She wrote to Charlotte in glowing terms, the letter full of exhortations of motherly love and good wishes for 'every bliss that can attend a union so felicitous in its prospects'.[47]

In Charlotte's future there seemed to be nothing but the promise of happiness; she was adored, and she loved her husband in turn. They were made for one another, and when news of Charlotte's pregnancy was announced, the future of the House of Hanover looked to be assured.

In fact, the pregnancy ended in tragedy when the princess died after giving birth to a stillborn son.

'Our blooming, our beloved Princess, is no more!!! After a protracted labour, and the delivery of a still-born male child, her Royal Highness expired this morning at half past Two o'clock. [...]

We never remember to have seen a deeper gloom than this sad catastrophe has thrown over the public countenance. There is a general disinclination to business, and the chief topic of discourse, or object of attention, seems to be the national loss. The situation of Prince Leopold is distressing in the extreme.'[48]

As the royal household[49] was plunged into despair and the nation echoed its deep mourning, Caroline did not even know of her loss. The Prince Regent did nothing to inform his estranged wife of the sad event and, unthinkably, she discovered the fate of her daughter quite by accident.

George sent a note to the pope to inform him that the princess was dead and, by chance, that messenger travelled through Pesaro, Caroline's adopted

47. Princess Charlotte of Wales and Caroline, Princess of Wales (1820). *Royal Correspondence, or, Letters between Her Late Royal Highness the Princess Charlotte, and Her Royal Mother, Queen Caroline*. London: Jones and Company, p.115.
48. *Jackson's Oxford Journal* (Oxford, England), Saturday, 8 November, 1817; Issue 3368, p.4.
49. Sir Richard Croft, the obstetrician who delivered Princess Charlotte's child, was so distraught at his role in her death that he never recovered from the experience. Three months after she died, he took his own life.

home. So it was that, in the middle of one of her no-doubt contented days of: 'Cheerful repast, plays, music in her private theatre'[50], the news of her only child's death shattered the idyllic life of the Princess of Wales. Great Britain had lost its heir, the succession now looked unsettled in the extreme and Caroline was plunged into a grief from which she never quite emerged. No doubt tormented by the thoughts of their restricted contact, the long years spent apart, the battling over custody, there was no chance that Caroline would be able to attend her daughter's funeral.

This tragedy was the beginning of the end for George and Caroline, and the princess was soon bound for England once more.

Back to Britain

Far away in Great Britain, the Prince Regent brooded and mused on the fate of his wife. Surrounded by the evidence gathered by his spies, mourning his daughter and his mother too, the prince knew nothing but a wish to be avenged on the spouse he believed had humiliated him. She was happy with Pergami and all the intelligence suggested that they were lovers, that they bathed together, shared a bed and generally behaved in a most wanton fashion. It was time, he decided, to put an end to the marriage he had never wanted in the first place.

There was no longer a king to refuse him this wish, with George III living as a virtual prisoner at Windsor, blind and insane, nor was Queen Charlotte able to calm his nerves, for she had died in 1818. Now there was only the capricious Prince Regent and he was determined to get his own back once and for all.

In 1818 George convened the Milan Commission. It was charged with cataloging and assessing the intelligence gathered by the agents who had followed Caroline on her travels, the most explosive of which was held in an infamous *green bag*. Much of this evidence was heresy and rumour, but it was all George had, and he was determined to make it stick.

Brougham, meanwhile, began to consider what Caroline's best course of action would be, well aware that he would be called upon as her advisor once

---

50. *The Morning Chronicle* (London, England), Saturday, 17 May, 1817; Issue 14990, p.3.

more should the prince's plans come to fruition. The regent didn't just want a divorce – he was also determined to secure an admission of adultery from the wife he hated.

He would have a long wait.

The endgame in this messy affair began with the death of George III on 29 January 1820. Now the Prince Regent was George IV, and his estranged wife was a queen. She was also, as he knew better than anybody else, not a woman who believed in backing down. Now more than ever, he *needed* that divorce and when word reached him that Caroline was on her way back to London, he was determined to get it.

Caroline was heartbroken at the news of George III's death and insulted when she learned that her husband had already moved to have her name struck from the liturgy. She was in Rome at the moment the exclusion from the liturgy became known, and the pope immediately withdrew her guard of honour, as well as all other privileges that would be afforded to a visiting royal, effectively rendering her treatment that of a private citizen. This was too much to countenance and with her annoyance came rage, as well as the reminder of the daughter and grandchild she had lost, not to mention all the bad blood that had been drawn over those past two decades.

Brougham dispatched his brother, James, to Italy to seek Caroline's assurances that she had *not* committed adultery and others in England were soon getting in touch too. Caroline began corresponding with British radicals including William Cobbett, who saw her as a rallying point for their cause. They became even more convinced that Caroline's case to be crowned queen had merit when Parliament offered her an increased annuity of £50,000 if she would give up her titles and stay away from England. Her advisors countered that Caroline would also need a promise that she would be neither divorced nor pursued for adultery. The king wouldn't agree to her terms and she wouldn't agree to his wish for a divorce, which would mean that she must admit adultery. With no common ground, the discussions collapsed and Caroline travelled for the coast.

The queen arrived in England on 5 June 1820 and reached the capital the following day in the company of Sir Matthew Wood, Alderman of the City of London and Member of Parliament. He was also the sort of man who knew how to raise eyebrows, as Charles Greville noted when he went to view the spectacle.

> 'The Queen arrived in London yesterday at seven o'clock, I rode as far as Greenwich to meet her. The road was thronged with an immense multitude the whole way from Westminster Bridge to Greenwich. Carriages, carts, and horsemen followed, preceded, and surrounded her coach the whole way. She was everywhere received with the greatest enthusiasm. Women waved pocket handkerchiefs, and men shouted wherever she passed. She travelled in an open landau, Alderman Wood sitting by her side and Lady Ann Hamilton and another woman opposite. Everybody was disgusted at the vulgarity of Wood in sitting in the place of honour, while the Duke of Hamilton's sister was sitting backwards in the carriage.'[51]

The route was lined with celebratory crowds who were delighted to see Caroline return to stick it to the unloved new king. He was cast as the enemy, she the damsel in distress and with revolution in France still a terrible memory, George feared where all of this might lead. Indeed, when someone smashed the windows of his lover Lady Hertford's home, no doubt the king felt the sting more than ever.

Let us look to *The Bristol Mercury*, its journalists ably summing up the mood of those who *loudly* rallied to the call of 'Queen Caroline', who was soon receiving visits and messages of support from all over the nation at her residence of Brandenburg House.

> 'Had not the Queen of Great Britain been disavowed, neglected, insulted abroad, she had not been forced to throw herself upon the justice and humanity of her People at home. Harassed, persecuted, slandered, she had no alternative left to her but to turn upon her pursuers [...]

51. Greville, Charles (1899). *A Journal of the Reign of King George IV, King William IV and Queen Victoria, Vol I*. London: Longmans, Green, and Co, p.29.

The entry of the Queen into London, greeted by immense multitudes of the people, without preparation, and almost contrary to expectation, came like an electric shock upon the inhabitants of the Metropolis.'[52]

The moment of truth had arrived and that *green bag* full of evidence was now in the hands of Parliament, awaiting its moment in court.

A Queen on Trial

'The Order of the day being read, for the further consideration and second reading of the Bill, intituled [sic], An Act to deprive Her Majesty Caroline Amelia Elizabeth of the title, prerogatives, rights, privileges, and exemptions of Queen Consort of this Realm; and to dissolve the Marriage between His Majesty and the said *Caroline Amelia Elizabeth*.'[53]

The Pains and Penalties Bill, an unprecedented move in Parliament, shocked Britain to the core. It effectively placed the queen on trial for adultery in the House of Lords and should Caroline lose, the cost to her would be immense. At stake was not only her reputation, but her British titles, rank and privileges and she was determined to fight it to her very last breath, with Brougham at her side. Although Caroline would have been happy to say goodbye to her husband, she simply wasn't willing to admit to adultery and, with George equally unwilling to admit to the charge both were most likely guilty of, it was up to the Lords to decide.

King George IV had learned nothing.

Yes, the behaviour Caroline was accused of was scandalous, treasonous, utterly unthinkable for a *queen* and yet, the people decided, *accusations* were all that the king had, and what weight could be placed against the accusations of a man so distrusted, so utterly and inarguably immoral as George IV? She was the wronged woman, pushed to breaking by rumours of

---

52. *The Bristol Mercury* (Bristol, England), Monday, 12 June, 1820; Issue 1577, p.3.
53. Anonymous (1819). *The Journals of the House of Commons, Volume 75*. London: HM Stationery Office, p.479.

Maria Fitzherbert, by the open cavorting of her husband and his mistresses, by Lady Jersey's constant presence when she was trying to make her home in England. Her daughter had been torn from her, she had been dragged through the mire of scandal, her reputation held up for ridicule and even her charitable adoption of a helpless child used to try and tarnish her name.

The Queen of Hearts, indeed.

Caroline's advisors encouraged her to play the role of wounded wife to the hilt and she or *someone* on her team penned a heartfelt open letter to the king. Over the course of several pages, she outlined each and every complaint against him, making her protests at the indignity of a trial clear even as she vowed to fight him tooth and nail. It is a strongly worded piece and one that her adoring public couldn't help but lap up.

'You have cast upon me every slur to which the female character is liable. Instead of loving, honouring, and cherishing me, [...] you have pursued me with hatred and scorn. [...] You wrested from me my child, and with her my only comfort and consolation. You sent me sorrowing through the world, and even in my sorrows pursued me with unrelenting persecution.'[54]

There can be no underestimating the impact of the bill on the nation and it really was one of the most infamous events of the Georgian era. It wasn't necessarily that the public believed that Caroline was innocent, more that they believed her husband was guilty of all manner of wrongdoing, and supporting *her* was an excellent way of hurting *him*. They lapped up reports of the proceedings in the press as the prosecution, led by Solicitor General Sir John Copley, heard tales of shared intimacy, of the queen admitting that Pergami slept in her bedroom but only because she was afraid of being poisoned, of riding together in carriages, sharing a bath and cavorting without care. Yet throughout all of this scandal, the people stayed true to their queen. After all, George behaved outrageously at home in England and it cost a *lot* more than Caroline was spending on her continental love life!

---

54. Wilks, John (1822). *Memoirs of Her Majesty Queen Caroline Amelia Eliz, Vol. I*. London: Sherwood, Neely and Jones, p.502.

On her appearances in court, Caroline didn't always seem particularly interested in the proceedings and after she dozed off, Lord Holland wryly noted, 'she sins not with courtiers, but sleeps with the lords'. Of course, let us not be misled into thinking that Caroline didn't care, but she had never been a lady who liked to sit still and all of this legal wrangling must, at times, have left her bored. Although she didn't always stay in the chamber of the Lords she did like to be present and could often be found waiting in an ante-room for the latest update. Brougham, meanwhile, might have been Caroline's advisor, but he was no admirer of his client. He told his friends that she was not so much pure innocent as 'pure in-no-sense'!

Central to the prosecution were the witness statements of those members of Caroline's household who had agreed to speak against their mistress. These individuals, however, cowered before the terrifyingly swift legal mind of Brougham, and he took great delight in tearing their statements apart and casting them aside as though they were of no more importance than gossip in the alehouse. He cast doubt on the moral character and believability of all of the witnesses, reserving his particular distaste for the Italians who took the stand. This was a lead that the press was quick to follow, until they wondered whether any word spoken by a citizen of Italy could be trusted, especially the sort who peered through keyholes and examined the stained bedsheets of a royal lady!

It isn't very often that a trial finds its own catchphrase but this remarkable proceeding did and it was the oft-repeated answer given by prosecution's star witness, Theodore Majocchi, and his fellow Italians. It was odd, Brougham noted, that Majocchi and the other witnesses could recall every single detail for the prosecution, no matter how small, including the fact that two chamberpots were used in Caroline's chamber, and how full they were, yet, when the defence team attempted to dig deeper, they all chorused, 'non mi ricordo', or 'I don't remember'. Inspiring poetry, pamphleteers and caricature, Majocchi was nicknamed *Signor Non mi Ricordo* in the press, who mockingly surmized that the phrase would soon be 'substituted throughout England, years to come, on all merry and parting occasions, for the native one of "I don't remember"'.[55] Bit by bit these incidences of memory lapse

---

55. *The Examiner* (London, England), Sunday, 27 August, 1820; Issue 661, p.1.

piled up and each one further undermined the prosecution case, laying bare the hearsay and rumour on which it was built.

Of course, Caroline wasn't treated as an angel by everyone but the cartoons and comments that circulated were nothing compared to the vitriol hurled at the king. It was a messy and public embarrassment, and when the Lords voted on the Pains and Penalties Bill they passed it by a painfully small margin of just nine votes. At the thought of reliving this humiliation in the Commons where the bill was likely to be rejected, Prime Minister Lord Liverpool decided that there was no option but to withdraw it.

'The Earl of Liverpool rose immediately, and said, […] In the present state of the country [and] with the division of sentiment, so nearly balanced, just evinced by their Lordships, they had come to a determination not to proceed with it.'[56]

He believed that Caroline was guilty and that she should be treated as such yet, to all intents and purposes, the bill had failed; the queen was still the queen and there was to be no divorce. The press and people celebrated uproariously and the king, furious and humiliated, was left to lick the wound left by Caroline, the sharpest thorn in his portly side.

If Your Name's Not Down…

Positively glowing with triumph, Caroline returned to Brandenburg House and mused on her future. Her sense of victory must have been immense; she had gambled with the highest stakes in the crucible of the Lords itself and, somehow, emerged victorious from the best her husband could throw at her. She was still a wife and more importantly, still a queen.

But what was a queen without a crown?

What indeed?

When Caroline heard that her husband would be crowned at Westminster Abbey on 19 July 1821 she decided not to return to Italy, but to stake her

---

56. *Royal Cornwall Gazette, Falmouth Packet & Plymouth Journal* (Truro, England), Saturday, 18 November, 1820; Issue 908, p.4.

claim in the most public way possible. She would be beside George, she decided, and she would be crowned as his queen whether he liked it or not.

This was the first mistake Caroline had made for a long time. She had badly underestimated the strength of the public's support of her case as well as their loathing of her husband. As the months passed and her victory in the Lords became last year's scandal, the people of Britain weathered the long, cold winter and waited keenly for the summer to come. George IV loved to throw a party and his subjects were rather looking forward to the coronation, anticipating the knees up to end all knees ups. Caroline was yesterday's news and the fact that she chose to hang around did her public image no favours. The British people would much rather she had gone home to Italy yet instead here she was, shunned by high society and still hanging around even *after* she had accepted a £50,000 annuity from Parliament.

As Carlton House went on the PR offensive Caroline's own circle began to contract. Grown rather intoxicated by her triumphs, she seemed utterly blind to the way the wind had turned against her. When she began to discuss the possibility that she might make an appearance at Westminster Abbey, Brougham was quick to advise her against it but she wasn't about to be deterred. She wrote to George to tell him that she would be there for her crowning and expected to be attended by appropriate ladies on the big day.

'The Queen from circumstances being obliged to remain in England, she requests the King will be pleased to command those Ladies of the first Rank his Majesty may think most proper in this Realm, to attend the Queen on the day of the Coronation, of which her Majesty is informed is now fixed, and also to name such Ladies which will be required to bear her Majesty's Train on that day.

The Queen being particularly anxious to submit to the good Taste of his Majesty most earnestly entreats the King to inform the Queen in what Dress the King wishes the Queen to appear in, on that day, at the Coronation. Caroline R.'[57]

57. Melville, Lewis (1912). *An Injured Queen, Caroline of Brunswick: Vol I*. London: Hutchinson & Co, p.542.

Rather than reply, George passed the letter to Lord Liverpool. He in turn informed Caroline that she wasn't to come to the abbey and that, if she did, she wouldn't be welcome. Brougham redoubled his efforts to keep her from the coronation and the press echoed his warning, hoping that she would heed the words of the politician who had, so far, not failed her.

She didn't, of course.

Brougham had a suspicion that the headstrong lady might make her case in person. He wrote later that he had done his best to dissuade her, yet she wouldn't believe that 'the public feeling would not go along with her'.[58] Still, he noted, 'having an order, she could not be stopt when she insisted upon it,'[59] and so Caroline sallied forth at 6.00 am on the morning of the coronation, determined to get into the abbey.

Accompanied by the gallant if rather well-meaning Lord Hood, Caroline went from door to door at the abbey attempting to gain admission. Each time she was turned away and on one unpleasant occasion, the door was slammed shut in her face. Out for a good time, the crowd began to jeer and boo yet still she persisted, eventually being told by one of the doorkeepers that admission was by ticket only, regardless of who she was. Trying to make the best of a bad situation Lord Hood offered Caroline his own ticket so that she might at least see the procession, even if she couldn't be part of it. As she declined his offer, Lord Hood heard 'Some persons within the porch of the Abbey laughed, and uttered some expressions of disrespect.'[60] He was mortified and Caroline, no doubt feeling the public humiliation that was so unknown to her, had no choice but to flee.

'She flinched', wrote Brougham, 'for the first time in her life',[61] and it was the beginning of a swift end for Caroline of Brunswick.

---

58. Brougham, Henry (1871). *The Life and Times of Henry, Lord Brougham, Vol II*. Edinburgh: William Blackwood and Sons, p.422.
59. Ibid.
60. Urban, Sylvanus (1821). *The Gentleman's Magazine: 1821, Volume 91, Part 2*. London: John Nichols and Son, p.74.
61. Brougham, Henry (1871). *The Life and Times of Henry, Lord Brougham, Vol II*. Edinburgh: William Blackwood and Sons, p.422.

'I Be Tired of This Life'

Caroline had lost.

After all the years, all the struggles, the scandals and the silliness, she had overestimated how loved she was and the result was humiliating. Suddenly the husband she hated was the man of the hour and the rejoicing in the streets was for *him*, the fireworks and festivities all in the name of the king.

Caroline did her best to keep up appearances and continued to make her presence felt, even writing to let the Archbishop of Canterbury know that she wished 'to be crowned some days after the King, and before the arrangements were done away with, so that there might be no additional expense'.[62] The cleric replied that he couldn't be party to such an occasion without the express permission of the king. Of course, the king was never going to give that permission and so, finally, the door closed on the possibility of a coronation for Queen Caroline.

On 30 July Caroline was taken ill with abdominal pains during a trip to the theatre. She was whisked back to Brandenburg House to be seen by a team of doctors led by Dr Maton, who had previously treated the Duke of Kent. The queen, they decided, was suffering from an obstruction of her bowel and she began consuming opiates in an effort to combat the pain. This, Brougham surmized, only made matters worse and as the days passed and her condition declined, the prognosis for the queen was dark.

Convinced that death was merely days away and sleepless with agony, Caroline drew up her will. Her doctors believed that she had caused the obstruction herself thanks to a concoction of magnesia and laudanum that she had mixed on the first night of her illness, but of this we can't be sure. Caroline began to fear that she had been poisoned but if that were the case, then the person who administered the dose was herself. She had mixed the potion that the physicians now blamed for her worsening condition and none of their attempts to treat her seemed to be doing a bit of good. Perhaps Caroline had simply given up. When she discussed death with Brougham

---

62. Nightingale, Joseph (1822). *Memoirs of the Last Days of Her Late Most Gracious Majesty Caroline, Queen of Great Britain*. London: J Robins & Co, p.516.

just days before she drew her last breath she sighed, 'I shall not recover; and I am much better dead, for I be tired of this life.'[63]

Whether we should read some suicidal motive into this is a matter of conjecture. More likely, I think, that the queen had simply given up on self-care. She might well have suffered from mental health problems in her younger years but she was also a woman who seemed drawn to battling even insurmountable odds. Of course, we might speculate that she was unable to bear this final humiliation of being refused her crown, and chose instead to end her life, but I'm not quite convinced that this was the case.

Caroline of Brunswick, the uncrowned queen, died just after 10.00 pm on 7 August 1821.

'Yesterday evening, at twenty-five minutes after ten o'clock, the QUEEN departed this life after a short but painful illness, at Brandenburgh House, at Hammersmith.'[64]

Caroline wished to be buried with her family at Brunswick and for her coffin to bear a plate stating that she was the *injured queen of England*. Ordering the minimum period of mourning possible for his late wife, the king was happy to agree to the first request but rather less so to the second. As the coffin made its melancholy procession towards the coast, crowds gathered to watch the final departure of this most unusual woman and in London, rioting broke out.

One final drama occurred at Colchester where the procession came to rest. In the presence of the heartbroken Willikin, Stephen Lushington, Caroline's executor, succeeded in fastening the controversial plate to her coffin, proclaiming her the 'Injured Queen'. His triumph was temporary though and when the coffin continued on its journey, the official plate was in place once more.

Brougham was touched deeply by the scenes he saw on the road to Harwich and recorded the sense of a nation in mourning that followed the

---

63. Brougham, Henry (1871). *The Life and Times of Henry, Lord Brougham, Vol II*. Edinburgh: William Blackwood and Sons, p.423.
64. *The Morning Post* (London, England), Thursday, 9 August, 1821; Issue 15725, p.3.

coffin, especially the deep grief of those who had known Caroline. These scenes were echoed when she finally reached Brunswick where, amid great ceremony, the adventurous Caroline, Queen of the United Kingdom, was finally laid to rest.

Queen Caroline was, to put it mildly, a character. Married to a man who hated her and she came to loath in turn, she had embarked on life in England with every hope of a happy marriage, yet learned early on that such dreams were not destined to come true.

She wasn't blameless or course, and a lack of self-control was one of the particular character traits that she shared with George IV. Thanks to her marital travails, the marriages of the royal family became the entertainment of choice for the press and public, a situation that had never *quite* arisen before the Prince and Princess of Wales took their vows.

Nowadays we are used to private scandal becoming public drama, yet at a time it wasn't so common, Caroline was the public darling. This Queen of Hearts never knew when she was beaten; her life might have been happier if she had.

Afterword

And so, as Queen Caroline left Harwich bound for Brunswick, the last *legitimate* wife of King George IV left this world. He didn't remarry and her long shadow was soon fading into history, eventually replaced by William IV and Queen Adelaide, a lady who couldn't have been more different to Caroline if she had tried.

From the ill-fated Sophia Dorothea of Celle to the equally maligned Caroline of Brunswick via the politically inclined Caroline of Ansbach and the deceptively iron willed Charlotte of Mecklenburg-Strelitz, the four wives of the King Georges were each formidable characters in their own rights.

These were more than spouses, more than the women at the side of powerful men, but characters who live on, vibrant through the centuries. Their lives weren't always happy, not always long and definitely not without drama, yet through all the challenges they faced, even those that proved insurmountable, the three queens and the lady that never *quite* made it remained women to be reckoned with.

Thrice huzzah for them, one and all!

Bibliography

Adolphus, John (ed.). *A Correct, Full and Impartial Report, of the Trial of Her Majesty, Caroline, Queen Consort of Great Britain, Before the House of Peers*. London: Jones and Co, 1820.

Alexander, Marc. *Royal Murder*. UK: Willow Books, 2012.

Anonymous. *A Brief Account of the Coronation of His Majesty, George IV*. London: D Walther, 1821.

Anonymous. *Catalogue of Prints and Drawings in the British Museum. Political and Personal Satires, Volume 2*. London: The British Museum, 1873.

Anonymous. *George III: His Court and Family, Vol I*. London: Henry Colburn and Co, 1821.

Anonymous. *An Historical Account of the Life and Reign of King George the Fourth*. London: G Smeeton, 1830.

Anonymous. *The Important and Eventful Trial of Queen Caroline, Consort of George IV*. London: Geo Smeeton, 1820.

Anonymous. *The Journals of the House of Commons, Volume 75*. London: HM Stationery Office, 1819.

Anonymous. *Letters, in the Original, with Translations, and Messages, that Passed Between the King, Queen, Prince, and Princess of Wales*. London: S Osborn, 1737.

Anonymous. *The Life and Memoirs of Her Royal Highness Princess Charlotte of Saxe Coburg Saalfeld & C*. London: T. Kinnersley, 1818.

Anonymous. *A New Song: To the Tune of Packington's Pound*. London: F Giles, 1733.

Anonymous. *Oxford Magazine, Or, University Museum, Vols 3–4*. London: S Bladon, 1769.

Arkell, Ruby Lillian. *Caroline of Ansbach: George the Second's Queen*. Oxford: Oxford University Press, 1939.

Aspinall, Arthur (ed.). *The Correspondence of George, Prince of Wales: Vol I*. London: Cassell, 1963.

Aspinall, Arthur. *The Later Correspondence of George III.: December 1783 to January 1793, Vol II*. Cambridge: Cambridge University Press, 1962.

Aspinall, Arthur. *Letters of the Princess Charlotte 1811–1817*. London: Home and Van Thal, 1949.

Baker, Kenneth. *George III: A Life in Caricature*. London: Thames & Hudson, 2007.

Baker, Kenneth. *George IV: A Life in Caricature*. London: Thames & Hudson, 2005.

Baker-Smith, Veronica PM. *A Life of Anne of Hanover, Princess Royal.* Leiden: EJ Brill, 1995.

Bazalgette, Charles. *Prinny's Taylor: The Life and Times of Louis Bazalgette.* British Columbia: Tara Books, 2015.

Beacock Fryer, Mary, Bousfield, Arthur and Toffoli, Garry. *Lives of the Princesses of Wales.* Toronto: Dundurn Press, 1983.

Beatty, Michael A. *The English Royal Family of America, from Jamestown to the American Revolution.* Jefferson: McFarland & Co, 2003.

Bell, Robert. *The Life of the Rt. Hon. George Canning.* London: Harper, 1955.

Belsham, William. *Memoirs of the Kings of Great Britain of the House of Brunswic-Luneburg, Vol I.* London: C Dilly, 1793.

Belsham, William. *Memoirs of the Reign of George III to the Session of Parliament Ending AD 1793, Vol III.* London: GG and J Robinson, 1801.

Benjamin, Lewis Saul. *The First George in Hanover and England, Volume I.* London: Charles Scribner's Sons, 1909.

Berkeley, Helen (ed). *Memoirs of Madame D'Arblay.* London: James Mowatt & Co, 1844.

Black, Jeremy. *George III: America's Last King.* New Haven: Yale University Press, 2008.

Black, Jeremy. *The Hanoverians: The History of a Dynasty.* London: Hambledon and London, 2007.

Borman, Tracy. *King's Mistress, Queen's Servant: The Life and Times of Henrietta Howard.* London: Random House, 2010.

Brougham, Henry. *The Critical and Miscellaneous Writings of Henry Lord Brougham.* London: Lea & Blanchard, 1841.

Brougham, Henry. *The Life and Times of Henry, Lord Brougham, Vol II.* Edinburgh: William Blackwood and Sons, 1871.

Buckingham and Chandos, Duke of. *Memoirs of the Court of George IV, Vol I.* London: Hurst and Blackett, 1859.

Burney, Frances. *The Diary and Letters of Frances Burney, Madame D'Arblay, Vol II.* Boston: Little, Brown and Company, 1910.

Bury, Lady Charlotte Campbell. *Diary Illustrative of the Times of George the Fourth: Vol I.* London: Carey, Lea and Blanchard, 1838.

Bury, Lady Charlotte Campbell. *Diary Illustrative of the Times of George the Fourth: Vol II.* London: Carey, Lea and Blanchard, 1838.

Campbell Orr, Clarissa. *Queenship in Europe 1660–1815: The Role of the Consort.* Cambridge: Cambridge University Press, 2004.

Carroll, Leslie. *Royal Romances.* New York: New American Library, 2012.

Chambers, James. *Charlotte & Leopold: The True Story of The Original People's Princess.* London: Old Street Publishing, 2008.

Chapman, Frederic (trans.). *A Queen of Indiscretions, The Tragedy of Caroline of Brunswick, Queen of England.* London: John Lane, 1897.

Chapman, Hester W. *Caroline Matilda, Queen of Denmark, 1751–75*. London: Cape, 1971.

Chapman, Hester W. *Privileged Persons*. London: Reynal & Hitchcock, 1966.

Chauncey Woolsey, Sarah. *The Diary and Letters of Frances Burney, Vol II*. Boston: Little, Brown, and Company, 1910.

Childe-Pemberton, William Shakespear. *The Romance of Princess Amelia*. London: John Lane Company, 1911.

Clarke. *The Georgian Era: Volume I*. London, Vizetelly, Branston and Co., 1832.

Clarke, John, Godwin Ridley, Jasper and Fraser, Antonia. *The Houses of Hanover & Saxe-Coburg-Gotha*. Berkeley: University of California Press, 2000.

Cobbett, William and Jardine, David. *Cobbett's Complete Collection of State Trials, Vol XXII*. London: London, Hurst, Rees, Orme and Brown, 1817.

Courtney, William Leonard. *The Feminine Note in Fiction*. London: Chapman & Hall, 1904.

Cowper, Mary. *Diary of Mary, Countess Cowper, Lady of the Bedchamber to the Princess of Wales, 1714 -1720*. London: J Murray, 1865.

Coxe, William. *Memoirs of the Life and Administration of Robert Walpole*. London: Longman, Hurst, Rees, Orme & Brown, 1816.

Coxe, William. *Memoirs of the Life and Administration of Sir Robert Walpole, Earl of Orford: Vol II*. London: T Cadell, Jun and W Davies, 1800.

Craig, William Marshall. *Memoir of Her Majesty Sophia Charlotte of Mecklenburg Strelitz, Queen of Great Britain*. Liverpool: Henry Fisher, 1818.

David, Saul. *Prince of Pleasure*. New York: Grove Press, 2000.

De-la-Noy, Michael. *The King Who Never Was*. London: Peter Owen, 1996.

Delany, Mary and Hall, Augusta. *Autobiography and Correspondence of Mary Granville, Mrs Delany*. Cambridge: Cambridge University Press, 2011.

Delves Broughton, Vernon (ed.). *Court and Private Life in the Time of Queen Charlotte*. London: Richard Bentley, 1887.

Dickenson, Mary Hamilton. *Mary Hamilton: Afterwards Mrs. John Dickenson, at Court and at Home*. London: John Murray, 1925.

Donne, Bodham W (ed.). *The Correspondence of King George the Third With Lord North from 1768 to 1783: Vol I*. London: John Murray, 1867.

Doran, John. *Lives of the Queens of England of the House of Hanover, Volume 1*. New York: Redfield, 1855.

Duggan, JN. *Sophia of Hanover: From Winter Princess to Heiress of Great Britain, 1630–1714*. London: Peter Owen, 2013.

Edwards, Averyl. *Frederick Louis, Prince of Wales, 1701–1751*. London: Staples Press, 1947.

Field, Ophelia. *The Kit-Cat Club: Friends Who Imagined a Nation*. London: Harper Press, 2008.

Fitzgerald, Percy. *The Good Queen Charlotte*. London: Downey & Co, 1899.

Flower, Benjamin (ed.). *Flower's Political Review and Monthly Register, Vol III*. London: M Jones, 1813.

Fox, Charles James. *Speeches of the Right Honourable Charles James Fox, Vol V*. London: Longman, 1845.

Fox, Charles James. *Speeches of the Right Honourable Charles James Fox in the House of Commons, Vol III*. London: Longman, Hurst, Orme, and Brown, 1815.

Fraser, Flora. *Princesses: The Six Daughters of George III*. Edinburgh: A&C Black, 2012.

Fraser, Flora. *The Unruly Queen: The Life of Queen Caroline*. Edinburgh: A&C Black, 2012.

Georgiana, Duchess of Devonshire. *Georgiana: Extracts from the Correspondence of Georgiana, Duchess of Devonshire*. London: John Murray, 1955.

Gold, Claudia. *The King's Mistress*. London: Quercus, 2012.

Gossip, Giles. *Coronation Anecdotes*. London: Robert Jennings, 1828.

Graves, Charles. *Palace Extraordinary*. London: Cassell, 1963.

Gray, Denis. *Spencer Perceval: The Evangelical Prime Minister, 1762–1812*. Manchester: Manchester University Press, 1963.

Greenwood, William de Redman. *Love and Intrigues of Royal Courts*. London: T Werner Laurie, 1910.

Gregg, Edward. *Queen Anne*. New York: Yale University Press, 2014.

Greville, Charles. *A Journal of the Reign of King George IV, King William IV and Queen Victoria, Vol I*. London: Longmans, Green, and Co, 1899.

Hadlow, Janice. *The Strangest Family: The Private Lives of George III, Queen Charlotte and the Hanoverians*. London: William Collins, 2014.

Hansard, TC (ed.). *The Parliamentary Debates from the Year 1803 to the Present Time, Vol XXXV*. London: Hansard, 1817.

Harris, James. *Diaries and Correspondence of James Harris, First Earl of Malmesbury: Vol III*. London: Richard Bentley, 1844.

Hatton, Ragnhild. *George I*. London: Thames and Hudson. 1978.

Haywaed, A (ed.). *Diaries of a Lady of Quality from 1797 to 1844*. London: Longman, Green, Longman, Egberts & Green, 1864.

Heard, Kate. *High Spirits: The Comic Art of Thomas Rowlandson*. London: Royal Collection Trust, 2013.

Hedley, Owen. *Queen Charlotte*. London: J Murray, 1975.

Herman, Eleanor. *Sex with the Queen*. London: Harper Collins, 2009.

Hervey, John. *Lord Hervey's Memoirs*. London: Batsford, 1963.

Hervey, John and Croker, John Wilson (ed.). *Memoirs of the Reign of George the Second: Vol I*. London: John Murray, 1848.

Hervey, John and Croker, John Wilson (ed.). *Memoirs of the Reign of George the Second: Vol II*. London: John Murray, 1848.

Hetherington Fitzgerald, Percy. *The Life of George the Fourth*. London: Tinsley Brothers, 1881.

Hibbert, Christopher. *George III: A Personal History*. London: Viking, 1998.

Hibbert, Christopher. *George IV*. London: Penguin, 1998.

Hill, Constance. *Fanny Burney at the Court of Queen Charlotte*. London: John Lane, 1912.

Holt, Edward. *The Public and Domestic Life of His Late Most Gracious Majesty, George the Third, Vol I*. London: Sherwood, Neely and Jones, 1820.

Holt, Edward. *The Public and Domestic Life of His Late Most Gracious Majesty, George the Third, Vol II*. London: Sherwood, Neely and Jones, 1820.

Home, James A. *Letters of Lady Louisa Stuart to Miss Louisa Clinton*. Edinburgh: D Douglas, 1901.

Hoock, Holger. *Empires of the Imagination*. London: Profile Books, 2010.

Horrins, Johan. *Memoirs of a Trait in the Character of George III of These United Kingdoms*. London: W Edwards, 1835.

Howard, Jean, Sinfield, Alan and Smith, Lindsay. *Luxurious Sexualities: Textual Practice, Volume 11, Issue 3*. London: Routledge, 2005.

Huish, Robert. *Memoirs of George the Fourth: Vol I*. London: Thomas Kelly, 1830.

Huish, Robert. *Memoirs of Her Late Majesty Caroline, Queen of Great Britain*. London: T Kelly, 1821.

Hunt, Margaret. *Women in Eighteenth-Century Europe*. New York: Routledge, 2010.

Ilchester, Countess of & Stavordale, Lord (eds.). *The Life and Letters of Lady Sarah Lennox*. London: John Murray, 1902.

Inglis, Lucy. *Georgian London: Into the Streets*. London: Viking, 2013.

Irvine, Valerie. *The King's Wife: George IV and Mrs Fitzherbert*. London: Hambledon, 2007.

James, Edward T, James, Janet Wilson and Boyer, Paul S. *Notable American Women, 1607–1950: A Biographical Dictionary, Volume 2*. Cambridge: Harvard University Press, 1971.

Jenkinson, Robert Banks. *The Speech of the Right Hon. The Earl of Liverpool in the House of Lords*. London: John Hatchard and Son, 1820.

Jerrold, Clare. *The Story of Dorothy Jordan*. London: Eveleigh Nash, 1914.

Jesse Heneage, J. *Memoirs of the Life and Reign of King George the Third, Vol II*. London: Tinsley Brothers, 1867.

Jesse Heneage, J. *Memoirs of the Life and Reign of King George the Third, Vol III*. London: Richard Bentley, 1843.

Johnson, Samuel. *A Dictionary of the English Language: Vol I*. Heidelberg: Joseph Engelmann, 1828.

Kiste, John van der. *The Georgian Princesses*. Stroud: The History Press, 2013.

Kiste, John van der. *King George II and Queen Caroline*. Stroud: The History Press, 2013.

Kroll, Marie (ed.). *Letters from Liselotte*. London: Allison & Busby, 1842.

Lancelott, Francis. *The Queens of England and Their Times: Volume II*. New York: D Appleton and Co, 1859.

Langdale, Charles. *Memoirs of Mrs. Fitzherbert.* London: Richard Bentley, 1856.

Langford, Paul. *A Polite and Commercial People: England, 1727–1783.* Oxford: Clarendon Press, 1998.

Laquer, Thomas W. *The Queen Caroline Affair: Politics as Art in the Reign of George IV. The Journal of Modern History.* Vol. 54, No. 3 (Sep., 1982) , pp. 417–466

Lehman, H Eugene. *Lives of England's Reigning and Consort Queens.* Bloomington: AuthorHouse, 2011.

Leibniz, Gottfried Wilhelm Freiherr von, Clarke, Samuel and Alexander, Henry Gavin. *The Leibniz-Clarke Correspondence.* Manchester: Manchester University Press, 1956.

Leslie, Anita. *Mrs Fitzherbert: A Biography.* York: Scribner, 1960.

Leslie, CR. *Memoirs of the life of John Constable, R.A.* London: Longman, Brown, Green, and Longmans, 1845.

Leslie, Shane. *Mrs. Fitzherbert: A Life Chiefly from Unpublished Sources.* New York: Benziger Brothers, 1939.

Levey, Michael. *Sir Thomas Lawrence.* New Haven: Yale University Press, 2005.

Littell, E. *Littell's Living Age, Volume IV.* Boston: TH Carter and Company, 1845.

Littell, E. *Littell's Living Age, Volume 57.* New York: Littell, Son and Company, 1858.

Lloyd, Hannibal Evans. *George IV: Memoirs of His Life and Reign, Interspersed with Numerous Personal Anecdotes.* London: Treuttel and Würtz, 1830.

Lovat-Fraser, JA. *John Stuart Earl of Bute.* Cambridge: Cambridge University Press, 1912.

MacFarlane, Charles, and Thomson, Thomas. *The Comprehensive History of England; Civil and Military, Religious, Intellectual and Social, from the Earliest Period to the Suppression of the Sepoy Revolt, Vol III.* London: Blackie & Son, 1792.

Marschner, Joanna. *Queen Caroline: Cultural Politics at the Early Eighteenth Century Court.* New Haven: Yale University Press, 2014.

Mavor, William. *Universal History, Ancient and Modern.* London: Richard Phillips, 1803.

Melville, Lewis, *An Injured Queen, Caroline of Brunswick: Vol I.* London: Hutchinson & Co, 1912.

Minto, Emma Eleanor Elizabeth (ed.). *Life and Letters of Sir Gilbert Elliot First Earl of Minto from 1751 to 1806.* London: Longmans, 1874.

Molloy, J Fitzgerald. *Court Life Below Stairs of London Under the First Georges.* London: Downey & Co, 1897.

Morand, Paul. *The Captive Princess: Sophia Dorothea of Celle.* Florida: American Heritage Press, 1972.

Nightingale, Joseph. *Memoirs of Her Late Majesty Queen Caroline.* London: J Robins and Company, 1821.

Nightingale, Joseph. *Memoirs of the Last Days of Her Late Most Gracious Majesty Caroline, Queen of Great Britain, and Consort of King George the Fourth*. London: J Robins and Company, 1822.

Nightingale, Joseph. *Memoirs of the Public and Private Life of Her Most Gracious Majesty Caroline, Queen of Great Britain*. London: J Robins & Co, 1820.

Oulton, CW. *Authentic and Impartial Memoirs of Her Late Majesty: Charlotte Queen of Great Britain and Ireland*. London: Kinnersley, 1819.

Pearce, Charles E. *The Beloved Princess, Princess Charlotte of Wales*. London: Stanley Paul & Co, 1911.

Pearce, Edward. *The Great Man: Sir Robert Walpole: Scoundrel, Genius and Britain's First Prime Minister*. London: Random House, 2011.

Perceval, Spencer. *The Book, Complete*. London: Sherwood, Neely, & Jones, 1813.

Pergami, Bartolomeo. *Tales of the Baroni, or, Scenes in Italy*. London: J Bailey, 1820.

Plowden, Alison. *Caroline and Charlotte*. Stroud: The History Press, 2011.

Princess Charlotte of Wales and Caroline, Princess of Wales. *Royal Correspondence, or, Letters between Her Late Royal Highness the Princess Charlotte, and Her Royal Mother, Queen Caroline*. London: Jones and Company, 1820.

Reeve, Henry (ed.). *A Journal of the Reigns of King George IV and King William IV, Vol II*. London: Longmans, Green, and Co, 1874.

Ribeiro, Aileen. *Dress in Eighteenth-Century Europe*. London: BT Batsford, 1984.

Richardson, Joanne. *The Disastrous Marriage*. London: Jonathan Cape, 1960.

Robins, Jane. *The Trial of Queen Caroline: The Scandalous Affair that Nearly Ended a Monarchy*. New York: Simon and Schuster, 2006.

Robinson, Mary. *Memoirs of the Late Mrs Robinson*. London: Hunt and Clarke, 1827.

Rushton, Alan R. *Royal Maladies*. Victoria: Trafford Publishing, 2008.

Sanders, Margaret. *Intimate Letters of England's Queens*. Stroud: Amberley, 2014.

Saussure, Cesar de. *A Foreign View of England in the Reigns of George I & George II*. London: John Murray, 1902.

Shawe-Taylor, Desmond and Burchard, Wolf. *The First Georgians: Art and Monarchy 1714–1760*. London: Royal Collection Trust, 2014.

Sinclair-Stevenson, Christopher. *Blood Royal: The Illustrious House of Hanover*. London: Faber & Faber, 2012.

Smith, EA. *George IV*. New Haven: Yale University Press, 1999.

Somerset, Anne. *Ladies-in-Waiting: From The Tudors to the Present Day*. London: Castle Books, 2004.

Spencer, Sarah. *Correspondence of Sarah Spencer Lady Lyttelton 1787–1870*. London: John Murray, 1912.

Stuart, Lady Louisa. *Some Account of John, Duke of Argyll and His Family*. London: W Clowes & Sons, 1863.

Suffolk, Henrietta Hobart Howard. *Letters to and from Henrietta, Countess of Suffolk, Vol I*. London: John Murray, 1824.

Thackeray, William Makepeace. *The Works of William Makepeace Thackeray: Vol XIX*. London: Smith, Elder, & Co, 1869.

Thompson, Andrew C. *George II: King and Elector*. New Haven: Yale University Press, 2011.

Thomson, AT. *Memoirs of Sarah, Duchess of Marlborough: Vol I*. London: Henry Colburn, 1839.

Thomson, AT. *Memoirs of Sarah, Duchess of Marlborough: Vol II*. London: Henry Colburn, 1839.

Thomson, AT. *Memoirs of Viscountess Sundon: Vol I*. London: Henry Colburn, 1848.

Tillyard, Stella. *A Royal Affair: George III and his Troublesome Siblings*. London: Vintage, 2007.

Trench, Charles Chenevix. *George II*. London: Allen Lane, 1973.

Urban, Sylvanus, *The Gentleman's Magazine: Volume LXXXIII*. London: Nichols, Son, and Bentley, 1813.

Urban, Sylvanus. *The Gentleman's Magazine: 1821, Volume 91, Part 2*. London: John Nichols and Son, 1821.

Wallace, William. *Memoirs of the Life and Reign of George IV, Vol I*. London: Longman, Rees, Orme, Brown, and Green. 1831.

Wallace, William. *Memoirs of the Life and Reign of George IV, Vol III*. London: Longman, Rees, Orme, Brown, Green, & Longman. 1832.

Walpole, Horace and Doran, John (ed.). *Journal of the Reign of King George the Third*. London, Richard Bentley, 1859.

Walpole, Horace. *The Last Journals of Horace Walpole During the Reign of George III from 1771–1783*. London: John Lane, 1910.

Walpole, Horace. *Letters of Horace Walpole, Earl of Orford to Sir Horace Mann*. London: Richard Bentley, 1833.

Walpole, Horace. *The Letters of Horace Walpole: Vol I*. London: Lea and Blanchard, 1842.

Walpole, Horace. *The Letters of Horace Walpole: Vol II*. New York: Dearborn, 1832.

Walpole, Horace. *Memoirs of the Reign of King George the Second: Vol I*. London: Henry Colburn, 1846.

Walpole, Horace. *Memoirs of the Reign of King George the Third: Vol I*. Philadelphia: Lea & Blanchard, 1845.

Ward, Adolphus William. *The Electress Sophia and Hanoverian Succession*. London: Longmans, Green and Co, 1909.

Watkins, John. *Memoirs of Her Most Excellent Majesty Sophia-Charlotte, Queen of Great Britain*. London: Henry Colburn, 1819.

Wharncliffe, Lord. *The Letters and Works of Lady Mary Wortley Montagu: Vol I*. London: Richard Bentley, 1837.

Wilkins, William Henry. *Caroline, the Illustrious, Vol I*. London: J Murray, 1901.

Wilkins, William Henry. *Caroline, the Illustrious, Vol II*. London: Longmans, Green and Co, 1901.

Wilkins, William Henry. *The Love of an Uncrowned Queen*. London: Hutchinson & Co, 1900.

Wilkins, William Henry. *A Queen of Tears*. London: Longmans, Green & Co, 1904.

Wilks, John. *Memoirs of Her Majesty Queen Caroline Amelia Eliz, Vol. I*. London: Sherwood, Neely and Jones, 1822.

Williams, Kate. *Becoming Queen*. London: Random House, 2013.

Williams, Robert Folkestone. *Memoirs of Sophia Dorothea, Consort of George I, Vol I*. London: Henry Colburn, 1845.

Williams, Robert Folkestone. *Memoirs of Sophia Dorothea, Consort of George I, Vol II*. London: Henry Colburn, 1845.

Williams, Thomas. *Memoirs of Her Late Majesty Queen Charlotte*. London: W Simpkin and R Marshall, 1819.

Williams, Thomas. *Memoirs of His Late Majesty George III*. London: W Simpkin and R Marshall, 1820.

Worsley, Lucy. *Courtiers: The Secret History of the Georgian Court*. London: Faber and Faber, 2011.

Newspapers Cited

All British newspaper clippings are reproduced © The British Library Board; in addition to those cited, innumerable newspapers were consulted.

Bingley's Journal (London, England), February 8, 1772–15 February, 1772; Issue 89.

The Bristol Mercury (Bristol, England), Monday, 12 June, 1820; Issue 1577.

The Bury and Norwich Post: Or, Suffolk, Norfolk, Essex, Cambridge, and Ely Advertiser (Bury Saint Edmunds, England), Wednesday, 14 September,1814; Issue 1681.

Caledonian Mercury (Edinburgh, Scotland), Thursday, 26 June, 1806; Issue 13179.

Daily Advertiser (London, England), Monday, 5 May, 1783; issue 17249.

Daily Courant (London, England), Tuesday, 19 October, 1714; Issue 4052.

Daily Post (London, England), Thursday, 10 August, 1721; Issue 581.

Evening Mail (London, England), 6 January, 1796–8 January, 1796.

The Examiner (London, England), Sunday, 27 August, 1820; Issue 661.

General Evening Post (London, England), 8 September, 1761–10 September, 1761; Issue 4354.

Hampshire Telegraph and Sussex Chronicle etc (Portsmouth, England), Monday, 16 November, 1818; Issue 997.

Jackson's Oxford Journal (Oxford, England), Saturday, 4 May, 1816; issue 3289.

Jackson's Oxford Journal (Oxford, England), Saturday, 8 November, 1817; Issue 3368.

The Leeds Mercury (Leeds, England), Saturday, 2 July, 1814; Issue 2558.

London Chronicle (London, England), 13 August, 1782–15 August, 1782; Issue 4011.

London Chronicle (London, England), 20 August, 1782–22 August, 1782; issue 4014.

London Evening Post (London, England), 8 September, 1761–10 September,1761; Issue 5283.

London Evening Post (London, England), 10 August, 1762–12 August, 1762; Issue 5422.

London Gazette (London, England), 2 November, 1717–5 November, 1717; Issue 5587.

London Gazette (London, England), 6 March, 1722–10 March, 1722; Issue 6040.

London Journal (1720) (London, England), Saturday, 12 December, 1724.

London Packet or New Lloyd's Evening Post (London, England), 6 April, 1795–8 April, 1795; Issue 4001.

London Packet or New Lloyd's Evening Post (London, England), 8 April, 1795–10 April, 1795; Issue 4002.

Middlesex Journal or Chronicle of Liberty (London, England), 8 February, 1772–11 February, 1772; Issue 447.

The Morning Chronicle (London, England), Saturday, 17 May, 1817; Issue 14990.

The Morning Chronicle (London, England), Saturday, 8 November, 1817; Issue 15139.

The Morning Post (London, England), Thursday, 9 August, 1821; Issue 15725.

Oracle and Public Advertiser (London, England), Tuesday, 7 April, 1795; Issue 18 973.

Oracle and Public Advertiser (London, England), Thursday, 2 June, 1796; Issue 19 336.

Oracle and Public Advertiser (London, England), Wednesday, 8 June, 1796; Issue 19 341.

Post Man and the Historical Account (London, England), 13 December 1716–December 15, 1716; Issue 11520.

Royal Cornwall Gazette, Falmouth Packet & Plymouth Journal (Truro, England), Saturday, 18 November, 1820; Issue 908.

St. James's Chronicle or the British Evening Post (London, England), 31 March, 1795–2 April, 1795; Issue 5815.

St. James's Chronicle or the British Evening Post (London, England), 7 April, 1795–9 April, 1795; Issue 5818.

Star (London, England), Monday, 6 April, 1795; Issue 2068.

Sun (London, England), Monday 6 April, 1795: Issue 787.

True Briton (1793) (London, England), Friday, 14 April, 1797; Issue 1343.

Weekly Journal or Saturday's Post (London, England), Saturday, 8 February, 1718; Issue 61.

Weekly Miscellany (1732) (London, England), Friday, 25 November, 1737; Issue CCLVII.

Weekly Packet (London, England), November 9, 1717–16 November, 1717; Issue 280.

Whitehall Evening Post (1770) (London, England), 11 May, 1782–14 May, 1782; Issue 5639.

Websites Consulted

19th Century UK Periodicals (http://gale.cengage.co.uk/product-highlights/history/19th- (century-uk-periodicals-parts-1-and-2.aspx)

British and Irish Women's Letters and Diaries (www.bwl2.alexanderstreet.com)

British History Online (http://www.british-history.ac.uk)

British Newspapers 1600–1950 (http://gdc.gale.com/products/19th-century-british-library-newspapers-part-i-and-part-ii/)

Hansard (http://hansard.millbanksystems.com/index.html)

Historical Texts (http://historicaltexts.jisc.ac.uk)

House of Commons Parliamentary Papers (http://parlipapers.chadwyck.co.uk/marketing/index.jsp)

JSTOR (www.jstor.org)

The National Archives (http://www.nationalarchives.gov.uk)

Oxford Dictionary of National Biography (http://www.oxforddnb.com)

The Proceedings of the Old Bailey (http://www.oldbaileyonline.org)

The Times Digital Archive (http://gale.cengage.co.uk/times-digital-archive/times-digital-archive-17852006.aspx)

Index

Act of Settlement, 41, 54–55, 62
Albert, Frederick, 109
Amelia of Great Britain, Princess, 64, 97, 101
Amelia of the United Kingdom, Princess:
  Affair with Charles FitzRoy, 142–143
  Birth, 130–131
  Ill health and death of, 143–144
American War of Independence, 128
Anne, Princess Royal, 64, 72, 75–76, 81, 91
Anne, Queen of England, Scotland and
  Ireland, 10, 41–42, 55, 62, 64
  Death of, 42
Anthony Ulrich, Duke of Brunswick-
  Wolfenbüttel, 5–6, 9, 11–13, 29, 32
Augusta of Great Britain, Princess, 126–127,
  150–155
Augusta of Saxe-Gotha, Princess:
  See also, Frederick, Prince of Wales
  Children of, 96–97
  Death of, 115, 125–127
  Frederick II, Duke of Saxe-Gotha-
    Altenburg (father of), 92
  Magdalena Augusta of Anhalt-Zerbst
    (mother of), 92
  Marriage of, 92–93
    Widowed, 116
  Relationship with John Stuart, 3rd Earl of
    Bute, 106, 126
Augusta Sophia of the United Kingdom,
  Princess, 139–140
Augustus Frederick of Wolfenbüttel, Prince,
  5–6, 9
Austin, Sophia and Samuel, 177–178
Austin, William, 175–178, 185, 201
d'Auverquerque, Henry de Nassau, 1st Earl of
  Grantham, 70–71

Bar, Count Christian de, 42–44
Beauclerk, Diana, Duchess of St Albans, 67,
  69
Berkeley, George, 89
Bernstorff, Andreas Gottlieb von, 10–11, 29,
  36–37

Brougham, Henry, 1st Baron Brougham and
  Vaux, 180–182, 191–192, 194, 196, 198–202
Brougham, James, 192
Bury, Lady Charlotte Campbell, 152

Caroline of Ansbach, Queen Consort of Great
  Britain and Ireland: 47–102
  See also, George II, King of Great Britain
    and Ireland
  Birth and childhood of, 47–50
    Orphaned, 49
      Life at Prussian court, 49–50
  Children of, 61–62, 66–70, 72–77
    Feud with Frederick, Prince of Wales,
      90–93, 95–97, 99
  Coronation of, 82
  Eleonore Erdmuthe of Saxe-Eisenach,
    Princess (mother of), 48
  Illness and death, 92–93, 98–102
    Treatment by John Ranby, 99–100
  Infected with smallpox, 61
  John Frederick, Margrave of Brandenburg-
    Ansbach (father of), 47–48
  Marriage, 55–60
    Early plans, 51–52
    Relationship with Henrietta Howard,
      Countess of Suffolk, 63–64, 86–90
  Popularizes variolation, 77–80
  Possible conversion to Catholicism, 51–52
  Public reaction to, 65–66, 71–72
  Reaction to death of Sophia Charlotte of
    Hanover, 52–54
  Regent, 83, 95–96
  Relationship with George I, 62, 70–77
Caroline of Brunswick, Queen Consort of
  the United Kingdom of Great Britain and
  Ireland: 150–202
  See also Charlotte of Wales, George IV,
    King of the United Kingdom of Great
    Britain and Ireland:
  Augusta of Great Britain, Princess, (mother
    of), 126–127, 150–155
  Birth and childhood, 150–152

Charles William Ferdinand, Duke of
    Brunswick-Wolfenbüttel (father of),
    126–127, 150–154
Child of, 145, 171–172
Death of, 190–191
Coronation of George IV, 197–199
    Lord Hood's involvement, 199
Death of, 200–201
Eleonore von Münster (governess of), 155
Funeral of, 201–202
Ill health of, 152–154
Life in Europe, 145, 184–186
    Returns to England, 191–194
Marriage of, 138, 159–171
    See also, Delicate Investigation; Milan
        Commission; and Pains and Penalties
        Bill
    Potential suitors, 155
    Separation, 138, 172–181
    Relationship with Bartolomeo Pergami,
        186–188, 191, 195
    Romance with Irish soldier, 155–156
Caroline Matilda of Great Britain, Princess,
    128, 140
Cavendish, Georgiana, Duchess of
    Devonshire, 158
Charles II, Grand Duke of Mecklenburg, 144
Charles Louis Frederick, Duke of
    Mecklenburg, 103–105
Charles William Ferdinand, Duke of
    Brunswick-Wolfenbüttel, 126–127,
    150–154
Charlotte of Mecklenburg-Strelitz, Queen
    Consort of the United Kingdom of Great
    Britain and Ireland: 103–149
    See also George III, King of the United
        Kingdom of Great Britain and Ireland
    Alleged letter to Frederick the Great,
        105–106
    Birth and childhood of, 103–106
        Friderike Elisabeth de Grabow
            (governess of), 105
        Gottlob Burchard Genzmer (tutor of),
            104
        Caroline Vernon (lady in waiting of),
            123–124
        Sarah Wilson (maid of),123–125
    Charles Louis Frederick, Duke of
        Mecklenburg (father of), 103–105
    Children of, 117–119, 128–131
        Relationship with daughters, 134,
            139–144

Christiane, Duchess of Mecklenburg (sister
    of), 107
Coronation of, 113–115
Death of, 146–149
Elisabeth Albertine of Saxe-
    Hildburghausen, Princess (mother of),
    103, 105, 108
Frederick Albert (hairdresser of), 109
Johanna Louisa Hagedorn (lady-in-waiting
    of), 109
Juliana Elizabeth Schwellenberg (lady-in-
    waiting of), 109, 142
Marriage of, 106–113
    Reaction to madness of George III,
        119–120, 131–135, 138–149
    Philanthropic interests, 119–122, 146
Charlotte of Wales, Princess:
    See also, Delicate Investigation
    Birth of, 145, 171–172
    Death of, 190
    Marriage of, 145, 189–190
        Abandoned marriage plans to William of
            Orange, 182–183
    Mary Helen Dashwood (nurse of), 172
    Political interests of, 180–182
Charlotte, Princess Royal, 139–142
Christian VII, King of Denmark and Norway,
    140
Christiane, Duchess of Mecklenburg, 107
Churchill, Sarah, Duchess of Marlborough, 92
Cobbett, William, 192
Compton, Spencer, 1st Earl of Wilmington,
    81–82
Cornwallis, Charles, 2nd Marquess
    Cornwallis, 141
Cowper, Mary, Countess, 66–67, 76
Cowper, William, 1st Earl Cowper, 74
Craig, William Marshall, 121
Credé, Maurice, 187–188

Dalrymple, John, 2nd Earl of Stair, 102
Dalton, Michael, 124
Dashwood, Mary Helen, 172
Delicate Investigation:
    Accusations of infidelity, 174–180
    Adoption of children:
        Austin, Sophia and Samuel (parents of),
            177–178
        Austin, William, 175–178, 185, 201
Devall, William, 124
Douglas, Lady Charlotte, 175–177
Douglas, Lord John, 175

Edward, Duke of York and Albany, 109, 122
Eleonore Erdmuthe of Saxe-Eisenach,
    Princess, 48–49
Elisabeth Albertine of Saxe-Hildburghausen,
    Princess, 103, 105, 108
Elizabeth of the United Kingdom, Princess, 141
Elliot, Gilbert, 1st Earl of Minto, 135
Eltz, Baron Philipp Adam von, 57–59
Ernest Augustus, Duke of Brunswick-
    Lüneburg, 1–2, 6–10, 13–18, 28, 30–36,
    40, 65, 69
Excise Bill, 83–86

Fane, John, 7th Earl of Westmorland, 113
Ferdinand, Duke of Württemberg, 140
Finch, Lady Charlotte, 119, 129
Fitzherbert, Maria:
    Marriages of, 157
        George IV, 156–159, 165, 172, 195
Fitzroy, The Honourable Charles, 142–143
Fox, The Honourable Charles James, 133
Frederick Augustus I, King of Saxony, 28
Frederick I, King of Württemberg, 141
Frederick, Duke of York and Albany, 133,
    135–136, 153
Frederick, Prince of Wales:
    See also, Augusta of Saxe-Gotha, Princess
    Birth of, 61
    Childhood, 61–62, 64–65
    Children of, 96–97
        Illegitimate children of, 92
    Death of, 116
    Feud with parents, 90–93, 95–97, 99
    Hanoverian figurehead, 65
    Marriage of, 92–93
        Pursues Lady Diana Spencer, Duchess
            of Bedford, 92
        Pursues Wilhelmine of Prussia, 90
        Vane, Anne (mistress of), 92, 96
Frederick the Great, King of Prussia, 105–106
Frederick I of Prussia, King in Prussia, 49,
    51–52, 56–59
Frederick V, King of of Denmark, 140
Frederick William I, King in Prussia, 43
French Revolution, 137–138

Genzmer, Gottlob Burchard, 104
George I, King of Great Britain and Ireland:
    See also, Sophia Dorothea of Celle, Princess
    Birth and childhood, 2
    Children of, 18
        Feud with George II, 67–71, 74–77
    Death of, 45, 81
    Ernest Augustus, Duke of Brunswick-
        Lüneburg (father of), 1–2, 6–10, 13–18,
        28, 30–36, 40, 65, 69
        Adopts primogeniture, 16
        Death of, 40
        Meysenburg, Clara Elisabeth von
            (mistress of), 10, 16–20, 22, 24–31,
            34–36, 39–41
        Possible marriage to Anne, Queen of
            England, Scotland and Ireland, 10
    Karl Philipp, Duke of Brunswick-
        Lüneburg (brother of), 19–20
    Marriage of, 10–16
    Mistresses of:
        Kielmansegg, Sophia von, Countess of
            Darlington, 17, 34
        Schulenberg, Melusine von der,
            Duchess of Kendal, 17–18, 28, 34, 39,
            45, 89
    Sophia, Electress of Hanover (mother of),
        2–3, 6, 9–13, 15,–17, 25–26, 36, 41–42,
        50–51, 54–56, 61, 64
        Death of, 64
        Harling, Katharine von (Mistress of the
            Robes of), 16
    Sophia Charlotte of Hanover(sister of), 49,
        52–54, 56
    Travels to England, 64–65
George II, King of Great Britain and Ireland:
    See also, Caroline of Ansbach, Queen
        Consort of Great Britain and Ireland
    Birth and childhood of, 16
    Children of, 61–62, 66–70, 72–77
        Feud with Frederick, Prince of Wales,
            90–93, 95–97, 99
        Reaction to death of Frederick, Prince
            of Wales,
    Coronation of, 82
    Death of, 106
    Feud with father, 67–71, 74–77
    Infected with smallpox, 61
    Marriage of, 55–60
    Misses mother, 40–41, 45
    Mistresses of:
        Howard, Henrietta, Countess of Suffolk,
            45, 63–64, 70, 76, 81, 86–90, 92
        Berkeley, George Countess of Suffolk
            (husband of), 89
        Howard, Charles, 9th Earl of Suffolk
            (husband of), 63, 87

von Wallmoden, Amalie, Countess of
    Yarmouth, 89–90, 92, 95
    von Wallmoden, Johann (son of), 90
Travels to England, 64–65
George III, King of the United Kingdom of
    Great Britain and Ireland:
    See also, Charlotte of Mecklenburg-
        Strelitz, Queen Consort of the United
        Kingdom of Great Britain and Ireland
    Children of, 117–119, 128–131
    Coronation of, 113–115
    Death of, 192
    Ill health of, 119–120, 131–135, 138–149
        Simmons, Samuel (doctor of), 139
        Willis, Francis (doctor of), 131–133, 139
    Marriage of, 106–113
        Pursues Lady Sarah Lennox, 107, 113
    Relationship with John Stuart, 3rd Earl of
        Bute, 106–107
George IV, King of the United Kingdom of
    Great Britain and Ireland:
    See also, Caroline of Brunswick, Queen
        Consort of the United Kingdom of
        Great Britain and Ireland: and Charlotte
        of Wales, Princess
    Birth and childhood of, 118–119
    Children of, 145, 171–172
    Coronation of, 197–199
    Marriages of:
        Caroline of Brunswick, 138, 159–171
            Separation, 138, 172–181
            See also, Delicate Investigation; Milan
                Commission; and Pains and
                Penalties Bill
        Maria Fitzherbert, 157–159, 165, 172,
            195
    Mistresses of:
        Frances Villiers, Countess of Jersey,
            159–160, 162–164, 167–168, 171–175,
            195
        Isabella Ingram-Seymour-Conway,
            Marchioness of Hertford, 193
George Frederick II, Margrave of
    Brandenburg-Ansbach, 49
George William, Duke of Brunswick
    Lüneburg, 1–3, 5–13, 27–29, 37, 42
George William of Great Britain, Prince,
    67–71, 73
Gordon, Lady Louisa, 141
Grabow, Friderike Elisabeth de, 105
Graeme, Colonel David, 107
Grenville, William, 1st Baron Grenville, 176,
    179

Greville, Charles, 193
Grosvenor, Richard, 1st Earl Grosvenor, 122

Hagedorn, Johanna Louisa, 109
Hamilton, Lady Anne, 193
Harcourt, Simon, 1st Earl Harcourt, 107–108,
    131
Harling, Katharine von, 16
Harris, James, 1st Earl of Malmesbury,
    160–165, 167–170
Hastings, Francis, 10th Earl of Huntingdon,
    118
Hatton, Ragnhild Marie, 15, 31–32
Henry, Duke of Cumberland and Strathearn,
    122
Herbert, Elizabeth, Countess of Pembroke
    and Montgomery, 132, 138
Hertefield, Luise von, 152
Hervey, John, 2nd Baron Hervey, 71, 87–89,
    92, 96–97, 99
Hesse, Captain Charles, 183
Hood, Henry, 2nd Viscount Hood, 199
Horton, Anne, Duchess of Cumberland, 122
Howard, Charles, 9th Earl of Suffolk, 63, 87
Howard, Henrietta, Countess of Suffolk, 45,
    63–64, 70, 76, 81, 86–90, 92
Huish, Robert, 151
Hunter, William, 118

Ingram-Seymour-Conway, Isabella,
    Marchioness of Hertford, 193

Jenkinson, Robert, 2nd Earl of Liverpool,
    184, 197, 199
John Frederick, Duke of Brunswick-
    Lüneburg, 8
John Frederick, Margrave of Brandenburg-
    Ansbach, 47–48
John George IV, Elector of Saxony, 48,

Karl Philipp, Duke of Brunswick-Lüneburg,
    19–20
Kent, William, 98
Kielmansegg, Sophia von, Countess of
    Darlington, 17, 34
Ker, John, 3rd Duke of Roxburghe, 108
Knesebeck, Eléonore von dem (lady-in-
    waiting of) 18, 20, 30, 32–33, 38
Königsmarck, Countess Aurora von (sister
    of), 20, 26
Königsmarck, Count Philip Christoph von, 4,
    12, 18–39, 45

Leibniz, Gottfried, 50–54, 81
Lennox, Lady Sarah, 107, 113
Leopold I, Holy Roman Emperor, 3
Leopold of Saxe-Coburg-Saalfeld, Prince,
    183, 189–190
Lesparre, Armand de Madaillan de, Marquess
    de Lassay, 16–17
Louisa of Great Britain, Princess, 122
Louis Philippe I, King of the French, 141
Lushington, Stephen, 201

Maitland, Charles, 78–79
Majocchi, Theodore, 196
Manby, Thomas, 175
Manners-Sutton, Charles, Archbishop of
    Canterbury, 200
Marie Antoinette, Queen Consort of France
    and Navarre, 137–138
Maton, George, 200
Meysenburg, Clara Elisabeth von, Countess
    of Platen and Hallermund 10, 16–20, 22,
    24–31, 34–36, 39–41
Milan Commission, 191
Montagu, Lady Mary Wortley, 59, 63, 77
Montalbano, Don Nicolò, 32
Moyle, General John, 94
Münster, Eleonore von, 155

Neidschütz, Magdalena Sibylla von, Countess
    of Rochlitz, 48

Octavius of the United Kingdom, Prince,
    129–130, 139
d'Olbreuse, Éléonore Desmier, Duchess
    Consort of Brunswick-Lüneburg, 2–13, 15,
    18, 20, 28, 37, 42
Ompteda, Christian Friedrich Wilhelm
    Freiherr von, 187–188
Orban, Ferdinand, 51–52, 104

Pains and Penalties Bill, 194–197
    Findings of, 197
    Majocchi, Theodore (witness at), 196
    Public reaction to, 195–197
Parker, Thomas, 1st Earl of Macclesfield, 74
Pelham-Holles, Thomas, 1st Duke of
    Newcastle, 69–70
Perceval, The Right Honourable Spencer,
    176, 178–180
Pergami, Bartolomeo, 186–188, 191, 195
Peter the Wild Boy, 80
Pitt the Younger, The Right Honourable
    William, 133–135

Platen, Count Franz Ernst von, 10, 22, 36, 38
Porteous, Captain John, 93–94
Porteous Riots, 93–95

Ranby, John, 99–100
Regency Bill, 119, 131, 134
Rodolph Augustus, Duke of Brunswick-
    Lüneburg, 8
Royal Marriages Act, 122, 158

Schnath, George, 31–32
Schulenberg, Melusine von der, Duchess of
    Kendal, 17–18, 28, 34, 39, 45, 89
Schwellenberg, Juliana Elizabeth, 109, 142
Secker, Thomas, Archbishop of Canterbury,
    111
Seven Years' War, 122
Simmons, Samuel, 139
Smith, Sidney, 174–175
Sophia Charlotte of Hanover, Princess, 49,
    52–54, 56
Sophia, Electress of Hanover, 2–3, 6, 9–17,
    25–26, 36, 41–42, 50–51, 54–56, 61, 64
Sophia Dorothea of Celle, Princess: 2–46
    See also, George I, King of Great Britain
        and Ireland:
    Birth and childhood of, 3–5
    Children of, 18
    Death of, 44–46
    Éléonore Desmier d'Olbreuse (mother of),
        2–13, 15, 18, 20, 28, 37, 42
    Eléonore von dem Knesebeck (lady-in-
        waiting of), 18, 20, 30, 32–33, 38
    George William, Duke of Brunswick
        Lüneburg (father of), 1–3, 5–13, 27–29,
        37, 42
    Imprisonment of, 37–44
    Legitimacy of, 3, 6
    Marriage of, 10–16
        Dissolution of, 36–38
    Proposed marriage to Augustus Frederick
        of Wolfenbüttel, 5–9
    Relationship with Armand de Madaillan de
        Lesparre, Marquess de Lassay, 16–17
    Relationship with Philip Christoph von
        Königsmarck, 4, 12, 18–39, 45
    Codes employed in correspondence,
        20–21
Sophia of Gloucester, Princess, 136
Spencer, Diana, Duchess of Bedford, 92
Stanhope, Philip, 4th Earl of Chesterfield, 102
Stanley, John, 1st Baron Stanley of Alderley,
    154

Struensee, Johann Friedrich, 128, 140
Stuart, John, 3rd Earl of Bute, 106–107, 115, 126

Talbot, Captain William, 125
Thackeray, William Makepeace, 33
Tour d'Auvergne, Marie de la, Duchess of Thouars, 2

Vane, The Honourable Anne, 92, 96
Vernon, Caroline, 123–124
Vernon, Elizabeth, Countess of Harcourt, 131
Villiers, Frances, Countess of Jersey, 159–160, 162–164, 167–168, 171–175, 195

Wake, William, Archbishop of Canterbury, 68
Wallmoden, Amalie von, Countess of Yarmouth, 89–90, 92, 95
Wallmoden von, Count Johann, 90
Walpole, Horace, 4th Earl of Orford, 32–33, 95, 107, 110–111, 126–127

Walpole, Maria, Duchess of Gloucester, 122, 136
Walpole, Robert, 1st Earl of Orford, 71, 73–77, 81–86, 92–95, 101
Wilhelmine of Prussia, Princess, 90
Wilkins, William Henry, 13, 20
William IV, King of the United Kingdom of Great Britain and Ireland, 168
William, Duke of Cumberland, 80
William Frederick, Duke of Gloucester and Edinburgh, 177
William Frederick, Margrave of Brandenburg-Ansbach, 64
William Henry, Duke of Gloucester and Edinburgh, 122, 136
Willis, Francis, 131–133, 139
Wilson, Andrew, 93
Wilson, Sarah, 123–125
Wood, Alderman Matthew, 192